WORD BY WORD

Second Edition

ENGLISH/SPANISH

DICCIONARIO ILUSTRADO DE INGLÉS

Steven J. Molinsky • Bill Bliss

Herlinda Charpentier Saitz, Translator

Illustrated by
Richard E. Hill

PEARSON
Longman

Dedicated to Janet Johnston in honor of her wonderful contribution
to the development of our textbooks over three decades.

Steven J. Molinsky
Bill Bliss

Word by Word Picture Dictionary, International English/Spanish, second edition

Copyright © 2007 by Prentice Hall Regents
Pearson Education, Inc.

Pearson Education, 10 Bank Street, White Plains, NY 10606

Editorial director: Pam Fishman
Vice president, director of design and production: Rhea Banker
Director of electronic production: Aliza Greenblatt
Director of manufacturing: Patrice Fraccio
Senior manufacturing manager: Edith Pullman
Marketing manager: Carol Brown
Editorial assistant: Katherine Keyes
Senior digital layout specialist: Wendy Wolf
Text design: Wendy Wolf
Cover design: Tracey Munz Cataldo
Realia creation: Warren Fischbach, Paula Williams
Illustrations: Richard E. Hill
Contributing artists: Steven Young, Charles Cawley, Willard Gage, Marlon Violette
Reviewers: Marta E. Luján, The University of Texas at Austin; Carmen Schlig, Georgia State University;
Project management by TransPac Education Services, Victoria, BC, Canada
with assistance from Yu Jian Yo, Studio G, Robert Zacharias, & Susa Oñate

ISBN 0-13-242874-1

Longman on the Web
Longman.com offers online resources for teachers and students. Access our Companion Websites, our online
catalog, and our local offices around the world.

Visit us at longman.com.

Printed in the United States of America
1 2 3 4 5 6 7 8 9 10 – RRD – 11 10 09 08 07 06

CONTENTS

ÍNDICE/CONTENIDO

¡Bienvenidos(as) a la segunda edición del Diccionario ilustrado de inglés **WORD BY WORD** !
Nuestro propósito es que el aprendizaje del vocabulario de inglés adquiera vida en experiencias comunicativas dinámicas que preparen a los/las estudiantes a tener éxito en el uso del inglés tanto en la vida diaria como en la comunidad, la escuela y el trabajo.

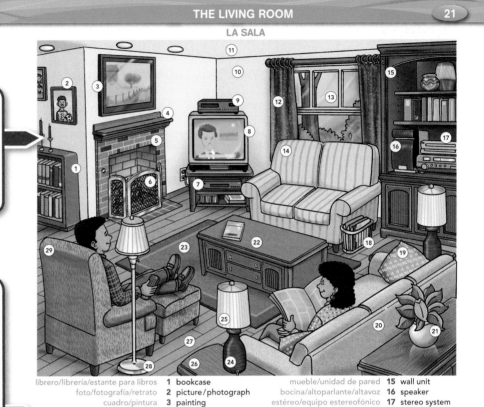

THE LIVING ROOM 21

LA SALA

Las claras, vibrantes y sencillas ilustraciones están diseñadas con la intención de ofrecer un claro y fácil manejo de las lecciones a estudiantes de cualquier nivel.

Más de 4.000 palabras y 138 tópicos están presentados en una cuidadosa y bien documentada secuencia, a través de lecciones que integran la gramática y el vocabulario para un mayor rendimiento en el aprendizaje de los mismos.

Las conversaciones modelo ilustran contextos y situaciones donde las palabras aparecen llenas de significado. Los/las estudiantes se compenetran en comunicaciones recíprocas y dinámicas a la vez que crean nuevas conversaciones basadas en los modelos que usan la lista de palabras de la lección.

librero/librería/estante para libros	1	bookcase
foto/fotografía/retrato	2	picture/photograph
cuadro/pintura	3	painting
manto de la chimenea/del hogar	4	mantel
hogar/chimenea	5	fireplace
pantalla/rejilla de la chimenea	6	fireplace screen
DVD/reproductor de video digital	7	DVD player
televisor/TV/televisión/tele	8	television/TV
videocasetera/videograbadora	9	VCR/video cassette recorder
pared/muro/tapia	10	wall
cielo raso/techo	11	ceiling
cortinas	12	drapes
ventana	13	window
confidente/canapé/sofá	14	loveseat

mueble/unidad de pared	15	wall unit
bocina/altoparlante/altavoz	16	speaker
estéreo/equipo estereofónico	17	stereo system
revistero	18	magazine holder
cojín	19	(throw) pillow
sofá	20	sofa/couch
mata/planta	21	plant
mesa de centro	22	coffee table
alfombra/alfombrilla/tapete	23	rug
lámpara	24	lamp
pantalla	25	lampshade
mesita/esquinera/mesilla	26	end table
piso	27	floor
lámpara de pie	28	floor lamp
sillón/silla de brazos/butaca	29	armchair

A. Where are you?
B. I'm in the living room.
A. What are you doing?
B. I'm dusting* the **bookcase**.

* dusting/cleaning

A. You have a very nice living room!
B. Thank you.
A. Your _____ is/are beautiful!
B. Thank you for saying so.

A. Uh-oh! I just spilled coffee on your _____!
B. That's okay. Don't worry about it.

Tell about your living room.
(In my living room there's ....)

Las conversaciones adicionales ayudan a que los/las estudiantes utilicen el vocabulario en contextos más amplios y ofrecen prácticas con claves de destreza comunicativa funcional tales como expresar halago, pedir disculpas o hacer preguntas.

Las preguntas para escribir y generar discusión están presentes con el fin de estimular al/a la estudiante a que relacione el vocabulario y los temas de cada lección con su experiencia personal, sus pensamientos, sus opiniones e información sobre sí mismos(as), su cultura y su país.

Estrategias para la enseñanza

Las estrategias para la enseñanza son una guía que ofrece, en una visión de conjunto, algunas sugerencias para presentar y practicar el vocabulario en cada lección del Diccionario ilustrado de inglés *Word by Word*. A continuación se enumeran, paso a paso, algunas de estas estrategias:

1▷ Reconocimiento de vocabulario: Haga que los/las estudiantes reconozcan las palabras que ya conocen escribiéndolas en la pizarra, mostrándoselas en las transparencias o haciendo que las identifiquen en las ilustraciones de la lección.

2▷ Presentación del vocabulario nuevo: Mediante el uso de las transparencias o la ilustración de la lección, señale la figura que corresponde a cada palabra, diga la palabra y haga que la clase la repita en coro e individualmente. (También puede hacer que escuchen la lista de las palabras poniendo el audio casette o CD en la sección de la lección correspondiente). Verifique que los/las estudiantes estén pronunciando y entendiendo lo que repiten.

3▷ Práctica de vocabulario: Haga que los/las estudiantes practiquen el vocabulario en coro, en pares o en grupos pequeños. Diga o escriba una palabra y haga que ellos señalen la figura o digan el número que le corresponde a dicha palabra. O bien, señale una figura o diga un número y haga que digan la palabra a la que corresponde la figura o el número.

4▷ Práctica de la conversación modelo: Algunas lecciones tienen conversaciones modelo que utilizan la primera palabra de la lista del vocabulario. Otros modelos son esquemas estructurales del diálogo que se pueden completar con otras palabras del vocabulario de la lección. Para la práctica de la conversación modelo se recomiendan los siguientes pasos:

  a. Haga que los/las estudiantes observen la ilustración en el modelo e imaginen quiénes podrán ser los/las que hablan y dónde tiene lugar la conversación.

  b. Presente el modelo o ponga el audio casette o CD en la sección correspondiente una o varias veces y verifique que hayan comprendido la situación y el vocabulario.

  c. Haga que los estudiantes repitan cada línea de la conversación en coro o individualmente.

  d. Haga que practiquen el modelo en parejas.

  e. Escoja una pareja para que presente la conversación basada en el modelo utilizando otras palabras de las que están en la lista del vocabulario de la lección.

  f. Indique a los/las estudiantes que practiquen en parejas varias conversaciones basadas en el modelo utilizando otras palabras de la lista del vocabulario de la lección.

  g. Haga que varias parejas presenten su conversación a la clase.

5▷ Práctica de conversación adicional: Muchas lecciones ofrecen dos esquemas de diálogo adicionales para afianzar la práctica de la conversación con el vocabulario. Haga que los/las estudiantes practiquen y presenten estas conversaciones usando la palabra que quieran. Antes de practicar las conversaciones adicionales usted puede hacer que escuchen las conversaciones modelo adicionales poniendo el audio casette o CD en la sección de la lección correspondiente.

6▷ Práctica de ortografía: Haga que los/las estudiantes deletreen las palabras en coro, en pares o en grupos pequeños. Diga una palabra y haga que la deletreen en voz alta, la escriban, o utilizando la transparencia, señale una figura y haga que escriban la palabra.

7▷ Temas de discusión, composición, diarios y portafolios: Haga que los/las estudiantes respondan a las preguntas (al pie de la página) en coro, en pares o en grupos pequeños. O bien, haga que escriban sus respuestas en casa, compartan su trabajo escrito con otros(as) compañeros(as) e intercambien ideas con el resto de la clase, en pares o en grupos pequeños. Los/las estudiantes pueden llevar un diario de su trabajo escrito. Estas composiciones pueden servir como ejemplo de su progreso.

8▷ Ejercicios de afianzamiento: Esta Guía del/de la profesor(a) proporciona recursos didácticos muy variados, que reforzarán el aprendizaje y aumentarán el vocabulario del estudiante.

Bienvenidos(as) a la segunda edición del diccionario ilustrado WORD BY WORD! Este texto presenta un vocabulario de más de 4.000 palabras que, a través de vibrantes ilustraciones, lecciones sencillas y accesibles, y un diseño claro, ofrece al estudiante de todos los niveles un fácil manejo de las lecciones para el aprendizaje del inglés. Nuestro objetivo es ayudar a que practiquen el inglés usado en la vida diaria, la comunidad, la escuela, el trabajo y los viajes internacionales de una manera dinámica y entretenida.

Word by Word organiza el vocabulario en 17 unidades temáticas que proporcionan una cuidadosa secuencia de lecciones basada en investigaciones con el objetivo de enseñar de manera integral el control de la gramática y el vocabulario a través de temas que comienzan con el mundo inmediato del estudiante y progresivamente avanzan hacia el mundo en general. Las primeras lecciones, sobre la familia, la casa y las actividades diarias, conducen a otras sobre la comunidad, la escuela, el trabajo, ir de compras, la recreación y otros temas. El texto también sirve como un programa general que integra el desarrollo del vocabulario, las habilidades orales y auditivas y la expresión de ideas con temas para la escritura y la conversación.

Cada lección en el diccionario Word by Word es autónoma y puede usarse ya sea en secuencia lógica o en cualquier orden deseado. Para mayor conveniencia, las lecciones se presentan de dos maneras: en el Índice/Contenido como secuencia lógica preestablecida, y en el Índice temático en orden alfabético. Estos índices, en combinación con el Glosario en el Apéndice, permiten tanto al estudiante como al/a la profesor(a) ubicar rápida y fácilmente todas las palabras y temas del Diccionario ilustrado.

El Diccionario ilustrado Word by Word es el núcleo del Programa de desarrollo de vocabulario Word by Word completo, el cual ofrece una amplia selección de recursos auxiliares impresos y audiovisuales para suplementar la instrucción en todos los niveles.

Los diferentes niveles de los libros de ejercicios ofrecen opciones flexibles para cumplir con las necesidades del aprendizaje. Los libros de ejercicios de vocabulario en los niveles principiante e intermedio sobresalen por sus estimulantes secciones de vocabulario, gramática y práctica auditiva. El libro de ejercicios de alfabetización proporciona prácticas para todos los niveles, especialmente adecuadas para aquellos(as) que no están familiarizados(as) con el alfabeto o necesitan una introducción previa al nivel de principiante en lo referente al vocabulario, la lectura y la escritura del inglés.

La Guía del/de la profesor(a) y el Libro para planear lecciones con disco compacto CD-ROM incluyen sugerencias para la organización de las lecciones, las actividades en la comunidad, los enlaces en Internet y las láminas reproducibles con el fin de ahorrar tiempo a los/las profesores(as) en la preparación de las lecciones. La Guía del/de la profesor(a) incluye un Manual de actividades con estrategias para la enseñanza que ofrece paso a paso actividades de desarrollo para el vocabulario esencial.

El programa audio-oral incluye todas las palabras y conversaciones para la práctica interpersonal e interactiva y—como material adicional—una selección musical de canciones con letras para aplicar el vocabulario de una manera entretenida.

Otros materiales suplementarios adicionales incluyen transparencias en color, tarjetas de juegos de vocabulario y un programa de pruebas. También hay ediciones bilingües disponibles.

Estrategias para la enseñanza

El diccionario Word by Word presenta las palabras en contexto. Las conversaciones modelo contienen situaciones que se usan en intercambios comunicativos llenos de significado. Los modelos sirven de ejemplo para que los estudiantes se compenetren en prácticas de conversación interpersonales y dinámicas. Además, las preguntas para contestar por escrito y para la discusión en grupo en cada lección sirven de estímulo para que relacionen el vocabulario y los temas a sus propias vidas conforme vayan hablando sobre sus experiencias, ideas, opiniones e información sobre sí mismos(as), su cultura y sus países. De esta manera, se van conociendo unos(as) a otros(as) "palabra por palabra".

Al usar el diccionario *Word by Word*, es recomendable desarrollar métodos y estrategias que sean compatibles con su propio estilo de enseñanza y las necesidades y aptitudes de los estudiantes. A continuación se enumeran algunas estrategias que pueden ser útiles al presentar y practicar el vocabulario de cada lección.

1. **Reconocimiento de vocabulario:** haga que los/las estudiantes reconozcan las palabras que ya conocen escribiéndolas en la pizarra, mostrándoselas en las transparencias o haciendo que las identifiquen en las ilustraciones de la lección.

2. **Presentación del vocabulario nuevo:** mediante el uso de las transparencias o la ilustración de la lección, señale la figura que corresponde a cada palabra, diga la palabra y haga que la clase la repita en coro e individualmente. (También puede hacer que escuchen la lista de palabras poniendo el audio casette o CD en la sección de la lección correspondiente). Verifique que los/las estudiantes estén pronunciando y entendiendo lo que repiten.

3. **Práctica de vocabulario:** haga que los/las estudiantes practiquen el vocabulario en coro, en pares o en grupos pequeños. Diga o escriba una palabra y haga que señalen la figura o digan el número que le corresponde a dicha palabra. O bien, señale una figura o diga un número y haga que digan la palabra a que corresponde la figura o el número.

4. **Práctica de la conversación modelo:** algunas lecciones tienen conversaciones modelo que utilizan la primera palabra de la lista del vocabulario. Otros modelos son esquemas estructurales del diálogo que se pueden completar con otras palabras del vocabulario de la lección. (En muchos esquemas estructurales del diálogo, hay números en corchetes que indican las palabras que se pueden usar para practicar la conversación. Si no hay números en corchetes, se podrán usar todas las palabras de la lección).

Para la práctica de la conversación modelo se recomiendan los siguientes pasos:

a. Haga que los/las estudiantes observen la ilustración en el modelo e imaginen quiénes podrán ser los/las que hablan y dónde tiene lugar la conversación.

b. Presente el modelo o ponga el audio casette o CD en la sección correspondiente una o varias veces y verifique que hayan comprendido la situación y el vocabulario.

c. Haga que los/las estudiantes repitan cada línea de la conversación en coro o individualmente.

d. Haga que practiquen el modelo en parejas.

e. Escoja una pareja para que presente la conversación basada en el modelo utilizando otras palabras de las que están en la lista del vocabulario de la lección.

f. Indíque a los/las estudiantes que practiquen en parejas varias conversaciones basadas en el modelo utilizando otras palabras de la lista del vocabulario de la lección.

g. Haga que varias parejas presenten su conversación a la clase.

5. **Práctica de conversación adicional:** Muchas lecciones ofrecen dos esquemas de diálogo adicionales para afianzar la práctica de la conversación con el vocabulario. (Estas se encuentran en el área sombreada en amarillo al pie de la página). Haga que los/las estudiantes practiquen y presenten estas conversaciones usando cualquier palabra que quieran. Antes de practicar las conversaciones adicionales usted puede hacer que escuchen las conversaciones modelo adicionales poniendo el audio casette o CD en la sección de la lección correspondiente.

6. **Práctica de ortografía:** haga que los/las estudiantes deletreen las palabras en coro, en pares o en grupos pequeños. Diga una palabra y haga que la deletreen en voz alta o la escriban. O bien, utilizando las transparencias, señale una figura y haga que escriban la palabra.

7. **Temas para discusión, composición, diarios y portafolios:** cada lección del diccionario *Word by Word* proporciona una o más preguntas para la discusión y composición. (Estas se encuentran en el área sombreada en azul al pie de la página). Haga que los/las estudiantes respondan a las preguntas en coro, en pares o en grupos pequeños. O bien, haga que escriban sus respuestas en casa, compartan su trabajo escrito con otros(as) compañeros(as) e

intercambien ideas con el resto de la clase, en pares o en grupos pequeños.

Es posible que quieran escribir un diario de su trabajo escrito. Si el tiempo lo permite y usted lo desea, puede escribirle a cada uno(a) una respuesta en su diario, expresando sus propias opiniones y experiencias, a la vez que sus reacciones a lo que haya escrito el/la estudiante. Si usted guarda los portafolios, estas composiciones servirán como ejemplos excelentes de su avance al aprender inglés.

8. Actividades de comunicación: La Guía del/de la profesor(a) de Word by Word y el Libro para planear lecciones con disco compacto CD-ROM ofrecen una gran gama de juegos, tareas, ejercicios de discusión en grupo, actividades de movimiento, dibujo y dramatización haciendo papeles donde imitan situaciones reales y otras actividades, creadas con el fin de atender a los diferentes estilos de aprendizaje y las aptitudes y capacidades particulares de cada estudiante. Para cada lección, seleccione una o más de estas actividades para afianzar el aprendizaje del vocabulario de una manera estimulante, creativa y amena.

El diccionario *WORD BY WORD* tiene como objetivo enseñar el vocabulario del inglés de una manera comunicativa, significativa y animada. Al proporcionarle la esencia de nuestro programa, esperamos que también le hayamos dado la clave: aprender vocabulario puede ser una actividad genuinamente dinámica e interpersonal, relacionada directamente a la vida de nuestros(as) estudiantes, que responde a sus diferentes estilos, aptitudes y capacidades personales y que además, . . . ¡puede ser divertido!

Steven J. Molinsky
Bill Bliss

Welcome to the second edition of the WORD BY WORD Picture Dictionary! This text presents more than 4,000 vocabulary words through vibrant illustrations and simple accessible lesson pages that are designed for clarity and ease-of-use with learners at all levels. Our goal is to help students practice English used in everyday life, in the community, in school, at work, and in international travel.

WORD BY WORD organizes the vocabulary into 17 thematic units, providing a careful research-based sequence of lessons that integrates students' development of grammar and vocabulary skills through topics that begin with the immediate world of the student and progress to the world at large. Early lessons on the family, the home, and daily activities lead to lessons on the community, school, workplace, shopping, recreation, and other topics. In addition to developing students' vocabulary, the text also serves as a comprehensive communication skills program that integrates vocabulary learning, listening and speaking skills, and themes for writing and discussion.

Since each lesson in *Word by Word* is self-contained, it can be used either sequentially or in any desired order. For users' convenience, the lessons are listed in two ways: sequentially in the Table of Contents, and alphabetically in the Thematic Index. These resources, combined with the Glossary in the appendix, allow students and teachers to quickly and easily locate all words and topics in the Picture Dictionary.

The *Word by Word* Picture Dictionary is the centerpiece of the complete *Word by Word* Vocabulary Development Program, which offers a wide selection of print and media support materials for instruction at all levels.

Workbooks at different levels offer flexible options to meet students' needs. Vocabulary Workbooks at Beginning and Intermediate levels feature motivating vocabulary, grammar, and listening practice. A Literacy Workbook provides all-skills practice especially appropriate for learners who are not familiar with the alphabet or who need a pre-Beginning-level introduction to English vocabulary, reading, and writing.

The Teacher's Guide and Lesson Planner with CD-ROM includes lesson-planning suggestions, community tasks, Internet weblinks, and reproducible masters to save teachers hours of lesson preparation time. An Activity Handbook with step-by-step teaching strategies for key vocabulary development activities is included in the Teacher's Guide.

The Audio Program includes all words and conversations for interactive practice and —as bonus material—an expanded selection of WordSongs for entertaining musical practice with the vocabulary.

Additional ancillary materials include Color Transparencies, Vocabulary Game Cards, a Testing Program, and ExamView CD-ROM. Bilingual Editions are also available.

Teaching Strategies

Word by Word presents vocabulary words in context. Model conversations depict situations in which people use the words in meaningful communication. These models become the basis for students to engage in dynamic, interactive practice. In addition, writing and discussion questions in each lesson encourage students to relate the vocabulary and themes to their own lives as they share experiences, thoughts, opinions, and information about themselves, their cultures, and their countries. In this way, students get to know each other "word by word."

In using *Word by Word*, we encourage you to develop approaches and strategies that are compatible with your own teaching style and the needs and abilities of your students. You may find it helpful to incorporate some of the following techniques for presenting and practicing the vocabulary in each lesson.

1. **Preview the Vocabulary:** Activate students' prior knowledge of the vocabulary by brainstorming with students the words in the lesson they already know and writing them on the board, or by having students look at the transparency or the illustration in *Word by Word* and identify the words they are familiar with.

2. **Present the Vocabulary:** Using the transparency or the illustration in the Picture Dictionary, point to the picture of each word, say the word, and have the class repeat it chorally and individually. (You can also play the word list on the Audio Program.) Check students' understanding and pronunciation of the vocabulary.

3. **Vocabulary Practice:** Have students practice the vocabulary as a class, in pairs, or in small groups. Say or write a word, and have students point to the item or tell the number. Or, point to an item or give the number, and have students say the word.

4. **Model Conversation Practice:** Some lessons have model conversations that use the first word in the vocabulary list. Other models are in the form of skeletal dialogs, in which vocabulary words can be inserted. (In many skeletal dialogs, bracketed numbers indicate which words can be used for practicing the conversation. If no bracketed numbers appear, all the words in the lesson can be used.)

The following steps are recommended for Model Conversation Practice:

a. Preview: Have students look at the model illustration and discuss who they think the speakers are and where the conversation takes place.

b. The teacher presents the model or plays the audio one or more times and checks students' understanding of the situation and the vocabulary.

c. Students repeat each line of the conversation chorally and individually.

d. Students practice the model in pairs.

e. A pair of students presents a conversation based on the model, but using a different word from the vocabulary list.

f. In pairs, students practice several conversations based on the model, using different words on the page.

g. Pairs present their conversations to the class.

5. **Additional Conversation Practice:** Many lessons provide two additional skeletal dialogs for further conversation practice with the vocabulary. (These can be found in the yellow-shaded area at the bottom of the page.) Have students practice and present these conversations using any words they wish. Before they practice the additional conversations, you may want to have students listen to the sample additional conversations on the Audio Program.

6. **Spelling Practice:** Have students practice spelling the words as a class, in pairs, or in small groups. Say a word, and have students spell it aloud or write it. Or, using the transparency, point to an item and have students write the word.

7. **Themes for Discussion, Composition, Journals, and Portfolios:** Each lesson of *Word by Word* provides one or more questions for discussion and composition. (These can be found in a blue-shaded area at the bottom of the page.) Have students respond to the questions as a class, in pairs, or in small groups. Or, have students write their responses at home, share their written work with other students, and discuss as a class, in pairs, or in small groups.

Students may enjoy keeping a journal of their written work. If time permits, you may want to write a response in each student's journal, sharing your own opinions and experiences as well as reacting to what the student has written. If you are keeping portfolios of students' work, these compositions serve as excellent examples of students' progress in learning English.

8. **Communication Activities:** The *Word by Word* Teacher's Guide and Lesson Planner with CD-ROM provides a wealth of games, tasks, brainstorming, discussion, movement, drawing, miming, role-playing, and other activities designed to take advantage of students' different learning styles and particular abilities and strengths. For each lesson, choose one or more of these activities to reinforce students' vocabulary learning in a way that is stimulating, creative, and enjoyable.

WORD BY WORD aims to offer students a communicative, meaningful, and lively way of practicing English vocabulary. In conveying to you the substance of our program, we hope that we have also conveyed the spirit: that learning vocabulary can be genuinely interactive . . . relevant to our students' lives . . . responsive to students' differing strengths and learning styles . . . and fun!

Steven J. Molinsky

Bill Bliss

Registration Form

Name _____ Gloria _____ P. _____ Sánchez _____
First · Middle Initial · Last

Address _____ 95 _____ Garden Street _____ 3G _____
Number · Street · Apartment Number
Los Angeles _____ CA _____ 90036 _____
City · State · Zip Code

Telephone _____ 323-524-3278 _____ Cell Phone _____ 323-695-1864 _____

E-Mail Address _____ gloria97@ail.com _____ SSN 227-93-6185 Sex M__ F X

Date of Birth _____ 5/12/88 _____ Place of Birth _____ Centerville, Texas _____

nombre completo	**1** name	código/zona postal	**11** zip code
nombre de pila	**2** first name	código/prefijo telefónico/clave telefónica	**12** area code
inicial del segundo nombre	**3** middle initial	número de teléfono	**13** telephone number/ phone number
apellidos (paterno y materno)	**4** last name/family name/ surname	número de teléfono celular/móvil	**14** cell phone number
domicilio	**5** address	dirección de correo electrónico	**15** e-mail address
número de la casa	**6** street number	número de seguro social	**16** social security number
calle	**7** street	sexo	**17** sex
número del apartamento	**8** apartment number	fecha de nacimiento	**18** date of birth
ciudad	**9** city	lugar de nacimiento	**19** place of birth
estado/provincia/ departamento	**10** state		

A. What's your **name**?
B. Gloria P. Sánchez.

A. What's your _____?
B. ....
A. Did you say ....?
B. Yes. That's right.

A. What's your last name?
B. ....
A. How do you spell that?
B. ....

Tell about yourself:
My name is ....
My address is ....
My telephone number is ....

Now interview a friend.

esposo **1** husband	**hijos** **children**	**abuelos** **grandparents**
esposa **2** wife	hija **5** daughter	abuela **10** grandmother
	hijo **6** son	abuelo **11** grandfather
padres **parents**	bebé/nene(a) **7** baby	
padre/papá **3** father		**nietos** **grandchildren**
madre/mamá **4** mother	**hermanos(as)** **siblings**	nieta **12** granddaughter
	hermana **8** sister	nieto **13** grandson
	hermano **9** brother	

A. Who is he?
B. He's my **husband**.
A. What's his name?
B. His name is *Jack*.

A. Who is she?
B. She's my **wife**.
A. What's her name?
B. Her name is *Nancy*.

A. I'd like to introduce my _____.
B. Nice to meet you.
C. Nice to meet you, too.

A. What's your _____'s name?
B. His/Her name is ....

Who are the people in your family?
What are their names?

Tell about photos of family members.

LA FAMILIA (PARIENTES) II

Helen • Walter • Jack • Nancy • Frank • Linda • Jennifer • Timmy • Alan

tío	**1**	uncle
tía	**2**	aunt
sobrina	**3**	niece
sobrino	**4**	nephew
primo/prima	**5**	cousin

suegra	**6**	mother-in-law
suegro	**7**	father-in-law
yerno	**8**	son-in-law
nuera	**9**	daughter-in-law
cuñado	**10**	brother-in-law
cuñada	**11**	sister-in-law

1. Jack is Alan's ____.
2. Nancy is Alan's ____.
3. Jennifer is Frank and Linda's ____.
4. Timmy is Frank and Linda's ____.
5. Alan is Jennifer and Timmy's ____.

6. Helen is Jack's ____.
7. Walter is Jack's ____.
8. Jack is Helen and Walter's ____.
9. Linda is Helen and Walter's ____.
10. Frank is Jack's ____.
11. Linda is Jack's ____.

A. Who is he/she?
B. He's/She's my _____.
A. What's his/her name?
B. His/Her name is _____.

A. Let me introduce my _____.
B. I'm glad to meet you.
C. Nice meeting you, too.

Tell about your relatives:
What are their names?
Where do they live?

Draw your family tree and tell about it.

EL SALÓN/LA SALA DE CLASES/EL AULA

maestro(a)	**1**	teacher	reloj	**11**	clock
asistente/auxiliar	**2**	teacher's aide	mapa	**12**	map
alumno(a)/estudiante	**3**	student	cartelera/tablero/tablilla/mural/de anuncios	**13**	bulletin board
pupitre/escritorio	**4**	desk			
silla/banco	**5**	seat/chair	sistema de altavoz/altoparlante	**14**	P.A. system/loudspeaker
mesa	**6**	table	pizarra/pizarrón/tablero para marcadores	**15**	whiteboard/board
computadora/ordenador	**7**	computer	globo terráqueo/del mundo	**16**	globe
retroproyector/proyector de transparencias	**8**	overhead projector	librera/librero/librería/estante para libros	**17**	bookcase/bookshelf
pantalla	**9**	screen	escritorio de la maestra/del maestro	**18**	teacher's desk
pizarra/pizarrón/tablero	**10**	chalkboard/board	papelera/cesto/canasta de papeles	**19**	wastebasket

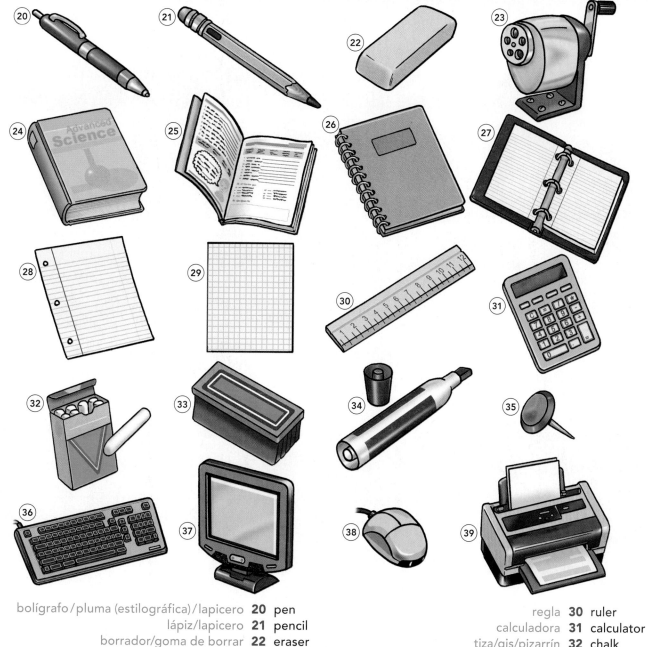

bolígrafo/pluma (estilográfica)/lapicero	20	pen
lápiz/lapicero	21	pencil
borrador/goma de borrar	22	eraser
sacapuntas	23	pencil sharpener
libro/texto	24	book/textbook
cuaderno/manual de ejercicios/de actividades	25	workbook
cuaderno/carpeta con espiral	26	spiral notebook
carpeta/portafolios	27	binder/notebook
papel para carpetas/para portafolios	28	notebook paper
papel cuadriculado	29	graph paper
regla	30	ruler
calculadora	31	calculator
tiza/gis/pizarrín	32	chalk
borrador	33	eraser
marcador	34	marker
tachuela/chinche/chincheta	35	thumbtack
teclado	36	keyboard
pantalla/monitor	37	monitor
ratón	38	mouse
impresora	39	printer

A. Where's the **teacher**?
B. The **teacher** is *next to* the **board**.

A. Where's the **globe**?
B. The **globe** is *on* the **bookcase**.

A. Is there a/an _____ in your classroom?*
B. Yes. There's a/an _____
   next to/on the _____.

A. Is there a/an _____ in your classroom?*
B. No, there isn't.

Describe your classroom.
(There's a/an ....)

* With 28, 29, 32 use: Is there _____ in your classroom?

ACCIONES EN EL SALÓN/LA SALA DE CLASES/EL AULA

Diga(n) su nombre.	1	Say your name.
Repita(n) su nombre.	2	Repeat your name.
Deletree(n) su nombre.	3	Spell your name.
Escriba(n) su nombre.	4	Print your name.
Firme(n).	5	Sign your name.
Levánte(n)se.	6	Stand up.
Vaya(n) a la pizarra/al pizarrón/al tablero.	7	Go to the board.
Escriba(n) en la pizarra/el pizarrón/el tablero.	8	Write on the board.
Borre(n) la pizarra/el pizarrón/el tablero.	9	Erase the board.
Siénte(n)se/Tome(n) asiento.	10	Sit down./Take your seat.
Abra(n) el libro.	11	Open your book.
Lea(n) la página diez.	12	Read page ten.
Estudie(n) la página diez.	13	Study page ten.
Cierre(n) el libro.	14	Close your book.
Guarde(n) el libro.	15	Put away your book.
Levante(n)/Alce(n) la mano.	16	Raise your hand.
Haga(n) una pregunta./Pregunte(n).	17	Ask a question.
Escuche(n) la pregunta.	18	Listen to the question.
Conteste(n) la pregunta.	19	Answer the question.
Escuche(n) la respuesta.	20	Listen to the answer.
Haga(n) su tarea/sus deberes.	21	Do your homework.
Traiga(n) su tarea/sus deberes.	22	Bring in your homework.
Revise(n) las respuestas/las contestaciones.	23	Go over the answers.
Corrija(n) sus errores.	24	Correct your mistakes.
Entregue(n) su tarea.	25	Hand in your homework.
Comparta(n) un libro.	26	Share a book.
Discuta(n) la pregunta.	27	Discuss the question.
Ayúdense.	28	Help each other.
Trabajen juntos(as).	29	Work together.
Comparta(n) con la clase.	30	Share with the class.

Consulte(n) el diccionario.	**31**	Look in the dictionary.	Conteste(n) las preguntas.	**48**	Answer the questions.
Busque(n) una palabra.	**32**	Look up a word.	Revise(n) sus respuestas/ sus contestaciones.	**49**	Check your answers.
Pronuncie(n) la palabra.	**33**	Pronounce the word.			
Lea(n) la definición.	**34**	Read the definition.	Entregue(n) los exámenes/las pruebas.	**50**	Collect the tests.
Copie(n) la palabra.	**35**	Copy the word.			
Trabaje(n) individualmente.	**36**	Work alone./ Do your own work.	Escoja(n)/Elija(n) la respuesta correcta.	**51**	Choose the correct answer.
Trabajen en parejas/pares.	**37**	Work with a partner.	Encierre(n) en un círculo la respuesta correcta.	**52**	Circle the correct answer.
Divídanse en equipos/ grupos pequeños.	**38**	Break up into small groups.	Llene(n) el espacio.	**53**	Fill in the blank.
Trabaje(n) en grupos/equipos.	**39**	Work in a group.	Rellene(n) el círculo.	**54**	Mark the answer sheet./ Bubble the answer.
Trabajen con toda la clase.	**40**	Work as a class.	Relacione(n)/Paree(n) las palabras.	**55**	Match the words.
Baje(n) las persianas.	**41**	Lower the shades.			
Apague(n) las luces.	**42**	Turn off the lights.	Subraye(n) la palabra.	**56**	Underline the word.
Mire(n) la pantalla.	**43**	Look at the screen.	Tache(n) la palabra.	**57**	Cross out the word.
Tome(n) notas.	**44**	Take notes.			
Prenda(n)/Ponga(n)/ Encienda(n)/las luces.	**45**	Turn on the lights.	Ordene(n)/acomode(n) las letras de la palabra.	**58**	Unscramble the word.
Saque(n) un papel.	**46**	Take out a piece of paper.	Ordene(n)/acomode(n) las palabras.	**59**	Put the words in order.
Pase(n) los exámenes/las pruebas.	**47**	Pass out the tests.	Escriba(n) en una hoja aparte.	**60**	Write on a separate sheet of paper.

You're the teacher! Give instructions to your students!

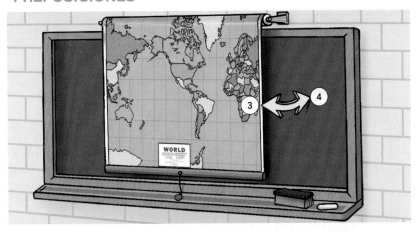

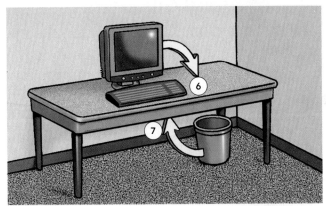

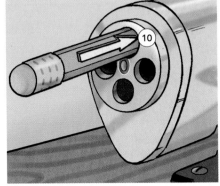

arriba	**1**	above	junto a	**5**	next to	en/dentro (de)	**10**	in
abajo	**2**	below	sobre	**6**	on			
			bajo/debajo (de)	**7**	under	entre	**11**	between
enfrente/	**3**	in front of						
delante (de)			a la izquierda de	**8**	to the left of			
detrás (de)	**4**	behind	a la derecha de	**9**	to the right of			

[1–10]
A. Where's the *clock*?
B. The *clock* is **above** the bulletin board.

[11]
A. Where's the *dictionary*?
B. The *dictionary* is **between** the *globe* and the *pencil sharpener*.

Tell about the classroom on page 4. Use the prepositions in this lesson.

Tell about your classroom.

HÁBITOS Y QUEHACERES DOMÉSTICOS I

me levanto	**1** get up		me desvisto	**11** get undressed
me baño/me ducho	**2** take a shower		me baño/me meto en la tina	**12** take a bath
me lavo/*me* cepillo los dientes	**3** brush *my** teeth		me acuesto	**13** go to bed
me afeito/me rasuro	**4** shave		me duermo	**14** sleep
me visto	**5** get dressed		hago/preparo el desayuno	**15** make breakfast
me lavo la cara	**6** wash *my** face		hago/preparo el almuerzo	**16** make lunch
me maquillo/me pinto	**7** put on makeup		hago/preparo la cena	**17** cook/make dinner
me cepillo el pelo/cabello	**8** brush *my** hair		desayuno	**18** eat/have breakfast
me peino el pelo/cabello	**9** comb *my** hair		almuerzo	**19** eat/have lunch
hago/tiendo la cama	**10** make the bed		ceno	**20** eat/have dinner

* my, his, her, our, your, their

A. What do you do every day?
B. I **get up**, I **take a shower**, and I **brush my teeth**.

A. What does he do every day?
B. He _____s, he _____s, and he _____s.

A. What does she do every day?
B. She _____s, she _____s, and she_____s.

What do you do every day? Make a list.

Interview some friends and tell about their everyday activities.

HÁBITOS Y QUEHACERES DOMÉSTICOS II

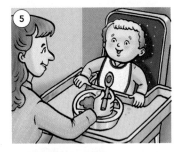

limpiar el apartamento/ departamento/la casa	**1** clean the apartment/ clean the house	estudiar	**8** study
lavar los platos/trastos	**2** wash the dishes	ir al trabajo	**9** go to work
lavar la ropa	**3** do the laundry	ir a la escuela/al colegio	**10** go to school
alisar con la plancha/planchar	**4** iron	manejar/conducir para ir al trabajo	**11** drive to work
darle de comer al bebé/ a la bebé/al nene/a la nena	**5** feed the baby	tomar el autobús/bus/ camión para ir a la escuela	**12** take the bus to school
darle de comer al gato	**6** feed the cat	trabajar	**13** work
pasear al perro	**7** walk the dog	salir del trabajo	**14** leave work
		ir a la tienda	**15** go to the store
		llegar a casa	**16** come home/get home

A. Hello. What are you doing?
B. I'm **clean**ing the **apartment**.

A. Hello, ... This is ....
What are you doing?

B. I'm _____ing. How about you?

A. I'm _____ing.

A. Are you going to _____ soon?

B. Yes. I'm going to _____ in a
little while.

What are you going to do tomorrow?
Make a list of everything you are
going to do.

ACTIVIDADES RECREATIVAS

ver la televisión/tele	**1** watch TV	tocar la guitarra	**9** play the guitar
oír/escuchar el/la radio	**2** listen to the radio	tocar el piano	**10** practice the piano
oír/escuchar música	**3** listen to music	hacer ejercicio	**11** exercise
leer un libro	**4** read a book	nadar	**12** swim
leer el periódico/diario	**5** read the newspaper	sembrar/plantar flores	**13** plant flowers
jugar	**6** play	usar la computadora/el ordenador	**14** use the computer
jugar barajas/a los naipes/las cartas	**7** play cards	escribir cartas	**15** write a letter
jugar baloncesto/básquetbol	**8** play basketball	descansar/relajarse	**16** relax

A. Hi. What are you doing?
B. I'm **watch**ing **TV**.

A. Hi, ... Are you
_____ing?

B. No, I'm not. I'm _____ing.

A. What's your (husband/wife/son/
daughter/. . .) doing?

B. He's/She's _____ing.

What leisure activities do you like to do?

What do your family members and
friends like to do?

EVERYDAY CONVERSATION

CONVERSACIONES DIARIAS

Greeting People   Saludos

Leave Taking   Despedidas

Hola.	**1** Hello. / Hi.	¿Qué hay de nuevo?/	**7** What's new?/
Buenos días.	**2** Good morning.	¿Qué te cuentas?	What's new with you?
Buenas tardes.	**3** Good afternoon.	Nada./No mucho.	**8** Not much. / Not too much.
Buenas noches./Buenas tardes.	**4** Good evening.	Adiós.	**9** Good-bye. / Bye.
¿Cómo está(s)?/¿Cómo te va?/	**5** How are you?/	Buenas noches.	**10** Good night.
¿Cómo le va?	How are you doing?	Hasta luego. /	**11** See you later. /
Bien./Bien, gracias.	**6** Fine. / Fine, thanks. / Okay.	Hasta pronto.	See you soon.

Introducing Yourself and Others   Presentaciones

Getting Someone's Attention
Expresiones para llamar la atención

Expressing Gratitude
Expresiones de agradecimiento

Saying You Don't Understand
Expresiones de duda

Calling Someone on the Telephone
En el teléfono

Hola. Me llamo	12	Hello. My name is ..../ Hi. I'm ....
Mucho gusto.	13	Nice to meet you.
El gusto es mío.	14	Nice to meet you, too.
Te/Le presento a	15	I'd like to introduce ..../ This is ....
Permiso./Disculpe(a).	16	Excuse me.
¿Puedo hacerle(te) una pregunta?	17	May I ask a question?
Gracias.	18	Thank you. / Thanks.
De nada./No hay de qué.	19	You're welcome.

¿Cómo?/No entiendo./ Disculpe(a). No entiendo.	20	I don't understand./ Sorry. I don't understand.
¿Repita(e), por favor?	21	Can you please repeat that?/ Can you please say that again?
Hola. Habla .... ¿Podría/Puedo hablar con ....?/ ¿Está ....?	22	Hello. This is .... May I please speak to ....?
Sí, un momento, por favor.	23	Yes. Hold on a moment.
Lo siento. .... no está aquí en este momento/ Lo siento. .... no se encuentra en este momento.	24	I'm sorry. .... isn't here right now.

Practice conversations with other students. Use all the expressions on pages 12 and 13.

EL ESTADO DEL TIEMPO

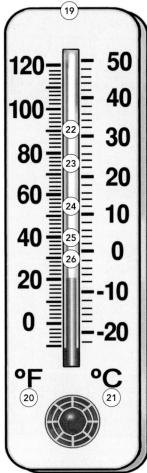

El estado del tiempo	Weather
está soleado	**1** sunny
está nublado/nuboso	**2** cloudy
está despejado/claro	**3** clear
hay bruma/calina	**4** hazy
hay niebla/neblina	**5** foggy
está contaminado	**6** smoggy
hace viento/está ventoso/sopla viento	**7** windy
está húmedo/pegajoso/bochornoso	**8** humid/muggy
llueve	**9** raining
llovizna	**10** drizzling
cae nieve/nieva	**11** snowing
graniza	**12** hailing
cellisquea/cae aguanieve/una helada	**13** sleeting

relámpagos/truenos/rayos	**14** lightning
tormenta de rayos/de truenos	**15** thunderstorm
tormenta de nieve	**16** snowstorm
tolvanera/polvareda	**17** dust storm
ola de calor	**18** heat wave

La temperatura	Temperature
termómetro	**19** thermometer
Fahrenheit	**20** Fahrenheit
Centígrados/Celsius	**21** Centigrade/Celsius
hace calor	**22** hot
es (un día/un clima) caluroso/cálido	**23** warm
hace fresco	**24** cool
hace frío	**25** cold
está helado	**26** freezing

[1–13]
A. What's the weather like?
B. It's _____.

[14–18]
A. What's the weather forecast?
B. There's going to be ___[14]___/
a ___[15–18]___.

[20–26]
A. How's the weather?
B. It's ___[22–26]___.
A. What's the temperature?
B. It's . . . degrees ___[20–21]___.

What's the weather like today? What's the temperature?   What's the weather forecast for tomorrow?

LOS NÚMEROS

Cardinal Numbers · Los números cardinales

0 zero	**11** eleven	**21** twenty-one	**101** one hundred (and) one
1 one	**12** twelve	**22** twenty-two	**102** one hundred (and) two
2 two	**13** thirteen	**30** thirty	**1,000** one thousand
3 three	**14** fourteen	**40** forty	**10,000** ten thousand
4 four	**15** fifteen	**50** fifty	**100,000** one hundred thousand
5 five	**16** sixteen	**60** sixty	**1,000,000** one million
6 six	**17** seventeen	**70** seventy	**1,000,000,000** one billion
7 seven	**18** eighteen	**80** eighty	
8 eight	**19** nineteen	**90** ninety	
9 nine	**20** twenty	**100** one hundred	
10 ten			

A. How old are you?
B. I'm _____ years old.

A. How many people are there in your family?
B. _____.

Ordinal Numbers · Los números ordinales (1°, 1ª; 2°, 2ª; etc.)

1st first	**11th** eleventh	**21st** twenty-first	**101st** one hundred (and) first
2nd second	**12th** twelfth	**22nd** twenty-second	**102nd** one hundred (and) second
3rd third	**13th** thirteenth	**30th** thirtieth	**1,000th** one thousandth
4th fourth	**14th** fourteenth	**40th** fortieth	**10,000th** ten thousandth
5th fifth	**15th** fifteenth	**50th** fiftieth	**100,000th** one hundred thousandth
6th sixth	**16th** sixteenth	**60th** sixtieth	**1,000,000th** one millionth
7th seventh	**17th** seventeenth	**70th** seventieth	**1,000,000,000th** one billionth
8th eighth	**18th** eighteenth	**80th** eightieth	
9th ninth	**19th** nineteenth	**90th** ninetieth	
10th tenth	**20th** twentieth	**100th** one hundredth	

A. What floor do you live on?
B. I live on the _____ floor.

A. Is this your first trip to our country?
B. No. It's my _____ trip.

How many students are there in your class?

How many people are there in your country?

What were the names of your teachers in elementary school?
(My *first*-grade teacher was Ms./Mrs./Mr. . . .)

TIME
LA HORA

two o'clock

two fifteen/
a quarter after *two*

two thirty/
half past *two*

two forty-five
a quarter to *three*

two oh five

two twenty/
twenty after *two*

two forty/
twenty to *three*

two fifty-five
five to *three*

A. What time is it?
B. It's _____.

A. What time does the movie
   begin?
B. At _____.

two A.M.

two P.M.

noon/
twelve noon

midnight/
twelve midnight

A. When does the train leave?
B. At _____.

A. What time will we arrive?
B. At _____.

Tell about your daily schedule:
   What do you do? When?
   (I get up at _____. I ....)

Do you usually have enough time to do
things, or do you "run out of time"?
Tell about it.

Tell about the use of time in different cultures or countries you know:
   Do people arrive on time for work? appointments? parties?
   Do trains and buses operate exactly on schedule?
   Do movies and sports events begin on time?
   Do workplaces use time clocks or timesheets to record employees' work hours?

EL DINERO

Coins
Moneda suelta/Suelto/Sencillo

Name	Value	Written as:	
1 penny	one cent	1¢	$ .01
2 nickel	five cents	5¢	$ .05
3 dime	ten cents	10¢	$ .10
4 quarter	twenty-five cents	25¢	$ .25
5 half dollar	fifty cents	50¢	$ .50
6 silver dollar	one dollar		$1.00

A. How much is a **penny** worth?
B. A **penny** is worth **one cent**.

A. *Soda* costs *ninety-five cents*. Do you have enough change?
B. Yes. I have a/two/three _____(s) and . . . .

Currency   Papel moneda

Name	We sometimes say:	Value	Written as:
7 (one-) dollar bill	a one	one dollar	$ 1.00
8 five-dollar bill	a five	five dollars	$ 5.00
9 ten-dollar bill	a ten	ten dollars	$ 10.00
10 twenty-dollar bill	a twenty	twenty dollars	$ 20.00
11 fifty-dollar bill	a fifty	fifty dollars	$ 50.00
12 (one-) hundred dollar bill	a hundred	one hundred dollars	$100.00

A. I'm going to the supermarket. Do you have any cash?
B. I have a **twenty-dollar bill**.
A. **Twenty dollars** is enough. Thanks.

A. Can you change a **five-dollar bill/a five**?
B. Yes. I have **five one-dollar bills/ five ones**.

Written as:	We say:
$1.30	a dollar and thirty cents
	a dollar thirty
$2.50	two dollars and fifty cents
	two fifty
$56.49	fifty-six dollars and forty-nine cents
	fifty-six forty-nine

Tell about some things you usually buy. What do they cost?

Name and describe the coins and currency in your country. What are they worth in U.S. dollars?

EL CALENDARIO

año	1	year
mes	2	month
semana	3	week
día	4	day
fin de semana	5	weekend

Los días de la semana **Days of the Week**

domingo	6	Sunday
lunes	7	Monday
martes	8	Tuesday
miércoles	9	Wednesday
jueves	10	Thursday
viernes	11	Friday
sábado	12	Saturday

Los meses del año **Months of the Year**

enero	13	January
febrero	14	February
marzo	15	March
abril	16	April
mayo	17	May
junio	18	June
julio	19	July
agosto	20	August
septiembre	21	September
octubre	22	October
noviembre	23	November
diciembre	24	December

3 de enero de 2012/ el tres de enero de dos mil doce	25	January 3, 2012 January third, two thousand twelve
cumpleaños	26	birthday
aniversario	27	anniversary
cita	28	appointment

A. What year is it?
B. It's _____.

[13–24]
A. What month is it?
B. It's _____.

[6–12]
A. What day is it?
B. It's _____.

A. What's today's date?
B. It's _____.

[26–28]
A. When is your _____?
B. It's on _____.

Which days of the week do you go to work/school?
(I go to work/school on _____.)

What do you do on the weekend?

What is your date of birth?
(I was born on ...... *month, day, year* ......)

What's your favorite day of the week? Why?

What's your favorite month of the year? Why?

EXPRESIONES DE TIEMPO Y LAS ESTACIONES

ayer	**1**	yesterday
hoy	**2**	today
mañana	**3**	tomorrow
por la mañana	**4**	morning
por la tarde	**5**	afternoon
por la tardecita/nochecita/al atardecer/al anochecer	**6**	evening
por la noche	**7**	night
ayer por la mañana	**8**	yesterday morning
ayer por la tarde	**9**	yesterday afternoon
ayer por la tardecita/nochecita/al atardecer/al anochecer	**10**	yesterday evening
anoche	**11**	last night
esta mañana	**12**	this morning
esta tarde	**13**	this afternoon
por la tardecita/nochecita/al atardecer/al anochecer	**14**	this evening
esta noche	**15**	tonight

mañana por la mañana	**16**	tomorrow morning
mañana por la tarde	**17**	tomorrow afternoon
mañana por la tardecita/nochecita/al atardecer/al anochecer	**18**	tomorrow evening
mañana por la noche	**19**	tomorrow night
la semana pasada	**20**	last week
esta semana	**21**	this week
la próxima semana/la semana entrante	**22**	next week
una vez a la semana	**23**	once a week
dos veces a la semana	**24**	twice a week
tres veces a la semana	**25**	three times a week
todos los días/a diario	**26**	every day

Las estaciones		**Seasons**
primavera	**27**	spring
verano	**28**	summer
otoño	**29**	fall/autumn
invierno	**30**	winter

What did you do yesterday morning/afternoon/evening? What did you do last night?

What are you going to do tomorrow morning/afternoon/evening/night?

What did you do last week?

What are your plans for next week?

How many times a week do you have English class?/go to the supermarket?/exercise?

What's your favorite season? Why?

TIPOS DE VIVIENDA Y COMUNIDADES

edificio de apartamentos/ departamentos	**1** apartment building	refugio/asilo para desvalidos/ albergue para desamparados	**9** shelter
casa	**2** house	hacienda/granja/finca	**10** farm
dúplex	**3** duplex/two-family house	rancho	**11** ranch
casas (de 2 o 3 plantas) en hileras	**4** townhouse/townhome	casa flotante	**12** houseboat
condominio/condo/piso	**5** condominium/condo	la ciudad	**13** the city
dormitorio/residencia estudiantil	**6** dormitory/dorm	los suburbios/las afueras	**14** the suburbs
casa prefabricada/móvil/rodante	**7** mobile home	el campo	**15** the country
asilo/casa de ancianos/de reposo	**8** nursing home	un pueblo/un poblado/una villa	**16** a town/village

A. Where do you live?

B. I live
- in a/an _____ [1–9] _____.
- on a _____ [10–12] _____.
- in _____ [13–16] _____.

[1–12]

A. Town Taxi Company.

B. Hello. Please send a taxi to
..... *(address)* .....

A. Is that a house or an apartment building?

B. It's a/an _____.

A. All right. We'll be there right away.

[1–12]

A. This is the Emergency Operator.

B. Please send an ambulance to
..... *(address)* .....

A. Is that a private home?

B. It's a/an _____.

A. What's your name and telephone number?

B. ....

Tell about people you know and where they live.

Discuss:
Who lives in dormitories?
Who lives in nursing homes?
Who lives in shelters?
Why?

LA SALA

librero/librería/estante para libros	**1** bookcase	mueble/unidad de pared	**15**	wall unit
foto/fotografía/retrato	**2** picture/photograph	bocina/altoparlante/altavoz	**16**	speaker
cuadro/pintura	**3** painting	estéreo/equipo estereofónico	**17**	stereo system
manto de la chimenea/del hogar	**4** mantel	revistero	**18**	magazine holder
hogar/chimenea	**5** fireplace	cojín	**19**	(throw) pillow
pantalla/rejilla de la chimenea	**6** fireplace screen	sofá	**20**	sofa/couch
DVD/reproductor de video digital	**7** DVD player	mata/planta	**21**	plant
televisor/TV/televisión/tele	**8** television/TV	mesa de centro	**22**	coffee table
videocasetera/videograbadora	**9** VCR/video cassette recorder	alfombra/alfombrilla/tapete	**23**	rug
		lámpara	**24**	lamp
pared/muro/tapia	**10** wall	pantalla	**25**	lampshade
cielo raso/techo	**11** ceiling	mesita/esquinera/mesilla	**26**	end table
cortinas	**12** drapes	piso	**27**	floor
ventana	**13** window	lámpara de pie	**28**	floor lamp
confidente/canapé/sofá	**14** loveseat	sillón/silla de brazos/butaca	**29**	armchair

A. Where are you?
B. I'm in the living room.
A. What are you doing?
B. I'm dusting* the **bookcase**.

* dusting/cleaning

A. You have a very nice living room!
B. Thank you.
A. Your _____ is/are beautiful!
B. Thank you for saying so.

A. Uh-oh! I just spilled coffee on your _____!
B. That's okay. Don't worry about it.

Tell about your living room.
(In my living room there's ....)

THE DINING ROOM
EL COMEDOR

mesa de comedor	**1**	(dining room) table	vajilla/vajilla de	**12**	china	pimentero	**22** pepper shaker
silla de comedor	**2**	(dining room) chair	porcelana/loza			mantel	**23** tablecloth
aparador	**3**	buffet	ensaladera	**13**	salad bowl	servilleta	**24** napkin
bandeja/charola	**4**	tray	sopera/	**14**	serving bowl	tenedor/trinche	**25** fork
tetera	**5**	teapot	fuente honda			plato	**26** plate
cafetera	**6**	coffee pot	bandeja	**15**	serving dish	cuchillo	**27** knife
azucarera	**7**	sugar bowl	florero/jarrón	**16**	vase	cuchara	**28** spoon
jarrita para la leche/crema	**8**	creamer	candela/vela	**17**	candle	plato hondo/tazón	**29** bowl
jarro(a)	**9**	pitcher	candelero	**18**	candlestick	taza	**30** mug
lámpara de araña/	**10**	chandelier	bandeja	**19**	platter	vaso	**31** glass
de techo/candil de techo			mantequillera	**20**	butter dish	taza	**32** cup
armario/alacena/	**11**	china cabinet	salero	**21**	salt shaker	plato pequeño/	**33** saucer
vitrina/chinero						platito/platillo	

A. This **dining room table** is very nice.
B. Thank you. It was a gift from my *grandmother*.*

*grandmother/grandfather/aunt/uncle/...

[In a store]

A. May I help you?
B. Yes, please. Do you have _____s?*
A. Yes. _____s* are right over there.
B. Thank you.

*With 12, use the singular.

[At home]

A. Look at this old _____ I just bought!
B. Where did you buy it?
A. At a yard sale. How do you like it?
B. It's VERY unusual!

Tell about your dining room.
(In my dining room there's
...............)

LA RECÁMARA/EL DORMITORIO

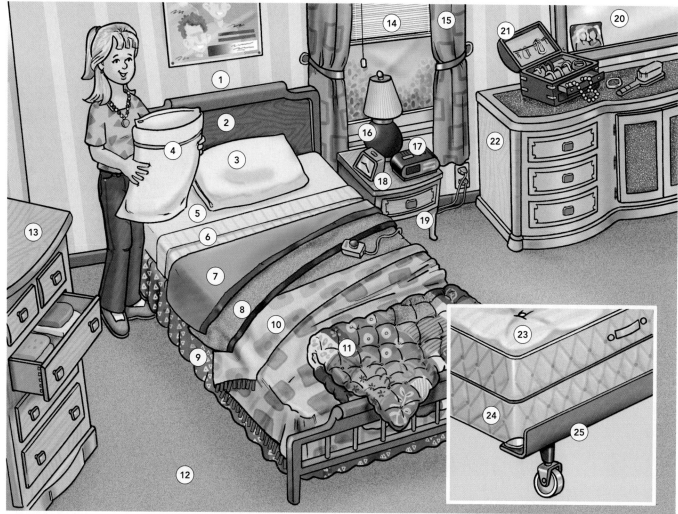

cama	**1**	bed	persianas	**14** blinds
cabecera	**2**	headboard	cortinas	**15** curtains
almohada	**3**	pillow	lámpara	**16** lamp
funda	**4**	pillowcase	despertador	**17** alarm clock
sábana ceñida	**5**	fitted sheet	radio reloj despertador	**18** clock radio
sábana	**6**	(flat) sheet	mesita/mesa de noche/buró	**19** night table/nightstand
manta/frazada/cobija/frisa	**7**	blanket	espejo	**20** mirror
manta/cobija/frisa eléctrica	**8**	electric blanket	joyero/alhajero	**21** jewelry box
volante/rodapié/pollera	**9**	dust ruffle	cómoda/tocador	**22** dresser/bureau
colcha/cubrecama/sobrecama	**10**	bedspread	colchón	**23** mattress
edredón/cobertor relleno	**11**	comforter/quilt	colchón de muelles	**24** box spring
alfombra	**12**	carpet	marco/armadura	**25** bed frame
chifonier/ropero/gavetero	**13**	chest (of drawers)		

A. Ooh! Look at that big bug!
B. Where?
A. It's on the **bed**!
B. I'LL get it.

[In a store]

A. Excuse me. I'm looking for
   a/an _____.*

B. We have some very nice _____s,
   and they're all on sale this week!

A. Oh, good!

* With 14 & 15, use: Excuse me. I'm looking for _____.

[In a bedroom]

A. Oh, no! I just lost my
   contact lens!

B. Where?

A. I think it's on the _____.

B. I'll help you look.

Tell about your bedroom.
(In my bedroom there's ....)

LA COCINA

refrigerador(a)/nevera	**1**	refrigerator	grifo/llave/pluma	**11**	faucet
congelador	**2**	freezer	fregadero/fregador	**12**	(kitchen) sink
cubo/bote de basura/	**3**	garbage pail	lavaplatos/lavavajillas	**13**	dishwasher
basurero/tinaco/zafacón			triturador de	**14**	(garbage)
batidora eléctrica/	**4**	(electric)	desperdicios		disposal
mezcladora eléctrica		mixer	trapo/paño/toalla de	**15**	dish towel
estante/armario/	**5**	cabinet	cocina/limpión		
gabinete			escurridor de	**16**	dish rack/
colgador para	**6**	paper towel	platos		dish drainer
papel toalla		holder	especiero/repisa	**17**	spice rack
envases/tarrones/	**7**	canister	para especias/		
recipientes para			condimentos		
harina, azúcar, té o sal			abrelatas eléctrico	**18**	(electric) can
mostrador	**8**	(kitchen)			opener
		counter	licuadora eléctrica	**19**	blender
jabón para el lavaplatos/	**9**	dishwasher	hornito/horno	**20**	toaster oven
lavavajillas		detergent	pastelero/tostador		
líquido de fregar/	**10**	dishwashing	horno microondas	**21**	microwave (oven)
lavar los platos		liquid	agarrador de ollas	**22**	potholder

tacho/hervidor	**23**	tea kettle
estufa/cocina	**24**	stove/range
quemador/fogón	**25**	burner
horno	**26**	oven
tostador/tostadora	**27**	toaster
cafetera	**28**	coffeemaker
compresor de	**29**	trash
basura		compactor
tablita/tabla para	**30**	cutting
picar/picador		board
libro de recetas	**31**	cookbook
de cocina		
molinillo/procesador	**32**	food
de alimentos		processor
silla	**33**	kitchen chair
mesa	**34**	kitchen table
individual/	**35**	placemat
mantelito		
individual		

A. I think we need a new **refrigerator**.
B. I think you're right.

[In a store]
A. Excuse me. Are your _____s still on sale?
B. Yes, they are. They're twenty percent off.

[In a kitchen]
A. When did you get this/these new _____(s)?
B. I got it/them last week.

Tell about your kitchen.
(In my kitchen there's ....)

Spanish	#	English	Spanish	#	English
osito	1	teddy bear	corral	16	playpen
intercomunicador/monitor de bebé	2	baby monitor/intercom	sonajero(a)/sonaja/maraquita	17	rattle
ropero/gavetero	3	chest (of drawers)	andadera/pollera/andador	18	walker
cuna	4	crib	cuna/cuna mecedora	19	cradle
orillero/paragolpes	5	crib bumper/bumper pad	carriola/cochecito	20	stroller
móvil	6	mobile	coche/carricoche	21	baby carriage
camilla/mesa para cambiar pañales	7	changing table	asiento para automóvil	22	car seat/safety seat
mameluco/pelele/pijamita de una pieza/mono	8	stretch suit	portabebé/sillita infantil	23	baby carrier
colchoneta/almohadilla para la mesa de cambiar pañales	9	changing pad	plato térmico para bebés	24	food warmer
			sillita elevadora	25	booster seat
cubo/bote/zafacón para pañales	10	diaper pail	portabebé/sillita infantil	26	baby seat
lamparita/lucecita de noche	11	night light	trona/silla alta	27	high chair
baúl para juguetes	12	toy chest	moisés/cuna portátil	28	portable crib
peluche	13	stuffed animal	bacinilla/bacenilla/bacín/bacinica	29	potty
muñeca	14	doll	portabebé/canguro	30	baby frontpack
columpio	15	swing	portabebé	31	baby backpack

A. Thank you for the **teddy bear**. It's a very nice gift.
B. You're welcome. Tell me, when are you due?
A. In a few more weeks.

A. That's a very nice _____.
Where did you get it?

B. It was a gift from ....

A. Do you have everything you need before the baby comes?

B. Almost everything. We're still looking for a/an _____ and a/an _____.

Tell about your country:
What things do people buy for a new baby?
Does a new baby sleep in a separate room, as in the United States?

EL BAÑO

Spanish	#	English
cesto/canasta	1	wastebasket
gabinete/mueble	2	vanity
jabón	3	soap
jabonera	4	soap dish
dispensador de jabón	5	soap dispenser
lavabo/lavamanos	6	(bathroom) sink
llave/pluma/grifo	7	faucet
botiquín/gabinete	8	medicine cabinet
espejo	9	mirror
vaso	10	cup
cepillo de dientes	11	toothbrush
portacepillos	12	toothbrush holder
cepillo de dientes eléctrico	13	electric toothbrush
secadora de cabello/pelo	14	hair dryer
repisa/tablilla	15	shelf
canasta/cesto para la ropa sucia	16	hamper

Spanish	#	English
ventilador	17	fan
toalla grande	18	bath towel
toalla para las manos	19	hand towel
toallita para la cara	20	washcloth/facecloth
barra para la toalla/colgador de toallas/toallero	21	towel rack
bomba destapacaños/desatascador	22	plunger
cepillo	23	toilet brush
papel higiénico/sanitario	24	toilet paper
desodorante/desodorizador/aromatizante ambiental	25	air freshener
excusado/retrete/inodoro	26	toilet

Spanish	#	English
asiento del excusado/redondela	27	toilet seat
regadera/ducha/baño	28	shower
regadera/ducha	29	shower head
cortina de baño	30	shower curtain
tina/bañera	31	bathtub/tub
parche antirresbalón/alfombrilla/estera de goma	32	rubber mat
desagüe/escurridor	33	drain
esponja	34	sponge
alfombra/alfombrilla/tapete de baño	35	bath mat
báscula/balanza	36	scale

A. Where's the **hair dryer**?
B. It's *on* the **vanity**.

A. Where's the **soap**?
B. It's *in* the **soap dish**.

A. Where's the **plunger**?
B. It's *next to* the **toilet brush**.

A. [Knock. Knock.] Did I leave my glasses in there?
B. Yes. They're on/in/next to the _____.

A. *Bobby*? You didn't clean up the bathroom! There's toothpaste on the _____, and there's powder all over the _____!
B. Sorry. I'll clean it up right away.

Tell about your bathroom. (In my bathroom there's ....)

EL EXTERIOR/FUERA DE LA CASA

El patio delantero	Front Yard	El patio trasero	Backyard
farol	1 lamppost	silla de jardín	17 lawn chair
buzón/casilla/casillero postal	2 mailbox	cortacésped/cortagrama	18 lawnmower
entrada	3 front walk	barraca/caseta para herramientas	19 tool shed
escalinatas	4 front steps	puerta con tela metálica	20 screen door
porche/portal/soportal	5 (front) porch	puerta trasera/de atrás	21 back door
contrapuerta	6 storm door	agarrador/tirador/perilla	22 door knob
puerta principal	7 front door	patio/cubierta/veranda	23 deck
timbre	8 doorbell	asador/parrilla/barbacoa	24 barbecue/ (outdoor) grill
luz de la entrada	9 (front) light	patio	25 patio
ventana	10 window	canal de desagüe/gotera	26 gutter
malla/tela metálica/mosquitero	11 (window) screen	desagüe/caño	27 drainpipe
contraventana/postigo	12 shutter	antena parabólica	28 satellite dish
tejado/techo	13 roof	antena de televisión	29 TV antenna
garaje/estacionamiento/cochera	14 garage	chimenea	30 chimney
puerta del garaje/ estacionamiento/de la cochera	15 garage door	puerta lateral	31 side door
entrada para el coche/carro	16 driveway	cerca(o)/valla	32 fence

A. When are you going to repair the **lamppost**?
B. I'm going to repair it next Saturday.

[On the telephone]
A. Harry's Home Repairs.
B. Hello. Do you fix _____s?
A. No, we don't.
B. Oh, okay. Thank you.

[At work on Monday morning]
A. What did you do this weekend?
B. Nothing much. I repaired my _____ and my _____.

Do you like to repair things?
What things can you repair yourself?
What things can't you repair? Who repairs them?

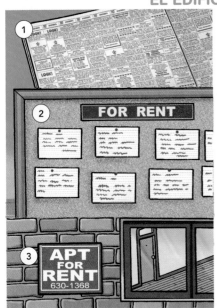

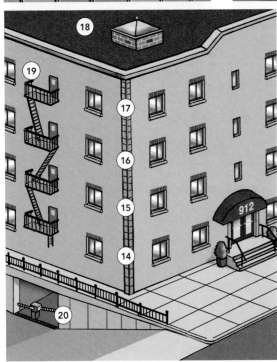

Búsqueda de apartamentos/ departamentos	**Looking for an Apartment**	La mudanza	**Moving In**	garaje/estacionamiento/ aparcamiento con techo	**20**	parking garage
anuncios/clasificados para apartamentos/ departamentos	**1** apartment ads/ classified ads	camión de mudanzas	**8** moving truck/ moving van	balcón	**21**	balcony
tablero/mural/ tablón de anuncios	**2** apartment listings	vecino(a)	**9** neighbor	patio	**22**	courtyard
letrero de vacante	**3** vacancy sign	conserje	**10** building manager	estacionamiento/ aparcamiento/ parqueadero	**23**	parking lot
		portero(a)	**11** doorman	espacio para estacionarse	**24**	parking space
Firma del contrato	**Signing a Lease**	llave	**12** key	piscina/alberca/ pileta	**25**	swimming pool
arrendatario(a)/ inquilino(a)	**4** tenant	cerradura/chapa	**13** lock	bañera/ tina de hidromasaje/ de terapia/tina-jacuzzi	**26**	whirlpool
arrendador(a)/ casero(a)	**5** landlord	primer piso	**14** first floor			
		segundo piso	**15** second floor			
contrato de alquiler	**6** lease	tercer piso	**16** third floor	basurero	**27**	trash bin
depósito	**7** security deposit	cuarto piso	**17** fourth floor	aire acondicionado	**28**	air conditioner
		techo	**18** roof			
		escalera de emergencia	**19** fire escape			

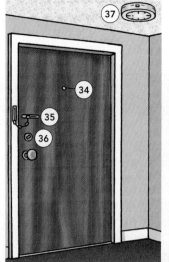

Vestíbulo/Lobby	**Lobby**
interfono/portero automático/eléctrico	**29** intercom/ speaker
timbre/chicharra	**30** buzzer
casilla/casillero postal/buzón	**31** mailbox
ascensor/elevador	**32** elevator
escalera	**33** stairway

Puerta de entrada	**Doorway**
mirilla	**34** peephole
cadena de seguridad/ antirrobo	**35** (door) chain
cerrojo dormido/ cerrojo/seguro	**36** dead-bolt lock
detector de humo	**37** smoke detector

Pasillo/Corredor	**Hallway**
salida/escalera de emergencia	**38** fire exit/ emergency stairway
alarma contra incendios	**39** fire alarm
extintor/sistema de aspersión contra incendios	**40** sprinkler system
superintendente/conserje/encargado(a)	**41** superintendent
disparador/tobogán/conducto/ chuta para la basura	**42** garbage chute/ trash chute

Sótano	**Basement**
depósito	**43** storage room
cuarto de almacenaje	**44** storage locker
lavandería/cuarto de lavado/lavadero	**45** laundry room
verja de seguridad	**46** security gate

[19–46]
A. Is there a **fire escape**?
B. Yes, there is. Do you want to see the apartment?
A. Yes, I do.

[19–46]

[Renting an apartment]
A. Let me show you around.
B. Okay.
A. This is the _____, and here's the _____.
B. I see.

[19–46]

[On the telephone]
A. Mom and Dad? I found an apartment.
B. Good. Tell us about it.
A. It has a/an _____ and a/an _____.
B. That's nice. Does it have a/an _____?
A. Yes, it does.

Do you or someone you know live in an apartment building? Tell about it.

PROBLEMAS DE MANTENIMIENTO Y REPARACIÓN DE LA CASA

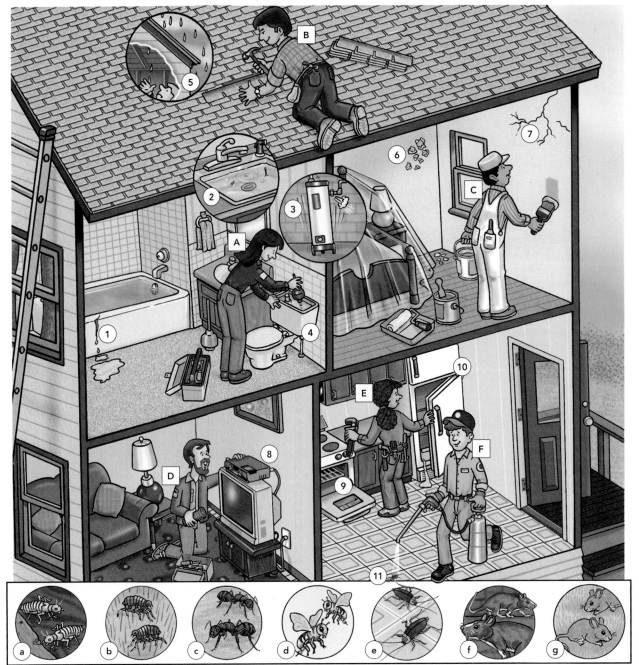

plomero(a)/fontanero(a)	**A plumber**	**reparador(a)/mecánico(a)**	**E appliance repairperson**
El agua de la tina/bañera se sale.	**1** The bathtub is leaking.	La estufa no funciona.	**9** The stove isn't working.
El lavabo/lavamanos está tapado.	**2** The sink is clogged.	El refrigerador está averiado/descompuesto.	**10** The refrigerator is broken.
El calentador de agua no funciona.	**3** The hot water heater isn't working.		
El excusado/retrete/inodoro/ está descompuesto.	**4** The toilet is broken.	**fumigador(a)**	**F exterminator/ pest control specialist**
reparador(a) de techos	**B roofer**	Hay ___ en la cocina.	**11** There are ___ in the kitchen.
El techo tiene goteras.	**5** The roof is leaking.	carcomas/comejenes/ termitas/termes	**a** termites
pintor(a)	**C (house) painter**	pulgas	**b** fleas
La pintura se está descascarillando.	**6** The paint is peeling.	hormigas	**c** ants
La pared está cuarteada.	**7** The wall is cracked.	abejas	**d** bees
compañía de televisión por cable	**D cable TV company**	cucarachas	**e** cockroaches
La señal no funciona.	**8** The cable TV isn't working.	ratas	**f** rats
		ratones	**g** mice

cerrajero(a)	**G**	**locksmith**		ayudante	**J**	**home repairperson/"handyman"**
La cerradura está rota.	**12**	The lock is broken.		Los azulejos del baño están flojos.	**17**	The tiles in the bathroom are loose.
electricista	**H**	**electrician**		carpintero(a)	**K**	**carpenter**
La luz de la entrada no prende/se enciende.	**13**	The front light doesn't go on.		Los escalones están rotos.	**18**	The steps are broken.
El timbre de la puerta no suena.	**14**	The doorbell doesn't ring.		La puerta no se abre.	**19**	The door doesn't open.
No hay luz en la sala.	**15**	The power is out in the living room.		servicio de calefacción y aire acondicionado	**L**	**heating and air conditioning service**
desollinador(a)	**I**	**chimneysweep**		La calefacción está descompuesta/rota.	**20**	The heating system is broken.
La chimenea está sucia.	**16**	The chimney is dirty.		El aire acondicionado no funciona.	**21**	The air conditioning isn't working.

A. What's the matter?
B. _____[1–21]_____.
A. I think we should call a/an _____[A–L]_____.

[1–21]

A. I'm having a problem in my apartment/house.
B. What's the problem?
A. _____.

[A–L]

A. Can you recommend a good _____?
B. Yes. You should call ....

What do you do when there are problems in your home? Do you fix things yourself, or do you call someone?

LA LIMPIEZA DE LA CASA

barrer el piso	**A**	sweep the floor
pasar la aspiradora	**B**	vacuum
trapear/fregar el piso	**C**	mop the floor
lavar las ventanas	**D**	wash the windows
sacudir/quitar el polvo	**E**	dust
encerar el piso	**F**	wax the floor
lustrar los muebles	**G**	polish the furniture
limpiar el (cuarto de) baño	**H**	clean the bathroom
sacar la basura	**I**	take out the garbage

escoba	**1**	broom
recogedor	**2**	dustpan
escobilla	**3**	whisk broom
barredor de alfombra	**4**	carpet sweeper
aspiradora	**5**	vacuum (cleaner)
accesorios para la aspiradora	**6**	vacuum cleaner attachments
bolsa para la aspiradora	**7**	vacuum cleaner bag
aspiradora de mano	**8**	hand vacuum

trapeador seco/mapo/mopa/mechudo	**9**	(dust) mop/(dry) mop
trapeador de esponja	**10**	(sponge) mop
trapeador/fregona	**11**	(wet) mop
papel toalla/papel absorbente	**12**	paper towels
líquido limpiaventanas	**13**	window cleaner
amoniaco/amoníaco	**14**	ammonia
limpión/trapo para limpiar/sacudir	**15**	dust cloth
plumero/sacudidor	**16**	feather duster
cera para el piso	**17**	floor wax
cera para muebles	**18**	furniture polish
limpiador en polvo/farola	**19**	cleanser
cepillo para limpiar el inodoro	**20**	scrub brush
esponja	**21**	sponge
cubo/cubeta	**22**	bucket/pail
basurero/bote para la basura/ tinaco/zafacón	**23**	trash can/ garbage can
contenedor de artículos renovables/reciclables	**24**	recycling bin

[A–I]
A. What are you doing?
B. I'm **sweep**ing **the floor**.

[1–24]
A. I can't find the **broom**.
B. Look over there!

[1–12, 15, 16, 20–24]
A. Excuse me. Do you sell _____(s)?
B. Yes. They're at the back of the store.
A. Thanks.

[13, 14, 17–19]
A. Excuse me. Do you sell _____?
B. Yes. It's at the back of the store.
A. Thanks.

What household cleaning chores do people do in your home?
What things do they use?

MATERIALES DE MANTENIMIENTO

metro/vara de una yarda	**1** yardstick	lubricante/aceite tres en uno	**15** oil
matamoscas	**2** fly swatter	goma de pegar/pegamento	**16** glue
bomba/destapacaños	**3** plunger	guantes de jardín	**17** work gloves
linterna/lámpara/faro de mano	**4** flashlight	insecticida/aerosol para	**18** bug spray/
extensión	**5** extension cord	matar insectos	insect spray
cinta de medir	**6** tape measure	matacucarachas	**19** roach killer
escalera	**7** step ladder	lija	**20** sandpaper
trampa para ratones/ratas/ratonera	**8** mousetrap	pintura	**21** paint
cinta para empacar/para pintores/ masking tape	**9** masking tape	disolvente/trementina/ aguarrás/terpina	**22** paint thinner
cinta aisladora/aislante/de empalme	**10** electrical tape	brocha	**23** paintbrush/brush
cinta gris para sellar	**11** duct tape	bandeja para la pintura	**24** paint pan
baterías/pilas	**12** batteries	rodillo	**25** paint roller
foco/bombilla(o)	**13** lightbulbs/bulbs	pistola para pintar	**26** spray gun
fusibles	**14** fuses		

A. I can't find the **yardstick**!
B. Look in the utility cabinet.
A. I did.
B. Oh! Wait a minute! I lent the **yardstick** to the neighbors.

[1–8, 23–26]

A. I'm going to the hardware store.
   Can you think of anything we need?

B. Yes. We need a/an _____.

A. Oh, that's right.

[9–22]

A. I'm going to the hardware store.
   Can you think of anything we need?

B. Yes. We need _____.

A. Oh, that's right.

What home supplies do you have?
How and when do you use each
one?

TOOLS AND HARDWARE
HERRAMIENTAS Y MATERIALES DE FERRETERÍA

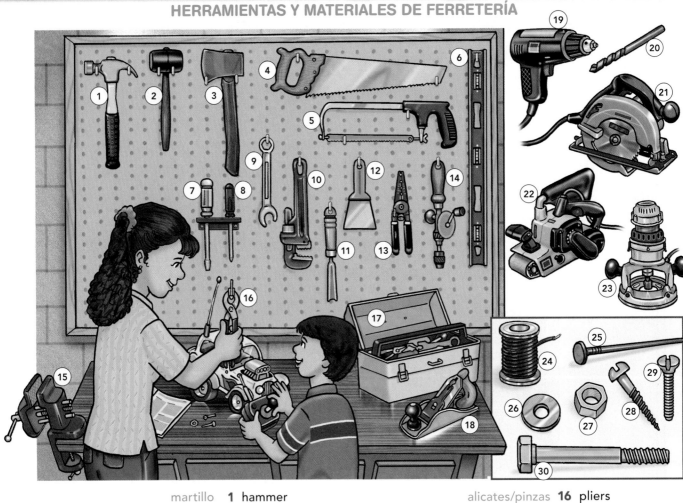

martillo	**1**	hammer	alicates/pinzas	**16** pliers
mazo de hule	**2**	mallet	caja de herramientas	**17** toolbox
hacha	**3**	ax	cepillo de carpintero/garlopa	**18** plane
serrucho	**4**	saw/handsaw	taladro eléctrico/barrena	**19** electric drill
sierra/serrucho	**5**	hacksaw	barrena/broca	**20** (drill) bit
nivel	**6**	level	sierra circular/cortadora eléctrica	**21** circular saw/
destornillador/desarmador	**7**	screwdriver		power saw
destornillador/de estrías/de cruz/	**8**	Phillips	lijadora eléctrica	**22** power sander
Phillips/desarmador de cruz		screwdriver	fresa/fresadora/	**23** router
llave/llave para tuercas	**9**	wrench	ranuradora eléctrica	
llave inglesa/	**10**	monkey wrench/	alambre	**24** wire
de cremallera/perico		pipe wrench	clavo	**25** nail
cincel	**11**	chisel	arandela/rondana	**26** washer
raspador/espátula	**12**	scraper	tuerca	**27** nut
pelador de cables	**13**	wire stripper	tornillo para madera	**28** wood screw
taladro de mano/taladradora	**14**	hand drill	tornillo para metal	**29** machine screw
torno/tornillo/prensa de banco	**15**	vise	perno	**30** bolt

A. Can I borrow your **hammer**?
B. Sure.
A. Thanks.

* *With 25–30, use:* Could I borrow some _____s?

[1–15, 17–24]

A. Where's the _____?

B. It's on/next to/near/over/under the _____.

[16, 25–30]

A. Where are the _____s?

B. They're on/next to/near/over/under the _____.

Do you like to work with tools? What tools do you have in your home?

cortar el césped/la grama/el zacate	**A**	mow the lawn
sembrar/plantar vegetales	**B**	plant vegetables
sembrar/plantar flores	**C**	plant flowers
regar las flores	**D**	water the flowers
barrer las hojas	**E**	rake leaves
recortar el seto	**F**	trim the hedge
podar los arbustos	**G**	prune the bushes
deshierbar	**H**	weed

cortacésped/cortagrama	**1**	lawnmower
lata/tanque de gasolina	**2**	gas can
cortadora de cordón/de línea	**3**	line trimmer
pala	**4**	shovel
semillas de vegetales	**5**	vegetable seeds
azadón/azada	**6**	hoe

palita de mano/jardín/palustre	**7**	trowel
carretilla	**8**	wheelbarrow
abono/fertilizante	**9**	fertilizer
manguera (de jardín)	**10**	(garden) hose
pitón/boca/boquilla	**11**	nozzle
rociador/regador/aspersor	**12**	sprinkler
regadera	**13**	watering can
rastrillo	**14**	rake
soplahojas	**15**	leaf blower
bolsa para la maleza/recortes de jardín	**16**	yard waste bag
tijeras de jardín	**17**	(hedge) clippers
podadora eléctrica	**18**	hedge trimmer
tijeras podadoras	**19**	pruning shears
escarda/escardilla(o)/almocafre	**20**	weeder

[A–H]
A. Hi! Are you busy?
B. Yes. I'm **mow**ing **the lawn**.

[1–20]
A. What are you looking for?
B. The **lawnmower**.

[A–H]
A. What are you going to do tomorrow?
B. I'm going to _____.

[1–20]
A. Can I borrow your _____?
B. Sure.

Do you ever work with any of these tools? Which ones? What do you do with them?

EN EL VECINDARIO I

panadería/pastelería/repostería	**1** bakery	guardería infantil	**9** child-care center / day-care center
banco	**2** bank	tintorería/lavandería en seco	**10** cleaners / dry cleaners
barbería/peluquería	**3** barber shop	clínica/consultorio	**11** clinic
librería	**4** book store	tienda de ropa	**12** clothing store
terminal de autobuses/camiones	**5** bus station	cafetería/café/cafetín	**13** coffee shop
confitería/tienda de confites/dulces	**6** candy store	tienda de computadoras/ordenadores	**14** computer store
agencia/distribuidora de carros	**7** car dealership	tienda/tiendita de abarrotes/colmado	**15** convenience store
puesto/tienda de tarjetas/ papelería	**8** card store	centro de fotocopias	**16** copy center

delicatessen/charcutería	17	delicatessen/deli
almacén	18	department store
tienda de descuentos	19	discount store
churrería/tienda de donas	20	donut shop
farmacia/droguería	21	drug store/pharmacy
tienda de electrónicos	22	electronics store
óptica/oculista	23	eye-care center/optician
cafetería/bar/merendero	24	fast-food restaurant
floristería/florería/florista	25	flower shop/florist
mueblería	26	furniture store
gasolinera/surtidor/estación/ bomba de gasolina	27	gas station/ service station
tienda/abarrotería/ bodega/colmado	28	grocery store

A. Where are you going?
B. I'm going to the **bakery**.

A. Hi! How are you today?
B. Fine. Where are you going?
A. To the _____. How about you?
B. I'm going to the _____.

A. Oh, no! I can't find my wallet/purse!
B. Did you leave it at the _____?
A. Maybe I did.

Which of these places are in your neighborhood?
(In my neighborhood there's a/an ....)

EN EL VECINDARIO II

salón de belleza/peluquería	**1**	hair salon
ferretería	**2**	hardware store
gimnasio/club	**3**	health club
hospital	**4**	hospital
hotel	**5**	hotel
heladería/refresquería/sorbetería	**6**	ice cream shop
joyería	**7**	jewelry store
lavandería pública/ automática/lavamático	**8**	laundromat
biblioteca	**9**	library
almacén/tienda de ropa de maternidad	**10**	maternity shop
motel	**11**	motel
cine	**12**	movie theater
almacén/tienda de música	**13**	music store
manicurista	**14**	nail salon
parque	**15**	park
tienda de mascotas	**16**	pet shop/ pet store

fotocentro/centro de revelado	**17** photo shop	galería/centro comercial	**23** (shopping) mall
pizzería	**18** pizza shop	supermercado	**24** supermarket
oficina de correos	**19** post office	juguetería	**25** toy store
restaurante	**20** restaurant	estación de trenes	**26** train station
escuela/instituto/colegio	**21** school	agencia de viajes	**27** travel agency
zapatería	**22** shoe store	videocentro	**28** video store

A. Where's the **hair salon**?
B. It's right over there.

A. Is there a/an _____ nearby?
B. Yes. There's a/an _____
   around the corner.
A. Thanks.

A. Excuse me. Where's the _____?
B. It's down the street, next to the _____.
A. Thank you.

Which of these places are in your neighborhood?
(In my neighborhood there's a/an
.............)

THE CITY
LA CIUDAD

juzgado/corte/tribunal	1	courthouse
taxi	2	taxi/cab/taxicab
parada de taxis/piquera	3	taxi stand
taxista/conductor/chofer de taxi	4	taxi driver/cab driver
hidrante/boca de riego	5	fire hydrant
basurero	6	trash container
palacio de gobierno/ayuntamiento/alcaldía	7	city hall
alarma contra incendios	8	fire alarm box
buzón	9	mailbox
alcantarilla/desagüe/drenaje	10	sewer
estación de policía	11	police station
cárcel	12	jail
acera/banqueta	13	sidewalk
calle	14	street
alumbrado/lámpara/farol/poste de luz	15	street light
estacionamiento/parqueadero/aparcamiento	16	parking lot
inspector(a) de estacionómetro/parquímetro	17	meter maid
estacionómetro/parquímetro	18	parking meter
camión de la basura	19	garbage truck
subterráneo/metro	20	subway
estación del metro	21	subway station

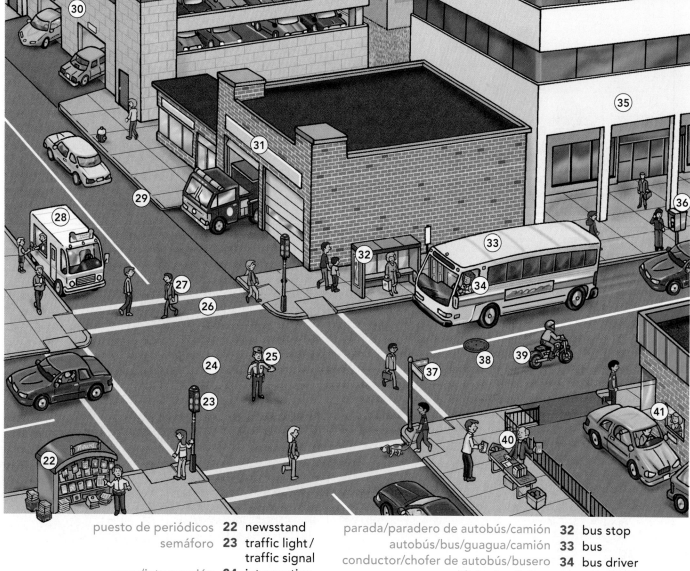

puesto de periódicos	**22**	newsstand
semáforo	**23**	traffic light / traffic signal
cruce/intersección	**24**	intersection
policía	**25**	police officer
cruce de peatones/línea de seguridad	**26**	crosswalk
peatón(a)	**27**	pedestrian
repartidor/carretilla de helados/ mantecados	**28**	ice cream truck
cuneta/empalme/bordillo/encintado	**29**	curb
estacionamiento/ parqueadero de niveles	**30**	parking garage
estación de bomberos/bomba	**31**	fire station
parada/paradero de autobús/camión	**32**	bus stop
autobús/bus/guagua/camión	**33**	bus
conductor/chofer de autobús/busero	**34**	bus driver
edificio de oficinas	**35**	office building
teléfono público	**36**	public telephone
letrero con el nombre de la calle	**37**	street sign
boca de la alcantarilla/ del desagüe/del drenaje	**38**	manhole
motocicleta/moto	**39**	motorcycle
buhonero/vendedor ambulante	**40**	street vendor
cajero/ventanilla de servicio rápido	**41**	drive-through window

A. Where's the _____?
B. On/In/Next to/Between/Across from/ In front of/Behind/Under/Over the _____.

[An Election Speech]

If I am elected mayor, I'll take care of all the problems in our city. We need to do something about our _____s. We also need to do something about our _____s. And look at our _____s! We REALLY need to do something about THEM! We need a new mayor who can solve these problems. If I am elected mayor, we'll be proud of our _____s, _____s, and _____s again! Vote for me!

Go to an intersection in your city or town. What do you see? Make a list. Then tell about it.

DESCRIPCIÓN FÍSICA DE LAS PERSONAS/LA GENTE

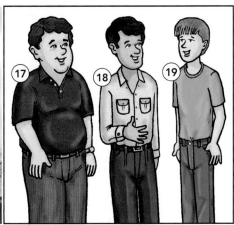

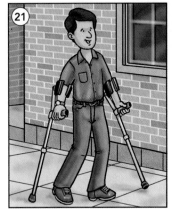

Spanish	#	English
niño(a)/niños(as)	1	**child–children**
bebé/nene(a)	2	baby/infant
niño(a) que empieza a hacer pinitos/a andar	3	toddler
niño	4	boy
niña	5	girl
adolescente	6	teenager
adulto	7	**adult**
hombre–hombres	8	man–men
mujer–mujeres	9	woman–women
persona mayor/ de edad avanzada/ de la tercera edad/ anciano(a)	10	senior citizen/ elderly person

Spanish	#	English
edad		**age**
joven	11	young
maduro(a)/cuarentón(a)/ cincuentón(a)	12	middle-aged
mayor/de edad avanzada	13	old/elderly
estatura		**height**
alto(a)	14	tall
estatura promedio/ mediana	15	average height
bajo(a)	16	short
peso		**weight**
gordo(a)	17	heavy
de peso mediano	18	average weight
delgado(a)/fino(a)/ esbelto(a)	19	thin/slim

Spanish	#	English
embarazada/ encinta	20	pregnant
discapacitado(a)	21	physically challenged
ciego(a)/tener problemas de la vista	22	vision impaired
sordo(a)/tener problemas de oído	23	hearing impaired

Descripción del pelo/cabello		Describing Hair			negro	**30**	black
largo	**24**	long			café/castaño/marrón	**31**	brown
hasta el hombro	**25**	shoulder length			rubio/mono/güero	**32**	blond
corto	**26**	short			pelirrojo	**33**	red
					cano/canoso/gris	**34**	gray
lacio/liso	**27**	straight					
ondulado	**28**	wavy			calvo(a)/pelón(a)	**35**	bald
rizado/ensortijado/crespo/	**29**	curly			barba	**36**	beard
encrespado/chino/grifo					bigote/mostacho	**37**	mustache

A. Tell me about *your brother*.
B. *He's a tall heavy boy* with *short curly brown* hair.

A. What does *your new boss* look like?
B. *She's average height*, and *she* has *long straight black* hair.

A. Can you describe *the person*?
B. *He's a tall thin middle-aged man*.
A. Anything else?
B. Yes. *He's bald*, and *he* has *a mustache*.

A. Can you describe *your grandmother*?
B. *She's a short thin elderly person* with *long wavy gray* hair.
A. Anything else?
B. Yes. *She's hearing impaired*.

Tell about yourself.

Tell about people in your family.

Tell about your favorite actor or actress or other famous person.

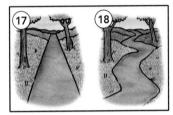

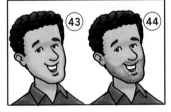

nuevo(a) – viejo(a)	1–2	new – old
joven – viejo(a)	3–4	young – old
alto(a) – bajo(a)	5–6	tall – short
largo(a) – corto(a)	7–8	long – short
grande – chiquito(a)/pequeño(a)	9–10	large/big – small/little
rápido(a) – lento(a)	11–12	fast – slow
gordo(a) - delgado(a)/flaco(a)	13–14	heavy/fat – thin/skinny
pesado(a) – liviano(a)	15–16	heavy – light
recto(a) – sinuoso(a)/curvo(a)	17–18	straight – crooked
liso(a) – rizado(a)/encrespado(a)	19–20	straight – curly
ancho(a) – angosto(a)/estrecho(a)	21–22	wide – narrow
grueso(a) – delgado(a)	23–24	thick – thin
oscuro(a) – claro(a)/con luz	25–26	dark – light
alto(a) – bajo(a)	27–28	high – low
flojo(a)/holgado(a) – estrecho(a)/apretado(a)	29–30	loose – tight
bueno(a) – malo(a)	31–32	good – bad
caliente – frío(a)	33–34	hot – cold
ordenado(a) – desordenado(a)	35–36	neat – messy
limpio(a) – sucio(a)	37–38	clean – dirty
suave – duro(a)	39–40	soft – hard
fácil – difícil/duro(a)	41–42	easy – difficult/hard
terso(a)/liso(a) – áspero(a)	43–44	smooth – rough
escandaloso(a) – quieto(a)/tranquilo(a)/callado(a)	45–46	noisy/loud – quiet
casado(a) – soltero(a)	47–48	married – single

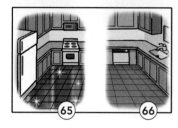   

rico(a) – pobre	**49–50**	rich/wealthy – poor	elegante – sencillo(a)	**63–64** fancy – plain
bonito(a) – feo(a)	**51–52**	pretty/beautiful – ugly	brillante – opaco(a)	**65–66** shiny – dull
guapo(a) – feo(a)	**53–54**	handsome – ugly	afilado(a) – romo(a)/desafilado(a)	**67–68** sharp – dull
mojado(a) – seco(a)	**55–56**	wet – dry	cómodo(a) –	**69–70** comfortable –
abierto(a) – cerrado(a)	**57–58**	open – closed	incómodo(a)	uncomfortable
lleno(a) – vacío(a)	**59–60**	full – empty	honesto(a)/honrado(a) –	**71–72** honest – dishonest
caro(a) – barato(a)	**61–62**	expensive – cheap/inexpensive	deshonesto(a)	

[1–2]
A. Is your car **new**?
B. No. It's **old**.

1–2	Is your car _____?	25–26	Is the room _____?	49–50	Is your uncle _____?
3–4	Is he _____?	27–28	Is the bridge _____?	51–52	Is the witch _____?
5–6	Is your sister _____?	29–30	Are the pants _____?	53–54	Is the pirate _____?
7–8	Is his hair _____?	31–32	Are your neighbor's children _____?	55–56	Are the clothes _____?
9–10	Is their dog _____?	33–34	Is the water _____?	57–58	Is the door _____?
11–12	Is the train _____?	35–36	Is your desk _____?	59–60	Is the pitcher _____?
13–14	Is your friend _____?	37–38	Are the windows _____?	61–62	Is that restaurant _____?
15–16	Is the box _____?	39–40	Is the mattress _____?	63–64	Is the dress _____?
17–18	Is the road _____?	41–42	Is the homework _____?	65–66	Is your kitchen floor _____?
19–20	Is her hair _____?	43–44	Is your skin _____?	67–68	Is the knife _____?
21–22	Is the tie _____?	45–46	Is your neighbor _____?	69–70	Is the chair _____?
23–24	Is the line _____?	47–48	Is your sister _____?	71–72	Is he _____?

A. Tell me about your ....
B. He's/She's/It's/They're _____.

A. Do you have a/an _____ ....?
B. No. I have a/an _____ ....

Describe yourself.

Describe a person you know.

Describe some things in your home.

Describe some things in your community.

DESCRIPCIÓN DE ESTADOS FÍSICOS Y EMOTIVOS/DE ÁNIMO

estar cansado(a)	**1**	tired
tener sueño/estar soñoliento(a)	**2**	sleepy
estar agotado(a)	**3**	exhausted
estar enfermo(a)	**4**	sick/ill
tener calor	**5**	hot
tener frío	**6**	cold
tener hambre	**7**	hungry
tener sed	**8**	thirsty

estar lleno(a)/satisfecho(a)	**9**	full
estar contento(a)	**10**	happy
estar triste	**11**	sad/unhappy
sentirse desgraciado(a)/infeliz	**12**	miserable
estar entusiasmado(a)/emocionado (a)	**13**	excited
estar decepcionado(a)	**14**	disappointed
estar contrariado(a)	**15**	upset
estar molesto(a)/contrariado(a)	**16**	annoyed

estar enfadado(a)/disgustado(a)/enojado(a)	**17** angry/mad
estar furioso(a)	**18** furious
estar harto(a)/colmado(a)/asqueado(a)	**19** disgusted
estar frustrado(a)	**20** frustrated
estar sorprendido(a)	**21** surprised
estar atónito(a)/turbado(a)/consternado(a)/ estupefacto(a)/pasmado(a)	**22** shocked
sentirse solo(a)	**23** lonely
echar de menos/tener morriña/nostalgia	**24** homesick
estar nervioso(a)	**25** nervous

estar preocupado(a)	**26** worried
estar asustado(a)/tener miedo	**27** scared/afraid
estar aburrido(a)	**28** bored
estar orgulloso(a)	**29** proud
estar avergonzado(a)	**30** embarrassed
estar celoso(a)	**31** jealous
estar confundido(a)/desconcertado(a)/ enredado(a)/hecho(a) un lío	**32** confused

A. You look _____.
B. I am. I'm VERY _____.

A. Are you _____?
B. No. Why do you ask? Do I LOOK _____?
A. Yes. You do.

What makes you happy? sad? mad?

What do you do when you feel nervous? annoyed?

Do you ever feel embarrassed? When?

LAS FRUTAS

manzana	**1** apple	higo	**12** fig
durazno/melocotón	**2** peach	coco	**13** coconut
pera	**3** pear	aguacate	**14** avocado
banana/guineo/plátano	**4** banana	melón	**15** cantaloupe
plátano verde/grande	**5** plantain	melón verde/dulce/chino/	**16** honeydew
ciruela	**6** plum	de Indias	(melon)
albaricoque/	**7** apricot	sandía/melón de agua	**17** watermelon
chabacano/damasco		piña	**18** pineapple
nectarina	**8** nectarine	toronja/pomelo	**19** grapefruit
kiwi	**9** kiwi	lima/limón (amarillo)	**20** lemon
papaya/fruta bomba	**10** papaya	lima/limón (verde)	**21** lime
mango	**11** mango	naranja/china	**22** orange

mandarina	**23** tangerine
uvas	**24** grapes
cerezas	**25** cherries
ciruelas pasas	**26** prunes
dátiles	**27** dates
uvas pasas/pasitas	**28** raisins
nueces	**29** nuts
frambuesas	**30** raspberries
arándanos	**31** blueberries
fresas	**32** strawberries

[1–23]
A. This **apple** is delicious!
   Where did you get it?
B. At *Sam's Supermarket.*

[24–32]
A. These **grapes** are delicious!
   Where did you get them?
B. At *Franny's Fruit Stand.*

A. I'm hungry. Do we have any fruit?
B. Yes. We have _____s* and
   _____s.*

* With 15–19, use:
   We have _____ and _____.

A. Do we have any more _____s?†
B. No. I'll get some more when I go
   to the supermarket.

† With 15–19 use:
   Do we have any more _____?

What are your favorite fruits?
Which fruits don't you like?

Which of these fruits grow where you live?

Name and describe other fruits you know.

LOS VEGETALES/LAS VERDURAS

apio	**1** celery	guisante/chícharo/ petit pois	**16** pea	alcachofa	**27** artichoke
maíz/elote	**2** corn	habichuelas tiernas/	**17** string bean/	papa/patata	**28** potato
brécol/brócoli	**3** broccoli	ejotes/judías verdes	green bean	batata dulce/camote	**29** sweet potato
coliflor	**4** cauliflower	haba	**18** lima bean	batata (anaranjada)	**30** yam
espinaca	**5** spinach	frijol negro	**19** black bean	pimiento verde	**31** green pepper/
perejil	**6** parsley	frijol rojo/colorado	**20** kidney bean		sweet pepper
espárrago	**7** asparagus	habichuelas coloradas		pimiento rojo/	**32** red pepper
berenjena	**8** eggplant	poroto		pimiento morrón	
lechuga	**9** lettuce	repollito/col de bruselas	**21** brussels sprout	chile/pimiento	**33** jalapeño
repollo/col	**10** cabbage	pepino/pepinillo	**22** cucumber	jalapeño	(pepper)
bok choy	**11** bok choy	tomate/jitomate	**23** tomato	chile colorado	**34** chili pepper
calabacita/	**12** zucchini	zanahoria	**24** carrot	remolacha/betabel	**35** beet
calabacín		rábano	**25** radish	cebolla	**36** onion
calabaza pequeña	**13** acorn squash	hongo/seta/	**26** mushroom	cebollino(a)/cebollín/	**37** scallion/
zapallo/güira(o)	**14** butternut squash	champiñón		escalonia	green onion
ajo	**15** garlic			nabo	**38** turnip

A. What do we need from the supermarket?
B. We need **celery*** and **pea**s.†

* 1–15   † 16–38

A. How do you like the
___[1–15]___ / ___[16–38]___s?
B. It's/They're delicious.

A. *Bobby?* Finish your vegetables!
B. But you KNOW I hate
___[1–15]___ / ___[16–38]___s!
A. I know. But it's/they're good for you!

Which vegetables do you like?
Which vegetables don't you like?

Which of these vegetables grow where you live?

Name and describe other vegetables you know.

CARNES, AVES, PESCADOS Y MARISCOS

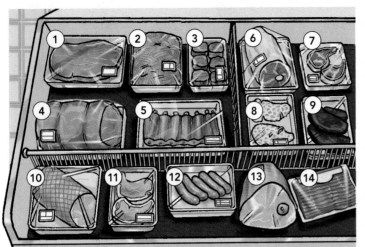

Carnes	**Meat**		pavo/guajolote	**20** turkey
filete/bistec/bisté/bife	**1** steak		pato	**21** duck
carne molida	**2** ground beef			
carne para guisar/cocer/estofado	**3** stewing beef		**Pescados y mariscos**	**Seafood**
carne para asar	**4** roast beef		PESCADOS	FISH
costillas	**5** ribs		salmón	**22** salmon
pierna de cordero	**6** leg of lamb		mero	**23** halibut
chuletas de cordero	**7** lamb chops		abadejo/bacalao	**24** haddock
tripa/mondongo/callos/menudo	**8** tripe		lenguado	**25** flounder
hígado	**9** liver		trucha	**26** trout
puerco/cerdo	**10** pork		bagro/bagre/barbo	**27** catfish
chuletas de puerco/de cerdo	**11** pork chops		filete de lenguado/de suela	**28** filet of sole
salchichones/chorizos/longaniza/salchichas	**12** sausages		MARISCOS	SHELLFISH
jamón	**13** ham		gambas/langostinos/camarones	**29** shrimp
tocino/tocineta/panceta/bacón/beicon	**14** bacon		conchuelas/vieiras/veneras/ callos de hacha	**30** scallops
Aves	**Poultry**		cangrejos	**31** crabs
pollo/gallina	**15** chicken		almejas	**32** clams
pechugas de pollo/gallina	**16** chicken breasts		mejillones	**33** mussels
muslos de pollo/gallina	**17** chicken legs/drumsticks		ostras	**34** oysters
alitas/alas de pollo/gallina	**18** chicken wings		langosta	**35** lobster
encuentros/caderas de pollo/gallina	**19** chicken thighs			

A. I'm going to the supermarket. What do we need?
B. Please get some **steak**.
A. **Steak**? All right.

A. Excuse me. Where can I find _____?
B. Look in the _____ Section.
A. Thank you.

A. This/These _____ looks/ look very fresh!
B. Let's get some for dinner.

Do you eat meat, poultry, or seafood? Which of these foods do you like?

Which of these foods are popular in your coun'

PRODUCTOS LÁCTEOS, JUGOS Y BEBIDAS

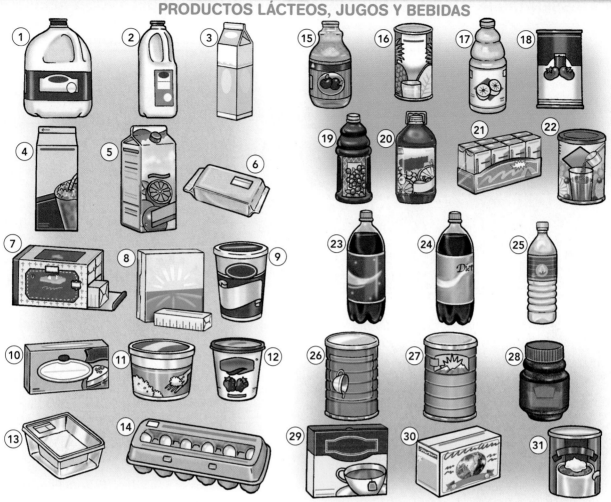

Productos lácteos	Dairy Products	Jugos/Zumos	Juices	Bebidas	Beverages
leche	1 milk	jugo de manzana	15 apple juice	soda/gaseosa/refresco	23 soda
leche baja en grasa	2 low-fat milk	jugo de piña	16 pineapple juice	soda de dieta	24 diet soda
leche descremada/desgrasada	3 skim milk	jugo de toronja/pomelo	17 grapefruit juice	agua embotellada	25 bottled water
leche con chocolate	4 chocolate milk	jugo de tomate	18 tomato juice		
jugo de naranja/de china*	5 orange juice*	jugo de uvas	19 grape juice	Café y té	Coffee and Tea
queso	6 cheese	ponche de frutas	20 fruit punch	café	26 coffee
mantequilla	7 butter	cartón/paquete de jugos	21 juice paks	café descafeinado	27 decaffeinated coffee/decaf
margarina	8 margarine	jugo/zumo/bebida en polvo/instantánea	22 powdered drink mix	café instantáneo	28 instant coffee
crema agria/crema	9 sour cream			té	29 tea
queso crema	10 cream cheese			tisana/infusión de hierbas/yerbas	30 herbal tea
requesón/cuajada	11 cottage cheese			chocolate en polvo	31 cocoa/hot chocolate mix
yogur/leche búlgara	12 yogurt				
soja/soya/tofu*	13 tofu*				
huevos	14 eggs				

*El jugo de naranja y el tofu no son productos lácteos, pero usualmente se les encuentra en esta sección.

A. I'm going to the supermarket to get some **milk**. Do we need anything else?
B. Yes. Please get some **apple juice**.

A. Excuse me. Where can I find _____?
B. Look in the _____ Section.
A. Thanks.

A. Look! _____ is/are on sale this week!
B. Let's get some!

Which of these foods do you like?
Which of these foods are good for you?
Which brands of these foods do you buy?

DELICATESSEN/CHARCUTERÍA: CARNES FRÍAS, PRODUCTOS CONGELADOS Y APERITIVOS

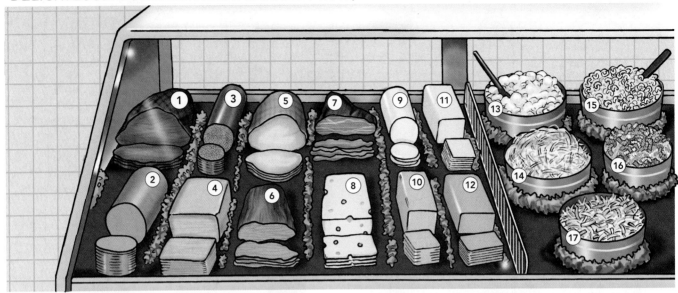

Delicatessen/Charcutería	Deli	
carne (de vaca) asada/rosbif	**1**	roast beef
mortadela	**2**	bologna
salami	**3**	salami
jamón	**4**	ham
pavo/guajolote	**5**	turkey
carne adobada/en salmuera/ salpresa/cornbif	**6**	corned beef
pastrami	**7**	pastrami
queso suizo	**8**	Swiss cheese
provolone	**9**	provolone
queso americano	**10**	American cheese
mozzarella	**11**	mozzarella
queso cheddar	**12**	cheddar cheese
ensalada de papas/patatas	**13**	potato salad
ensalada de repollo/col	**14**	cole slaw
ensalada de coditos	**15**	macaroni salad
ensalada de pasta	**16**	pasta salad
ensalada de mariscos	**17**	seafood salad

Productos congelados	Frozen Foods	
helado	**18**	ice cream
vegetales congelados	**19**	frozen vegetables
comida congelada /platos congelados	**20**	frozen dinners
concentrado de limonada congelada	**21**	frozen lemonade
concentrado de jugo de naranja/ de china congelado	**22**	frozen orange juice

Aperitivos/Botanas/Antojitos/ Pasabocas	Snack Foods	
papas/papitas/patatas fritas	**23**	potato chips
fritos de tortilla/totoposte/totopo	**24**	tortilla chips
pretzels	**25**	pretzels
nueces	**26**	nuts
palomitas/rosetas/hojuelas/ rositas de maíz	**27**	popcorn

A. Should we get some **roast beef**?
B. Good idea. And let's get some **potato salad**.

[1–17]
A. May I help you?
B. Yes, please. I'd like some _____.

[1–27]
A. Excuse me. Where is/are _____?
B. It's/They're in the _____ Section.

What kinds of snack foods are popular in your country?

Are frozen foods common in your country? What kinds of foods are in the Frozen Foods Section?

ABARROTES/PROVISIONES

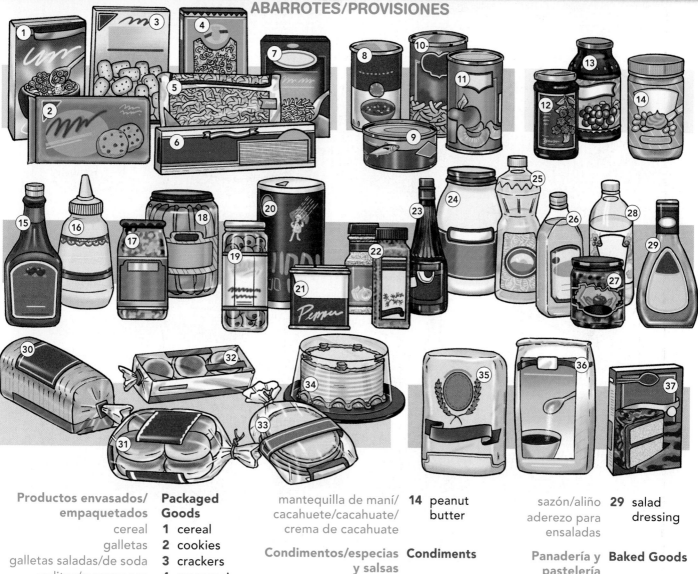

Productos envasados/ empaquetados	Packaged Goods
cereal	**1** cereal
galletas	**2** cookies
galletas saladas/de soda	**3** crackers
coditos/macarrones cortos	**4** macaroni
fideos/tallarines	**5** noodles
espaguetis	**6** spaghetti
arroz	**7** rice

Productos enlatados	Canned Goods
sopa	**8** soup
atún enlatado	**9** tuna (fish)
vegetales/verduras enlatados(as)	**10** (canned) vegetables
fruta enlatada	**11** (canned) fruit

Mermeladas y confituras	Jams and Jellies
mermelada	**12** jam
jalea	**13** jelly

mantequilla de maní/ cacahuete/cacahuate/ crema de cacahuate	**14** peanut butter

Condimentos/especias y salsas	Condiments
salsa de tomate/catsup	**15** ketchup
mostaza	**16** mustard
encurtido picado	**17** relish
encurtidos	**18** pickles
aceitunas	**19** olives
sal	**20** salt
pimienta	**21** pepper
especias/condimentos	**22** spices
salsa china/de soja/soya	**23** soy sauce
mayonesa	**24** mayonnaise
aceite para cocinar	**25** (cooking) oil
aceite de oliva	**26** olive oil
salsa	**27** salsa
vinagre	**28** vinegar

sazón/aliño aderezo para ensaladas	**29** salad dressing

Panadería y pastelería	Baked Goods
pan	**30** bread
bollos/ panecillos	**31** rolls
bollos/ panecillos	**32** English muffins
pan de pita	**33** pita bread
bizcocho/torta/ pastel/ponqué	**34** cake

Productos para hornear	Baking Products
harina	**35** flour
azúcar	**36** sugar
harina preparada para bizcocho	**37** cake mix

A. I got **cereal** and **soup**. What else is on the shopping list?
B. **Ketchup** and **bread**.

A. Excuse me. I'm looking for _____.
B. It's/They're next to the _____.

A. Pardon me. I'm looking for _____.
B. It's/They're between the _____ and the _____.

Which of these foods do you like?

Which brands of these foods do you buy?

ARTÍCULOS PARA EL HOGAR, EL BEBÉ Y LAS MASCOTAS

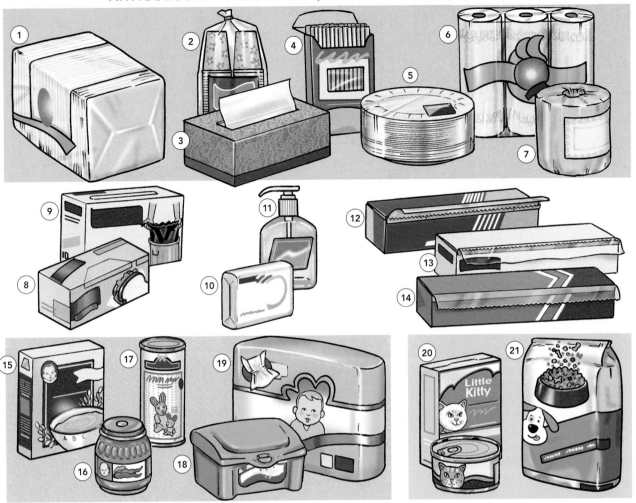

Productos de papel/desechables	Paper Products
servilletas	**1** napkins
vasos de cartón/desechables	**2** paper cups
pañuelos desechables/kleenex	**3** tissues
pajillas/popotes/carrizos/sorbetos	**4** straws
platos de cartón/desechables	**5** paper plates
papel toalla	**6** paper towels
papel higiénico/sanitario	**7** toilet paper

Artículos para el hogar	Household Items
bolsitas plásticas para sándwiches	**8** sandwich bags
bolsas para la basura	**9** trash bags
jabón	**10** soap
jabón líquido	**11** liquid soap
papel de aluminio	**12** aluminum foil
plástico para envolver	**13** plastic wrap
papel encerado/de cera	**14** waxed paper

Artículos para el bebé	Baby Products
cereal	**15** baby cereal
papillas/colados	**16** baby food
fórmula	**17** formula
toallitas húmedas desechables	**18** wipes
pañales desechables	**19** (disposable) diapers

Comida para mascotas	Pet Food
comida para gatos	**20** cat food
comida para perros	**21** dog food

A. Excuse me. Where can I find **napkins**?
B. **Napkins**? Look in Aisle *4*.

[7, 10–17, 20, 21]
A. We forgot to get _____!
B. I'll get it. Where is it?
A. It's in Aisle _____.

[1–6, 8, 9, 18, 19]
A. We forgot to get _____!
B. I'll get them. Where are they?
A. They're in Aisle _____.

What do you need from the supermarket?
Make a complete shopping list!

EL SUPERMERCADO

pasillo/corredor	**1**	aisle	empacador(a)	**14** bagger/packer
cliente	**2**	shopper/customer	caja rápida	**15** express checkout (line)
carretilla/carrito	**3**	shopping basket		
fila para pagar	**4**	checkout line	periódico	**16** tabloid (newspaper)
mostrador de chequeo/caja	**5**	checkout counter	revista	**17** magazine
cinta/banda transportadora	**6**	conveyor belt	lector óptico	**18** scanner
caja registradora	**7**	cash register	bolsa plástica/de plástico	**19** plastic bag
carrito/carretilla	**8**	shopping cart	frutas y verduras	**20** produce
chicle/goma de masticar	**9**	(chewing) gum	gerente	**21** manager
pastilla/caramelo/dulce	**10**	candy	empleado(a)	**22** clerk
cupones	**11**	coupons	pesa/balanza	**23** scale
cajero(a)	**12**	cashier	recicladora/reembolsadora para latas	**24** can-return machine
bolsa/cartucho/talego de papel	**13**	paper bag	recicladora/reembolsadora para botellas	**25** bottle-return machine

[1–8, 11–19, 21–25]
A. This is a gigantic supermarket!
B. It is! Look at all the **aisle**s!

[9, 10, 20]
A. This is a gigantic supermarket!
B. It is. Look at all the **produce**!

Where do you usually shop for food? Do you go to a supermarket, or do you go to a small grocery store? Describe the place where you shop.

Describe the differences between U.S. supermarkets and food stores in your country.

CONTAINERS AND QUANTITIES

ENVASES, RECIPIENTES Y MEDIDAS DE CANTIDAD

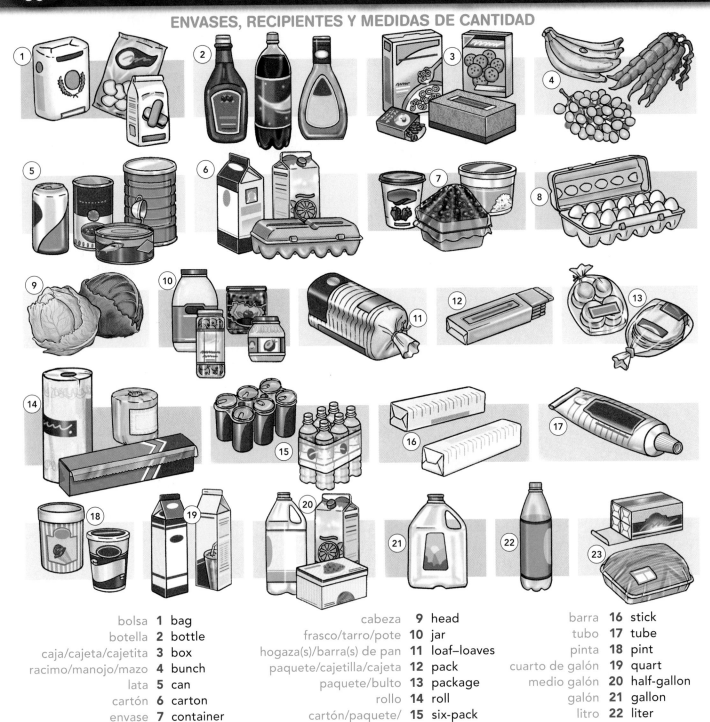

bolsa	**1**	bag		cabeza	**9**	head		barra	**16**	stick
botella	**2**	bottle		frasco/tarro/pote	**10**	jar		tubo	**17**	tube
caja/cajeta/cajetita	**3**	box		hogaza(s)/barra(s) de pan	**11**	loaf–loaves		pinta	**18**	pint
racimo/manojo/mazo	**4**	bunch		paquete/cajetilla/cajeta	**12**	pack		cuarto de galón	**19**	quart
lata	**5**	can		paquete/bulto	**13**	package		medio galón	**20**	half-gallon
cartón	**6**	carton		rollo	**14**	roll		galón	**21**	gallon
envase	**7**	container		cartón/paquete/	**15**	six-pack		litro	**22**	liter
docena	**8**	dozen*		bulto de seis artículos				libra	**23**	pound

* "a dozen eggs," NO "a dozen of eggs"

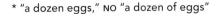

A. Please get a **bag** of *flour* when you go to the supermarket.
B. A **bag** of *flour*? Okay.

A. Please get two **bottles** of *ketchup* when you go to the supermarket.
B. Two **bottles** of *ketchup*? Okay.

[At home]

A. What did you get at the supermarket?
B. I got _____, _____, and _____.

[In a supermarket]

A. Is this the express checkout line?
B. Yes, it is. Do you have more than eight items?
A. No. I only have _____, _____, and _____.

Open your kitchen cabinets and refrigerator. Make a list of all the things you find.

What do you do with empty bottles, jars, and cans? Do you recycle them, reuse them, or throw them away?

PESOS Y MEDIDAS

cucharadita   teaspoon
cdta.   tsp.

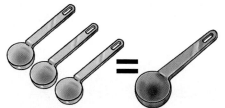

cucharada   tablespoon
cda.   Tbsp.

una onza   1 (fluid) ounce
1 oz. líquida   1 fl. oz.

una taza   cup
c.
8 ozs. líquidas   8 fl. ozs.

una pinta   pint
pt.
16 ozs. líquidas   16 fl. ozs.

un cuarto de galón   quart
qt.
32 ozs. líquidas   32 fl. ozs.

un galón   gallon
gal.
128 ozs. líquidas   128 fl. ozs.

A. How much water should I put in?
B. The recipe says to add one _____ of water.

A. This fruit punch is delicious! What's in it?
B. Two _____s of apple juice, three _____
of orange juice, and a _____ of grape juice.

una onza   an ounce

1 oz.   oz.

un cuarto   a quarter
de libra   of a pound
¼ lb.   1/4 lb.
4 ozs.   4 ozs.

media   half a
libra   pound
½ lb.   1/2 lb.
8 ozs.   8 ozs.

tres cuartos   three-quarters
de libra   of a pound
¾ lb.   3/4 lb.
12 ozs.   12 ozs.

una libra   a pound

1 lb.   lb.
16 ozs.   16 ozs.

A. How much roast beef would you like?
B. I'd like _____, please.
A. Anything else?
B. Yes. Please give me _____ of Swiss cheese.

A. This chili tastes very good! What did you put in it?
B. _____ of ground beef, _____ of beans, _____ of tomatoes, and _____ of chili powder.

RECETAS Y PREPARACIÓN DE ALIMENTOS

corte (a)	**1** cut (up)		cocine(a)	**14** cook
pique (pica)	**2** chop (up)		hornee(a)	**15** bake
corte(a)/rebane(a)	**3** slice		hierva(e)	**16** boil
ralle(a)	**4** grate		ase(a) a la parrilla	**17** broil
pele(a)/monde(a)	**5** peel		cuezca/cueza (cuece) al vapor	**18** steam
parta(e)	**6** break		fría(e)	**19** fry
bata(e)	**7** beat		guise(a)/saltee(a)	**20** saute
revuelva(e)	**8** stir		cuezca/cueza(cuece) a fuego lento	**21** simmer
eche(a)/vierta(e)	**9** pour		ase(a)/hornee(a)	**22** roast
añada(e)	**10** add		ase(a) a la parrilla	**23** barbecue / grill
combine(a) ____ y ____	**11** combine ____ and ____		saltee(a)/sofría(e)	**24** stir-fry
mezcle(a) ____ y ____	**12** mix ____ and ____		cuezca/cueza(cuece)/cocine(a) en el microondas	**25** microwave
ponga (pon) ____ en ____	**13** put ____ in ____			

A. Can I help you?
B. Yes. Please **cut up** the vegetables.

[1–25]

A. What are you doing?
B. I'm _____ing the ....

[14–25]

A. How long should I _____ the ....?
B. _____ the .... for .... minutes/seconds.

What's your favorite recipe? Give instructions and use the units of measure on page 57. For example:

Mix a cup of flour and two tablespoons of sugar.
Add half a pound of butter.
Bake at 350° (degrees) for twenty minutes.

UTENSILIOS DE COCINA

cuchara bola para servir helados	**1**	ice cream scoop	rejilla para cocer al vapor	**14**	steamer	minutero	**24**	kitchen timer
abrelatas	**2**	can opener	cuchillo	**15**	knife	rodillo/rolo	**25**	rolling pin
abrebotellas	**3**	bottle opener	triturador/ machacador de ajos	**16**	garlic press	molde para tartas	**26**	pie plate
mondador/ pelapapas	**4**	(vegetable) peeler	rallo/rallador	**17**	grater	mondador	**27**	paring knife
batidor de mano	**5**	(egg) beater	bandeja/fuente/ refractario	**18**	casserole dish	plancha/bandeja para hornear galletas	**28**	cookie sheet
tapadera/tapa	**6**	lid/cover/top	bandeja de asar/ hornear	**19**	roasting pan	molde de hacer galletas	**29**	cookie cutter
olla/cacerola/cazo	**7**	pot	parrilla de asar/ hornear/pavera	**20**	roasting rack	tazón/cuenco	**30**	(mixing) bowl
sartén	**8**	frying pan/ skillet	trinchante	**21**	carving knife	batidor de mano	**31**	whisk
olla de baño María	**9**	double boiler	cacerola	**22**	saucepan	taza de medir	**32**	measuring cup
wok/disco chino	**10**	wok	colador	**23**	colander	cuchara de medir	**33**	measuring spoon
cucharón	**11**	ladle				molde para bizcochos/ hornear/pasteles	**34**	cake pan
colador	**12**	strainer				cuchara de madera	**35**	wooden spoon
espátula	**13**	spatula						

A. Could I possibly borrow your **ice cream scoop**?
B. Sure. I'll be happy to lend you my **ice cream scoop**.
A. Thanks.

A. What are you looking for?
B. I can't find the _____.
A. Look in that drawer/in that cabinet/ on the counter/next to the _____/
....

[A Commercial]
Come to *Kitchen World*! We have everything you need for your kitchen, from _____s and _____s, to _____s and _____s. Are you looking for a new _____? Is it time to throw out your old _____? Come to *Kitchen World* today! We have everything you need!

What kitchen utensils and cookware do you have in your kitchen?

Which things do you use very often?

Which things do you rarely use?

COMIDA RÁPIDA/AL PASO/AL INSTANTE

hamburguesa	**1** hamburger		helado de yogur	**15** frozen yogurt
hamburguesa con queso/quesoburguesa	**2** cheeseburger		batido de leche/malteada	**16** milkshake
perro caliente/hot dog	**3** hot dog		soda/gaseosa	**17** soda
bocadillo/emparedado/sándwich de pescado	**4** fish sandwich		tapas	**18** lids
bocadillo/emparedado/sándwich de pollo	**5** chicken sandwich		vasos de cartón	**19** paper cups
pollo frito	**6** fried chicken		pajillas/popotes/carrizos/	**20** straws
papas fritas	**7** french fries		sorbetos	
nachos	**8** nachos		servilletas	**21** napkins
taco	**9** taco		cubiertos plásticos/de plástico	**22** plastic utensils
burrito	**10** burrito		salsa de tomate/catsup	**23** ketchup
pedazo de pizza	**11** slice of pizza		mostaza	**24** mustard
tazón de chile con carne	**12** bowl of chili		mayonesa	**25** mayonnaise
ensalada	**13** salad		encurtido de pepinillos	**26** relish
helado	**14** ice cream		sazón/aliño/aderezo para ensaladas	**27** salad dressing

A. May I help you?
B. Yes. I'd like a/an ___[1–5, 9–17]___ /
an order of ___[6–8]___ .

A. Excuse me. We're almost out of
___[18–27]___ .
B. I'll get some more from the
supply room. Thanks for telling
me.

Do you go to fast-food restaurants? Which ones?
How often? What do you order?

Are there fast-food restaurants in your country?
Are they popular? What foods do they have?

EN LA CAFETERÍA Y LOS SÁNDWICHES

churro/dona/buñuelo/llanta	**1**	donut
pan dulce/bollo/bollito	**2**	muffin
bagel	**3**	bagel
bollo/dulce/panecillo	**4**	bun
pan dulce danés	**5**	danish/pastry
bisquet/panecillo	**6**	biscuit
croissant/cuernito	**7**	croissant
huevos	**8**	eggs
panqueques/hot cakes	**9**	pancakes
waffles/gofres	**10**	waffles
pan tostado/tostada	**11**	toast
tocino/tocineta	**12**	bacon
chorizos/salchichas	**13**	sausages
papas estilo casero	**14**	home fries
café	**15**	coffee
café descafeinado	**16**	decaf coffee
té	**17**	tea
té frío/helado	**18**	iced tea
limonada	**19**	lemonade

chocolate caliente	**20**	hot chocolate
leche	**21**	milk
bocadillo/emparedado/sándwich de atún	**22**	tuna fish sandwich
bocadillo/emparedado/sándwich de huevo	**23**	egg salad sandwich
bocadillo/emparedado/sándwich de pollo	**24**	chicken salad sandwich
bocadillo/emparedado/ sándwich de jamón con queso	**25**	ham and cheese sandwich
bocadillo/emparedado/ sándwich de carne en salmuera/cornbif	**26**	corned beef sandwich
bocadillo/emparedado/ sándwich de tomate con lechuga y tocino	**27**	BLT/bacon, lettuce, and tomato sandwich
bocadillo/emparedado/ sándwich de carne (asada)/rosbif	**28**	roast beef sandwich
pan blanco/blando/suave/de molde/de agua	**29**	white bread
pan integral/de trigo	**30**	whole wheat bread
pan sirio/de pita	**31**	pita bread
pan integral de centeno/negro	**32**	pumpernickel
pan de centeno	**33**	rye bread
un panecito/panecillo/bollo	**34**	a roll
un mollete/pan de barra	**35**	a submarine roll

A. May I help you?
B. Yes. I'd like a _____[1–7]_____/an order of _____[8–14]_____, please.
A. Anything to drink?
B. Yes. I'll have a small/medium-size/large/extra-large _____[15–21]_____.

A. I'd like a _____[22–28]_____ on _____[29–35]_____, please.
B. What do you want on it?
A. Lettuce/tomato/mayonnaise/mustard/. . .

Do you like these foods? Which ones? Where do you get them? How often do you have them?

lleve los clientes a la mesa	**A** seat the customers		asiento elevador	**7** booster seat
vierta/sirva el agua	**B** pour the water		menú/carta	**8** menu
tome/anote la orden	**C** take the order		canasta/canastilla/cesta para pan	**9** bread basket
sirva la comida	**D** serve the meal		ayudante de camarero(a)	**10** busperson
			mesera/camarera	**11** waitress/server
anfitriona	**1** hostess		mesero/camarero	**12** waiter/server
anfitrión	**2** host		barra de ensaladas	**13** salad bar
cliente/comensal	**3** diner/patron/customer		comedor	**14** dining room
butaca/reservado/privado	**4** booth		cocina	**15** kitchen
mesa	**5** table		chef	**16** chef
silla alta/trona	**6** high chair			

[4–9]
A. Would you like a **booth**?
B. Yes, please.

[10–12]
A. Hello. My name is *Julie*, and I'll be your **waitress** this evening.
B. Hello.

[1, 2, 13–16]
A. This restaurant has a wonderful **salad bar**.
B. I agree.

limpie la mesa	**E**	clear the table		
pague la cuenta	**F**	pay the check		
deje una propina	**G**	leave a tip		
ponga/arregle la mesa	**H**	set the table		

cuarto para lavar platos	**17**	dishroom
lavaplatos/lavavajillas	**18**	dishwasher
bandeja/charola	**19**	tray
carrito de postres	**20**	dessert cart
cuenta	**21**	check
propina	**22**	tip
plato para la ensalada	**23**	salad plate
plato para el pan y la mantequilla	**24**	bread-and-butter plate
plato llano	**25**	dinner plate

plato hondo/sopero	**26**	soup bowl
vaso/copa para el agua	**27**	water glass
copa	**28**	wine glass
taza	**29**	cup
platito/platillo	**30**	saucer
servilleta	**31**	napkin

juego de cubiertos/cuchillería		**silverware**
tenedor/trinche para la ensalada	**32**	salad fork
tenedor	**33**	dinner fork
cuchillo	**34**	knife
cucharita/cucharilla/cuchara de té	**35**	teaspoon
cuchara para la sopa	**36**	soup spoon
cuchillo para la mantequilla	**37**	butter knife

[A–H]
A. Please _____.
B. All right. I'll _____ right away.

[23–37]
A. Excuse me. Where does the _____ go?
B. It goes {
  to the left of the _____.
  to the right of the _____.
  on the _____.
  between the _____ and the _____.
}

[1, 2, 10–12, 16, 18]
A. Do you have any job openings?
B. Yes. We're looking for a _____.

[23–37]
A. Excuse me. I dropped my _____.
B. That's okay. I'll get you another _____ from the kitchen.

Tell about a restaurant you know. Describe the place and the people. (Is the restaurant large or small? How many tables are there? How many people work there? Is there a salad bar? . . .)

UN MENÚ

coctel/copa de frutas	**1**	fruit cup/ fruit cocktail	antipasto/entremés	**10**	antipasto (plate)
jugo de tomate	**2**	tomato juice	ensalada estilo César	**11**	Caesar salad
coctel de camarones/ de gambas	**3**	shrimp cocktail	pastel/budín de carne molida	**12**	meatloaf
alitas de pollo	**4**	chicken wings	filete/bistec de costilla/ asado/bife/rosbif	**13**	roast beef/ prime rib
nachos	**5**	nachos	pollo al horno/asado	**14**	baked chicken
cáscaras de papa rellenas	**6**	potato skins	pescado a la parrilla	**15**	broiled fish
			espaguetis con albóndigas	**16**	spaghetti and meatballs
ensalada mixta	**7**	tossed salad/ garden salad	chuleta de ternera	**17**	veal cutlet
ensalada griega	**8**	Greek salad	una papa al horno/asada	**18**	a baked potato
ensalada de espinacas	**9**	spinach salad	puré de papas	**19**	mashed potatoes
			papas fritas	**20**	french fries
			arroz	**21**	rice

fideos	**22**	noodles
vegetales/ verduras mixtos(as)	**23**	mixed vegetables
bizcocho/torta/ pastel de chocolate	**24**	chocolate cake
pastel/tarta de manzanas	**25**	apple pie
helado	**26**	ice cream
gelatina	**27**	jello
pudín/budín	**28**	pudding
copa de helado/ mantecado especial/ sundae	**29**	ice cream sundae

[Ordering dinner]

A. May I take your order?
B. Yes, please. For the appetizer, I'd like the ___[1–6]___.
A. And what kind of salad would you like?
B. I'll have the ___[7–11]___.
A. And for the main course?
B. I'd like the ___[12–17]___, please.
A. What side dish would you like with that?
B. Hmm. I think I'll have ___[18–23]___.

[Ordering dessert]

A. Would you care for some dessert?
B. Yes. I'll have ___[24–28]___/an ___[29]___.

Tell about the food at a restaurant you know. What's on the menu?

What are some typical foods on the menus of restaurants in your country?

LOS COLORES

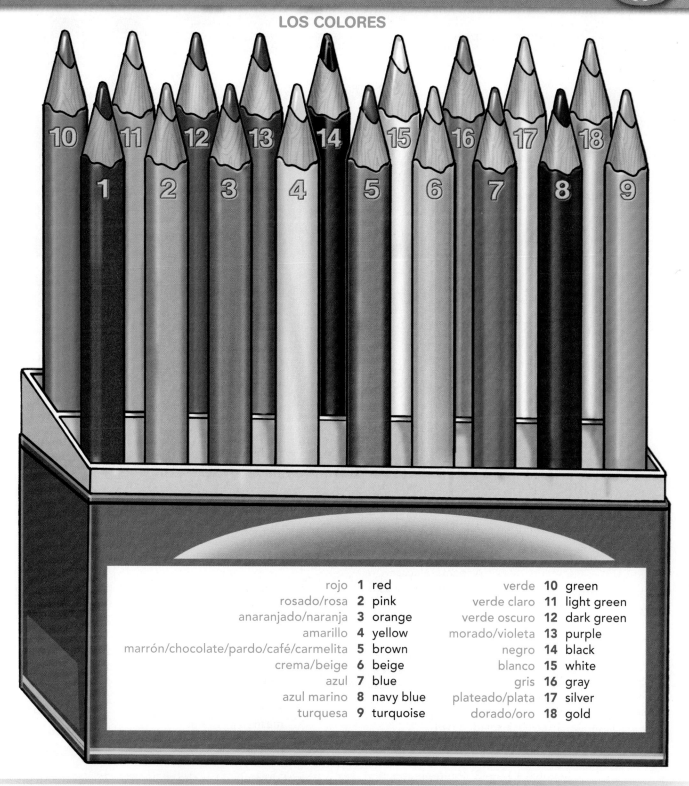

rojo	**1**	red	verde	**10**	green
rosado/rosa	**2**	pink	verde claro	**11**	light green
anaranjado/naranja	**3**	orange	verde oscuro	**12**	dark green
amarillo	**4**	yellow	morado/violeta	**13**	purple
marrón/chocolate/pardo/café/carmelita	**5**	brown	negro	**14**	black
crema/beige	**6**	beige	blanco	**15**	white
azul	**7**	blue	gris	**16**	gray
azul marino	**8**	navy blue	plateado/plata	**17**	silver
turquesa	**9**	turquoise	dorado/oro	**18**	gold

A. What's your favorite color?
B. **Red**.

A. I like your _____ shirt.
   You look very good in _____.

B. Thank you. _____ is my
   favorite color.

A. My TV is broken.

B. What's the matter with it?

A. People's faces are _____,
   the sky is _____, and the
   grass is _____!

Do you know the flags of different countries?
What are the colors of flags you know?

What color makes you happy? What color
makes you sad? Why?

LA ROPA

blusa	**1**	blouse	corbata	**14** tie/necktie
falda	**2**	skirt	uniforme	**15** uniform
camisa	**3**	shirt	camiseta/playera	**16** T-shirt
pantalones	**4**	pants/slacks	pantalones cortos/shorts	**17** shorts
camisa de mangas cortas	**5**	sport shirt	vestido/traje de maternidad	**18** maternity dress
pantalones vaqueros/jeans/ de mezclilla/mahones	**6**	jeans	mono/mameluco/overol/guardapolvo	**19** jumpsuit
polo/camisa/jersey de punto	**7**	knit shirt/jersey	chaleco	**20** vest
vestido/traje	**8**	dress	mameluco/trajecito júmper/júmper/mono	**21** jumper
suéter/con cuello de pico	**9**	sweater	blazer/chaqueta cruzada	**22** blazer
chaqueta/saco	**10**	jacket	túnica	**23** tunic
chaqueta/saco informal/ deportiva(o)/chaquetón/ campera/americana	**11**	sport coat/ sport jacket/ jacket	leotardos/mallas	**24** leggings
			overol/mono/mameluco	**25** overalls
			camisa de cuello de tortuga/cisne	**26** turtleneck
traje sastre/vestido de chaqueta/de dos piezas	**12**	suit	esmoquin/smóking	**27** tuxedo
			corbata de gato/de lazo/de pajarita/ mariquita/corbatín	**28** bow tie
conjunto/traje/ vestido de tres piezas/terno	**13**	three-piece suit	vestido/traje de noche/de fiesta/ formal/de etiqueta	**29** (evening) gown

A. I think I'll wear my new **blouse** today.
B. Good idea!

A. I really like your _____.
B. Thank you.
A. Where did you get it/them?
B. At ....

A. Oh, no! I just ripped my _____!
B. What a shame!

What clothing items in this lesson do you wear?

What color clothing do you like to wear?

What do you wear at work or at school? at parties? at weddings?

ROPA PARA RESGUARDARSE DEL TIEMPO

abrigo/gabán/sobretodo	**1** coat	paraguas/parasol/sombrilla	**15** umbrella
abrigo/gabán/sobretodo	**2** overcoat	poncho (de agua)/jorongo/sarape	**16** poncho
sombrero	**3** hat	capote corto/chamarra para lluvia/chubasquero	**17** rain jacket
chaqueta/cazadora/chompa/chamarra	**4** jacket	botas de goma/de caucho/hule/para la lluvia	**18** rain boots
bufanda	**5** scarf/muffler	gorro/gorra de esquiar	**19** ski hat
abrigo tejido/de punto/suéter abierto	**6** sweater jacket	abrigo/chaqueta para esquiar	**20** ski jacket
leotardos/mallas	**7** tights	guantes	**21** gloves
gorra/cachucha	**8** cap	máscara de esquiar/pasamontañas	**22** ski mask
chaqueta de cuero	**9** leather jacket	abrigo de plumas de ganso/acolchonado	**23** down jacket
gorra de béisbol	**10** baseball cap	mitones/guantes enteros	**24** mittens
chaqueta/impermeable contra el viento	**11** windbreaker	abrigo de invierno/pelliza/parka	**25** parka
capote/impermeable	**12** raincoat	anteojos/lentes/gafas para sol	**26** sunglasses
sombrero impermeable	**13** rain hat	orejeras	**27** ear muffs
gabardina/trinchera/impermeable	**14** trench coat	chaleco de plumas de ganso/ acolchonado/acojinado	**28** down vest

A. What's the weather like today?
B. It's cool/cold/raining/snowing.
A. I think I'll wear my _____.

[1–6, 8–17, 19, 20, 22, 23, 25, 28]

A. May I help you?
B. Yes, please. I'm looking for a/an _____.

[7, 18, 21, 24, 26, 27]

A. May I help you?
B. Yes, please. I'm looking for _____.

What do you wear outside when the weather is cool?/when it's raining?/when it's very cold?

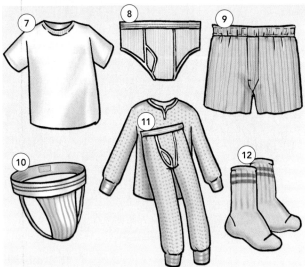

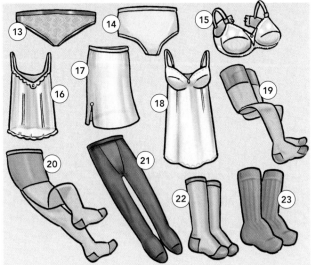

pijama/piyama	**1** pajamas	calzones largos/térmicos	**11** long underwear/ long johns
camisón	**2** nightgown	medias/tobilleras/calcetines/calcetas	**12** socks
camisa de dormir	**3** nightshirt	panty bikini/pantaleta bikini	**13** (bikini) panties
bata de baño/albornoz	**4** bathrobe/robe	panty/pantaleta/calzonario/ braga/bombacha	**14** briefs/ underpants
zapatillas/babuchas/ pantuflas/chinelas	**5** slippers	sostenedor/sostén/brassiere/bra	**15** bra
mameluco/pelele/ pijamita de una pieza	**6** blanket sleeper	camisola/justillo	**16** camisole
camiseta	**7** undershirt/T-shirt	peticote de falda/medio fondo/enagua	**17** half slip
calzoncillos/trusas	**8** (jockey) shorts/ underpants/briefs	peticote/fondo entero/enagua/combinación	**18** (full) slip
		medias	**19** stockings
calzoncillos bóxer/largos	**9** boxer shorts/boxers	pantimedias	**20** pantyhose
suspensorios	**10** athletic supporter/ jockstrap	leotardos/mallas	**21** tights
		calcetines	**22** knee-highs
		calcetines/medias/tobilleras/tobimedias largas	**23** knee socks

A. I can't find my new _____.
B. Did you look in the bureau/dresser/closet?
A. Yes, I did.
B. Then it's/they're probably in the wash.

What sleepwear items do you wear? What sleepwear items do people in your family wear?

ROPA DEPORTIVA Y CALZADO

camiseta sin mangas	1	tank top
pantalones/calzones cortos/ pantaloncillos/shorts	2	running shorts
vincha/bandana	3	sweatband
traje para correr/ traje deportivo/ chándal	4	jogging suit/ running suit/ warm-up suit
camiseta/playera	5	T-shirt
pantalones cortos/calzones/ pantaloncillos de Lycra/malla	6	lycra shorts/ bike shorts
sudadera	7	sweatshirt
pantalones de sudadera	8	sweatpants
batín	9	cover-up
vestido/traje de baño/ bañador	10	swimsuit/bathing suit
traje de baño/bañador	11	swimming trunks/ swimsuit/bathing suit
leotardo	12	leotard
zapatos	13	shoes
zapatos de tacón alto	14	(high) heels
zapatos de tacón bajo	15	pumps
mocasines	16	loafers
zapatillas deportivas/tenis	17	sneakers/athletic shoes
zapatillas para jugar tenis	18	tennis shoes
zapatillas para correr	19	running shoes
zapatillas de botín alto/ medio botín/tenis altos	20	high-tops/ high-top sneakers
sandalias	21	sandals
chancletas/chinelas/pantuflas	22	thongs/flip-flops
botas	23	boots
botas de trabajo	24	work boots
botas para escalar	25	hiking boots
botas de vaquero	26	cowboy boots
mocasines	27	moccasins

[1–12]
A. Excuse me. I found this/these _____ in the dryer. Is it/Are they yours?
B. Yes. It's/They're mine. Thank you.

[13–27]
A. Are those new _____?
B. Yes, they are.
A. They're very nice.
B. Thanks.

Do you exercise? What do you do?
What kind of clothing do you wear
when you exercise?

What kind of shoes do you wear when you go to work or to school?
when you exercise? when you relax at home?
when you go out with friends or family members?

anillo/sortija	1	ring
anillo de compromiso	2	engagement ring
anillo de matrimonio	3	wedding ring/wedding band
aretes/pendientes/pantallas	4	earrings
collar	5	necklace
collar de perlas	6	pearl necklace/pearls/ string of pearls
cadena	7	chain
collar de cuentas	8	beads
prendedor/broche	9	pin/brooch
dije/colgante/relicario	10	locket
pulsera/brazalete	11	bracelet
pasador/hebilla de cabello	12	barrette
gemelos/mancuernas/yuntas	13	cuff links

tirantes	14	suspenders
reloj/reloj de pulsera	15	watch/wrist watch
pañuelo	16	handkerchief
llavero	17	key ring/key chain
monedero	18	change purse
billetera/cartera	19	wallet
cinturón/correa	20	belt
bolso/bolsa/cartera	21	purse/handbag/pocketbook
carriel/bolsa de correa	22	shoulder bag
bolsa/bolsón	23	tote bag
maleta para libros/mochila	24	book bag
mochila/mochila de excursión	25	backpack
bolsa para maquillaje/necessaire	26	makeup bag
portafolios/maletín	27	briefcase

A. Oh, no! I think I lost my **ring**!
B. I'll help you look for it.

A. Oh, no! I think I lost my **earrings**!
B. I'll help you look for them.

[In a store]

A. Excuse me. Is this/Are these _____ on sale this week?
B. Yes. It's/They're half price.

[On the street]

A. Help! Police! Stop that man/woman!
B. What happened?!
A. He/She just stole my _____ and my _____!

Do you like to wear jewelry? What jewelry do you have?

In your country, what do men, women, and children use to carry their things?

DESCRIPCIÓN DE LA ROPA

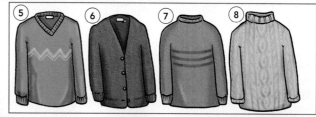

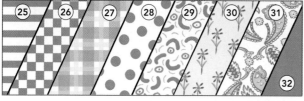
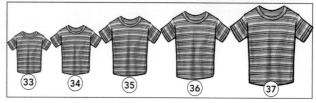

Tipos de ropa		Types of Clothing
camisa de mangas largas	**1**	long-sleeved shirt
camisa de mangas cortas	**2**	short-sleeved shirt
camisa sin mangas	**3**	sleeveless shirt
camisa de cuello de tortuga/cisne	**4**	turtleneck (shirt)
suéter con cuello en V/de pico	**5**	V-neck sweater
cárdigan/suéter abierto con botones	**6**	cardigan sweater
jersey/suéter con cuello cerrado	**7**	crewneck sweater
suéter con cuello de tortuga/cisne	**8**	turtleneck sweater
calcetines/medias/tobilleras/ tobimedias largas	**9**	knee-high socks
medias cortas/calcetas	**10**	ankle socks
medias/calcetines deportivas(os)	**11**	crew socks
aretes	**12**	pierced earrings
aretes de pinza/de presión	**13**	clip-on earrings

Tipos de material/tela		Types of Material
pantalones de pana/cordoncillo	**14**	corduroy pants
botas de cuero	**15**	leather boots
medias de nailon/nylon	**16**	nylon stockings
camiseta/playera de algodón	**17**	cotton T-shirt
chaqueta/chamarra de mezclilla	**18**	denim jacket

camisa de franela/lanilla	**19**	flannel shirt
blusa de poliéster	**20**	polyester blouse
vestido/traje de hilo/lino	**21**	linen dress
bufanda de seda	**22**	silk scarf
suéter de lana	**23**	wool sweater
sombrero de paja	**24**	straw hat

Patrones		Patterns
de rayas/de rayitas	**25**	striped
de cuadros/de cuadritos	**26**	checked
de diseño a cuadros escocés	**27**	plaid
punteado(a) de bolas/bolitas (motitas)	**28**	polka-dotted
estampado(a)	**29**	patterned/print
floreado(a)	**30**	flowered/floral
paisley/pesle	**31**	paisley
azul sólido	**32**	solid blue

Tallas/Tamaños		Sizes
petite/extra pequeño(a)	**33**	extra-small
pequeño(a)	**34**	small
mediano(a)	**35**	medium
grande	**36**	large
extra grande	**37**	extra-large

[1–24]
A. May I help you?
B. Yes, please. I'm looking for a *shirt*.*
A. What kind?
B. I'm looking for a *long-sleeved shirt*.

* With 9–16: I'm looking for _____.

[25–32]
A. How do you like this _____ tie/shirt/skirt?
B. Actually, I prefer that _____ one.

[33–37]
A. What size are you looking for?
B. _____.

Describe your favorite clothing items. For each item, tell about the color, the type of material, the size, and the pattern.

CLOTHING PROBLEMS AND ALTERATIONS
PROBLEMAS Y ARREGLOS DE LA ROPA

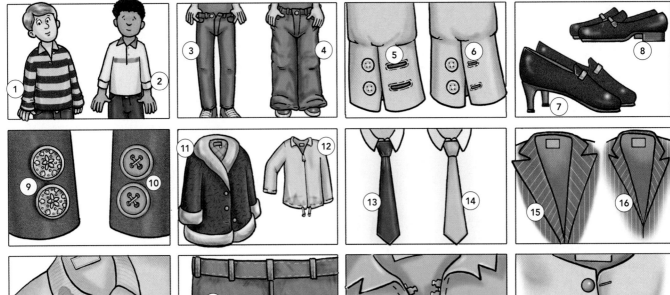

 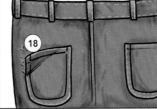  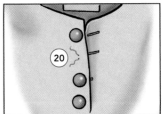

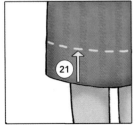    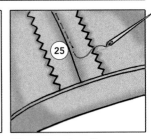

largo(a) – corto(a)	**1–2** long – short
estrecho(a) – ancho(a)/flojo(a)	**3–4** tight – loose/baggy
grande – chico(a)	**5–6** large/big – small
alto(a) – bajo(a)	**7–8** high – low
elaborado(a) – sencillo(a)	**9–10** fancy – plain
grueso(a)/pesado(a) –	**11–12** heavy – light
delgado(a)/liviano(a)	
oscuro(a) – claro(a)	**13–14** dark – light
ancho(a) – angosto(a)	**15–16** wide – narrow

cuello manchado	**17** stained *collar*
bolsillo desgarrado/roto	**18** ripped/torn *pocket*
cierre/cremallera roto(a)	**19** broken *zipper*
le falta *un botón*	**20** missing *button*
subirle la basta/el dobladillo a *la falda*	**21** shorten the *skirt*
alargar *las mangas*	**22** lengthen the *sleeves*
meterle a la costura de *la chaqueta*	**23** take in the *jacket*
sacarle a la costura de *los pantalones*	**24** let out the *pants*
remendar *la costura*	**25** fix/repair the *seam*

[1–2]
A. Are the sleeves too **long**?
B. No. They're too **short**.

1–2	Are the sleeves too _____?		9–10	Are the buttons too _____?
3–4	Are the pants too _____?		11–12	Is the coat too _____?
5–6	Are the buttonholes too _____?		13–14	Is the color too _____?
7–8	Are the heels too _____?		15–16	Are the lapels too _____?

[17–20]
A. What's the matter with it?
B. It has a **stained** *collar*.

[21–25]
A. Please **shorten** the *skirt*.
B. **Shorten** the *skirt*? Okay.

Tell about the differences between clothing people wear now and clothing people wore a long time ago.

LAVANDERÍA

separar la ropa	**A**	sort the laundry
meter la ropa en la lavadora	**B**	load the washer
sacar la ropa de la lavadora	**C**	unload the washer
meter la ropa en la secadora	**D**	load the dryer
colgar/tender la ropa en el tendedero	**E**	hang clothes on the clothesline
planchar	**F**	iron
doblar la ropa	**G**	fold the laundry
colgar la ropa	**H**	hang up clothing
guardar la ropa	**I**	put things away

ropa sucia	**1**	laundry
ropa clara	**2**	light clothing
ropa oscura	**3**	dark clothing
canasta para la ropa sucia	**4**	laundry basket
bolsa para la ropa sucia	**5**	laundry bag
lavadora/lavadora automática	**6**	washer/washing machine
detergente en polvo	**7**	laundry detergent
suavizador/suavizante	**8**	fabric softener
blanqueador/lejía/cloro	**9**	bleach

ropa mojada	**10**	wet clothing
secadora	**11**	dryer
filtro para la pelusa	**12**	lint trap
quitaestática	**13**	static cling remover
tendedero	**14**	clothesline
horquillas/ganchos/pinzas pinches para tender ropa	**15**	clothespin
plancha/planchar	**16**	iron
tabla de planchar	**17**	ironing board
ropa arrugada	**18**	wrinkled clothing
ropa planchada	**19**	ironed clothing
almidón en aerosol	**20**	spray starch
ropa limpia	**21**	clean clothing
clóset/armario/ropero	**22**	closet
gancho para colgar ropa	**23**	hanger
gaveta/cajón	**24**	drawer
repisa-repisas	**25**	shelf-shelves

[A–I]
A. What are you doing?
B. I'm _____ing.

[4–6, 11, 14–17, 23]
A. Excuse me. Do you sell _____s?
B. Yes. They're at the back of the store.
A. Thank you.

[7–9, 13, 20]
A. Excuse me. Do you sell _____?
B. Yes. It's at the back of the store.
A. Thank you.

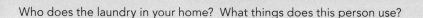

Who does the laundry in your home? What things does this person use?

EL ALMACÉN/LA TIENDA DE DEPARTAMENTOS

guía/directorio	**1**	(store) directory
Joyería	**2**	Jewelry Counter
Perfumería	**3**	Perfume Counter
escalera eléctrica/ automática/mecánica	**4**	escalator
ascensor/elevador	**5**	elevator
Sección de ropa de caballero	**6**	Men's Clothing Department
área de entrega de mercancía	**7**	customer pickup area
Sección de ropa de damas	**8**	Women's Clothing Department
Sección de ropa de niños	**9**	Children's Clothing Department

Sección de artículos para el hogar/ de cocina	**10**	Housewares Department
Sección de muebles	**11**	Furniture Department/ Home Furnishings Department
Sección de electrodomésticos	**12**	Household Appliances Department
Sección de electrónica/ aparatos electrónicos	**13**	Electronics Department
Mostrador de servicio al cliente	**14**	Customer Assistance Counter/ Customer Service Counter
servicios/baños para caballeros	**15**	men's room
servicios/baños para damas	**16**	ladies' room
fuente/bebedero	**17**	water fountain
cafetería/refresquería	**18**	snack bar
Mostrador para envolver regalos	**19**	Gift Wrap Counter

A. Excuse me. Where's the **store directory**?
B. It's over there, next to the **Jewelry Counter**.
A. Thanks.
B. You're welcome.

A. Excuse me. Do you sell *ties**?
B. Yes. You can find *ties** in the ____[6, 8–13]____ /at the ____[2, 3]____ on the first/second/third/fourth floor.
A. Thank you.

**ties/bracelets/dresses/toasters/. . .*

Describe a department store you know. Tell what is on each floor.

DE COMPRAS

comprar	**A**	buy
devolver	**B**	return
cambiar	**C**	exchange
probarse/ ponerse	**D**	try on
pagar	**E**	pay for
obtener información	**F**	get some information about

letrero para anuncio de ofertas/descuentos/rebajas	**1**	sale sign
etiqueta	**2**	label
etiqueta con el precio	**3**	price tag
recibo	**4**	receipt
descuento/rebaja	**5**	discount
talla/tamaño	**6**	size
material	**7**	material

cuidado de la ropa	**8**	care instructions
precio normal/regular	**9**	regular price
precio de descuento	**10**	sale price
precio	**11**	price
impuesto de ventas	**12**	sales tax
precio total	**13**	total price

A. May I help you?
B. Yes, please. I want to ___[A–F]___ this item.
A. Certainly. I'll be glad to help you.

A. { What's the ___[5–7, 9–13]___ ?
{ What are the ___[8]___ ?
B. _____.
A. Are you sure?
B. Yes. Look at the ___[1–4]___ !

Which stores in your area have sales? How often?

Tell about something you bought on sale.

EQUIPO DE VIDEO Y SONIDO

televisor/televisión	**1**	TV/television
televisor/televisión de plasma	**2**	plasma TV
televisor/televisión de cristal líquido	**3**	LCD TV
televisor/televisión de proyección	**4**	projection TV
televisor/televisión portátil	**5**	portable TV
control remoto	**6**	remote (control)
DVD/disco de video digital	**7**	DVD
reproductor de video digital/DVD	**8**	DVD player
video/videocasete/ videocinta	**9**	video/videocassette/ videotape
videocasetera/videograbadora/ videoreproductora	**10**	VCR/videocassette recorder
videocámara/ cámara de video	**11**	camcorder/ video camera
paquete de pilas/baterías	**12**	battery pack
cargador de pilas/baterías	**13**	battery charger
radio	**14**	radio
radio reloj despertador	**15**	clock radio
radio de onda corta	**16**	shortwave radio
grabadora de cintas magnetofónicas	**17**	tape recorder/ cassette recorder
micrófono	**18**	microphone
equipo estereofónico/de estéreo/ de estereofonía	**19**	stereo system/ sound system
disco	**20**	record
tornamesa/giradiscos/ tocadiscos	**21**	turntable
CD/disco compacto	**22**	CD/compact disc
reproductor de CD/discos compactos	**23**	CD player
sintonizador	**24**	tuner
audiocinta/audiocasete	**25**	(audio)tape/(audio)cassette
casetera	**26**	tape deck/cassette deck
bocinas/altavoces/ altoparlantes	**27**	speakers
equipo estereofónico portátil	**28**	portable stereo system/ boombox
reproductor de CD portátil	**29**	portable/personal CD player
tocacintas/ tocacasetes portátil	**30**	portable/personal cassette player
audífonos/auriculares	**31**	headphones
lector de MP3/reproductor de audio digital portátil	**32**	portable/personal digital audio player
sistema de videojuego	**33**	video game system
videojuego/cartucho/ paquete de videojuego	**34**	video game
videojuego manual	**35**	hand-held video game

A. May I help you?
B. Yes, please. I'm looking for a **TV**.

* With 27 & 31, use: I'm looking for _____.

A. I like your new _____. Where did you get it/them?
B. At .....*(name of store)*.....

A. Which company makes the best _____?
B. In my opinion, the best _____ is/are made by ....

What video and audio equipment do you have or want?

In your opinion, which brands of video and audio equipment are the best?

TELÉFONOS Y CÁMARAS

Spanish	#	English
teléfono	**1**	telephone/phone
teléfono portátil/inalámbrico	**2**	cordless phone
teléfono celular/móvil	**3**	cell phone/cellular phone
batería/pila	**4**	battery
cargador de baterías/pilas	**5**	battery charger
contestadora automática	**6**	answering machine
mensáfono/buscapersonas	**7**	pager
asistente digital personal/PDA	**8**	PDA/electronic personal organizer
máquina de fax/transmisor-receptor electrónico	**9**	fax machine
calculadora de bolsillo	**10**	(pocket) calculator
sumadora/calculadora	**11**	adding machine
regulador de voltaje	**12**	voltage regulator

Spanish	#	English
adaptador	**13**	adapter
cámara de 35 milímetros	**14**	(35 millimeter) camera
lente	**15**	lens
rollo de película/film	**16**	film
visor/lente zoom	**17**	zoom lens
cámara digital	**18**	digital camera
tarjeta de memoria	**19**	memory disk
trípode	**20**	tripod
flash removible	**21**	flash (attachment)
estuche de la cámara	**22**	camera case
proyector de transparencias/diapositivas	**23**	slide projector
pantalla	**24**	(movie) screen

A. Can I help you?
B. Yes. I want to buy a **telephone**.*

* With 16, use: I want to buy _____.

A. Excuse me. Do you sell _____s?*
B. Yes. We have a large selection of _____s.

* With 16, use the singular.

A. Which _____ is the best?
B. This one here. It's made by *(company)*
....

What kind of telephone do you use?

Do you have a camera? What kind is it?
What do you take pictures of?

Does anyone you know have an answering machine?
When you call, what message do you hear?

COMPUTADORAS/ORDENADORES

	Computer Hardware
Hardware/Equipo/Soporte físico	**Computer Hardware**
computadora/ordenador personal	**1** (desktop) computer
CPU/procesadora central/disco duro/base	**2** CPU/central processing unit
monitor/pantalla electrónica	**3** monitor/screen
lector de CD-ROM	**4** CD-ROM drive
disco CD-ROM	**5** CD-ROM
unidad de disquete	**6** disk drive
disquete	**7** (floppy) disk
teclado	**8** keyboard
ratón	**9** mouse
pantalla plana/de cristal líquido	**10** flat panel screen/LCD screen
microcomputadora/laptop/portátil	**11** notebook computer
palanca	**12** joystick
ratón fijo con pelota de barrido/trackball	**13** track ball
módem	**14** modem
protector de sobrevoltaje	**15** surge protector
impresora	**16** printer
escáner	**17** scanner
cable	**18** cable

Programa (informático)/de computadora	**Computer Software**
procesador de textos	**19** word-processing program
procesador de hoja de cálculo	**20** spreadsheet program
programa informático educativo	**21** educational software program
juego de computadora	**22** computer game

A. Can you recommend a good **computer**?
B. Yes. This **computer** here is excellent.

A. Is that a new _____?
B. Yes.
A. Where did you get it?
B. At .... *(name of store)* ....

A. May I help you?
B. Yes, please. Do you sell _____s?
A. Yes. We carry a complete line of _____s.

Do you use a computer? When?

In your opinion, how have computers changed the world?

LA JUGUETERÍA

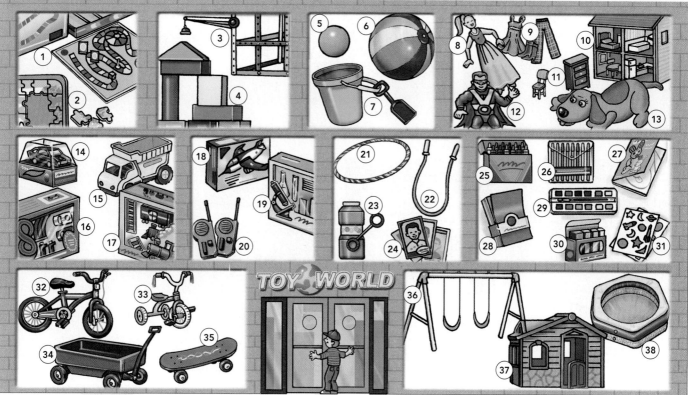

juego de mesa/tablero	**1**	board game	aro/hula hoop	**21** hula hoop
rompecabezas	**2**	(jigsaw) puzzle	cuerda/soga/reata/comba	**22** jump rope
juguete para armar/mecano	**3**	construction set	burbujas/pompas de jabón	**23** bubble soap
bloques/cubitos	**4**	(building) blocks	figuritas/estampas/tarjetas	**24** trading cards
pelota/balón	**5**	rubber ball	crayolas/lápices de cera/crayones	**25** crayons
pelota/balón de playa	**6**	beach ball	marcadores/lápices de felpa/	**26** (color) markers
cubito/cubeta y palita	**7**	pail and shovel	plumones	
muñeca	**8**	doll	cuaderno de dibujos/	**27** coloring book
ropa de muñeca	**9**	doll clothing	para pintar/colorear	
casa de muñecas	**10**	doll house	cartulina para actividades manuales	**28** construction paper
muebles para la casa	**11**	doll house	juego de pintura	**29** paint set
de muñecas		furniture	plastilina/masilla	**30** (modeling) clay
muñeco mecánico	**12**	action figure	calcomanía/pegatina	**31** stickers
peluche	**13**	stuffed animal	bicicleta	**32** bicycle
carrito de juguete	**14**	matchbox car	triciclo	**33** tricycle
camión de juguete	**15**	toy truck	vagón/vagoneta	**34** wagon
juego de carros de carrera	**16**	racing car set	monopatín/patineta	**35** skateboard
juego de trenes	**17**	train set	columpios	**36** swing set
modelo para armar	**18**	model kit	casa de juguete	**37** play house
juego de laboratorio/química	**19**	science kit	piscina/alberca/pileta infantil	**38** kiddie pool/
juego de intercomunicador/	**20**	walkie-talkie (set)	inflable/chapoteadero	inflatable pool
walki talki				

A. Excuse me. I'm looking for (a/an) _____(s) for my *grandson*.*
B. Look in the next aisle.
A. Thank you.

* *grandson/granddaughter/. . .*

A. I don't know what to get my
............-year-old son/daughter
for his/her birthday.
B. What about (a) _____?
A. Good idea! Thanks.

A. Mom/Dad? Can we buy
this/these _____?
B. No, *Johnny*. Not today.

What toys are most popular in your country?

What were your favorite toys when you were
a child?

THE BANK

EL BANCO

Spanish		English
hacer un depósito	A	make a deposit
sacar dinero/hacer un retiro	B	make a withdrawal
cambiar/cobrar un cheque	C	cash a check
comprar cheques de viajero	D	get traveler's checks
abrir una cuenta	E	open an account
pedir un préstamo	F	apply for a loan
cambiar divisas/dinero/efectivo	G	exchange currency
ficha de depósito	1	deposit slip
ficha de retiro	2	withdrawal slip
cheque	3	check

Spanish		English
cheques de viajero	4	traveler's check
libreta de banco	5	bankbook/passbook
tarjeta para cajero automático	6	ATM card
tarjeta de crédito	7	credit card
caja/caja fuerte/de caudales	8	(bank) vault
caja de seguridad	9	safe deposit box
cajero(a)	10	teller
guardia de seguridad	11	security guard
cajero automático	12	ATM (machine)/cash machine
funcionario(a) de banco	13	bank officer

[A–G]

A. Where are you going?
B. I'm going to the bank.
   I have to _____.

[5–7]

A. What are you looking for?
B. My _____. I can't find it anywhere!

[8–13]

A. How many _____s does the State Street Bank have?
B. ....

Do you have a bank account? What kind? Where? What do you do at the bank?

Do you ever use traveler's checks? When?

Do you have a credit card? What kind? When do you use it?

FINANZAS

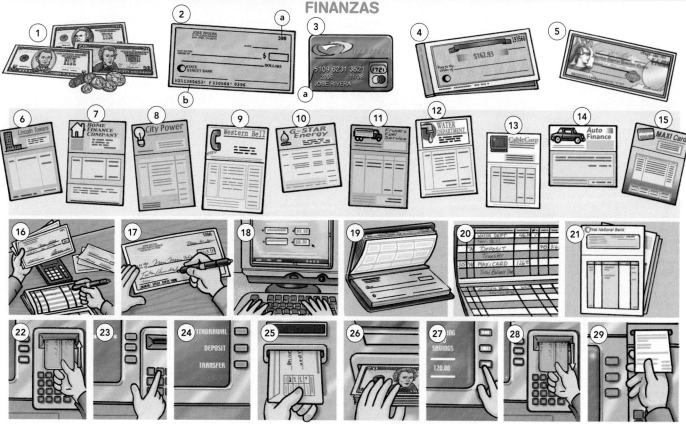

Formas de pago / Forms of Payment

dinero en efectivo — **1** cash
cheque — **2** check
número del cheque — **a** check number
número de la cuenta — **b** account number
tarjeta de crédito — **3** credit card
número de la tarjeta de crédito — **a** credit card number
orden de pago/giro postal/telegráfico — **4** money order
cheques de viajero — **5** traveler's check

Cuentas del hogar / Household Bills

renta/arriendo/alquiler — **6** rent
hipoteca — **7** mortgage payment
cuenta de la electricidad — **8** electric bill
cuenta del teléfono — **9** telephone bill
cuenta del gas — **10** gas bill
cuenta de la calefacción — **11** oil bill/heating bill
cuenta del agua — **12** water bill
cuenta de la televisión por cable — **13** cable TV bill
pago del automóvil — **14** car payment
cuenta de la tarjeta de crédito — **15** credit card bill

Finanzas familiares / Family Finances

reconciliar la cuenta de cheques — **16** balance the checkbook
hacer/escribir un cheque — **17** write a check
hacer banca en línea/banco virtual — **18** bank online
chequera/talonario de cheques — **19** checkbook
registro de cheques — **20** check register
estado de cuenta mensual — **21** monthly statement

Uso del cajero automático / Using an ATM Machine

inserte la tarjeta de cajero automático — **22** insert the ATM card
ingrese/teclee su número de identificación personal — **23** enter your PIN number/personal identification number
elija la transacción que desee realizar — **24** select a transaction
haga su depósito — **25** make a deposit
retire el dinero — **26** withdraw/get cash
transfiera fondos — **27** transfer funds
retire su tarjeta — **28** remove your card
retire el comprobante/recibo/resguardo de la transacción — **29** take your transaction slip/receipt

A. Can I pay by __[1, 2]__ / with a __[3–5]__ ?
B. Yes. We accept __[1]__ / __[2–5]__ s.

A. What are you doing?
B. { I'm paying the __[6–15]__ .
I'm __[16–18]__ ing.
I'm looking for the __[19–21]__ .

A. What should I do?
B. __[22–29]__ .

What household bills do you receive? How much do you pay for the different bills?

Who takes care of the finances in your household? What does that person do?

Do you use ATM machines? If you do, how do you use them?

LA OFICINA DE CORREOS

Spanish	#	English
carta	1	letter
tarjeta postal	2	postcard
aerograma	3	air letter/ aerogramme
paquete	4	package/parcel
primera clase	5	first class
urgente	6	priority mail
entrega inmediata/ expreso	7	express mail/ overnight mail
paquete postal/encomienda	8	parcel post
correo certificado	9	certified mail
sello postal/estampilla/timbre	10	stamp
pliego de sellos/estampillas	11	sheet of stamps
rollo de sellos/estampillas	12	roll of stamps
libreta de sellos/estampillas	13	book of stamps
giro/giro postal/telegráfico	14	money order
formulario de cambio de domicilio	15	change-of-address form

Spanish	#	English
formulario para registro en el servicio militar	16	selective service registration form
formulario para solicitar pasaporte	17	passport application form
sobre	18	envelope
remitente	19	return address
destinatario	20	mailing address
código/área postal	21	zip code
sello postal/matasellos	22	postmark
sello postal/estampilla/timbre	23	stamp/postage
buzón	24	mail slot
empleado(a) de correos	25	postal worker/postal clerk
báscula	26	scale
máquina de estampillas	27	stamp machine
cartero(a)	28	letter carrier/mail carrier
camión de correos	29	mail truck
buzón	30	mailbox

[1–4]
A. Where are you going?
B. To the post office. I have to mail a/an _____.

[5–9]
A. How do you want to send it?
B. _____, please.

[10–17]
A. Next!
B. I'd like a _____, please.
A. Here you are.

[19–21, 23]
A. Do you want me to mail this letter?
B. Yes, thanks.
A. Oops! You forgot the _____!

How often do you go to the post office? What do you do there?

Tell about the postal system in your country.

LA BIBLIOTECA

catálogo en línea	**1** online catalog		CD/discos compactos	**17** CDs
catálogo/tarjetero/fichero	**2** card catalog		videocintas	**18** videotapes
autor	**3** author		programa de computadora/informático	**19** (computer) software
título	**4** title		disco de video digital/DVD	**20** DVDs
carnet/tarjeta de identificación	**5** library card		sección de lenguas/	**21** foreign language
fotocopiadora	**6** copier/photocopier/		idomas extranjeros(as)	section
	copy machine		libros en lenguas/	**22** foreign language
estantes/librero/librería	**7** shelves		idiomas extranjeros(as)	books
sección infantil	**8** children's section		sección de referencias/consultas	**23** reference section
libros infantiles	**9** children's books		microfilm	**24** microfilm
sección de publicaciones	**10** periodical section		lector de microfilm	**25** microfilm reader
periódicas/revistas académicas			diccionario	**26** dictionary
boletines/revistas académicas	**11** journals		enciclopedia	**27** encyclopedia
revistas	**12** magazines		atlas	**28** atlas
periódicos	**13** newspapers		mostrador de la sección de consultas	**29** reference desk
sección audiovisual	**14** media section		bibliotecario(a) de la sección de consulta	**30** (reference) librarian
libros grabados/hablantes	**15** books on tape		mostrador de préstamos	**31** checkout desk
audiocintas/audiocasetes	**16** audiotapes		empleado(a) de biblioteca	**32** library clerk

[1, 2, 6–32]
A. Excuse me. Where's/Where are the _____?
B. Over there, at/near/next to the _____.

[8–23, 26–28]
A. Excuse me. Where can I find a/an __[26–28]__ / __[9, 11–13, 15–20, 22]__ ?
B. Look in the __[8, 10, 14, 21, 23]__ over there.

A. I'm having trouble finding a book.
B. Do you know the __[3–4]__ ?
A. Yes. ....

A. Excuse me. I'd like to check out this __[26–28]__/these __[11–13]__.
B. I'm sorry. It/They must remain in the library.

Do you go to a library? Where? What does this library have?

Tell about how you use the library.

INSTITUCIONES COMUNITARIAS

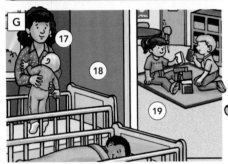

comisaría/estación/cuartel de policía	**A** police station	bombero(a)	**5** firefighter
cuartel/estación de bomberos	**B** fire station	sala de emergencias	**6** emergency room
hospital/sanatorio	**C** hospital	paramédico	**7** EMT/paramedic
palacio de gobierno/ayuntamiento	**D** town hall/city hall	ambulancia	**8** ambulance
centro recreativo	**E** recreation center	alcalde/intendente municipal	**9** mayor/city manager
basurero público	**F** dump	sala de reuniones	**10** meeting room
guardería infantil	**G** child-care center	gimnasio	**11** gym
centro para personas mayores	**H** senior center	director de actividades	**12** activities director
iglesia	**I** church	salón de juegos	**13** game room
sinagoga	**J** synagogue	piscina/pileta/alberca	**14** swimming pool
mezquita	**K** mosque	recogedor de basura	**15** sanitation worker
templo	**L** temple	centro de reciclaje/reutilización	**16** recycling center
		auxiliar de guardería infantil	**17** child-care worker
telefonista para llamadas de emergencia	**1** emergency operator	guardería infantil	**18** nursery
policía	**2** police officer	cuarto de juegos	**19** playroom
radiopatrulla/patrulla/coche de policía	**3** police car	enfermero(a) geriátrico(a)/	**20** eldercare worker/
vehículo autobomba	**4** fire engine	especialista en adultos mayores	senior care worker

[A–L]
A. Where are you going?
B. I'm going to the _____.

[1, 2, 5, 7, 12, 15, 17, 20]
A. What do you do?
B. I'm a/an _____.

[3, 4, 8]
A. Do you hear a siren?
B. Yes. There's a/an _____ coming up behind us.

What community institutions are in your city or town? Where are they located?

Which community institutions do you use? When?

CRÍMENES Y EMERGENCIAS

choque/accidente	**1** car accident	asesinato	**12** murder
incendio	**2** fire	apagón	**13** blackout/power outage
explosión	**3** explosion	escape/fuga de gas	**14** gas leak
robo	**4** robbery	tubería de agua principal rota	**15** water main break
robo a una casa	**5** burglary	cable eléctrico roto	**16** downed power line
atraco	**6** mugging	derrame de sustancias químicas	**17** chemical spill
secuestro	**7** kidnapping	descarrilamiento de trenes	**18** train derailment
niño(a) perdido(a)	**8** lost child	vandalismo	**19** vandalism
robo de automóvil/carro/coche	**9** car jacking	violencia de pandillas	**20** gang violence
robo a un banco	**10** bank robbery	conductores ebrios	**21** drunk driving
asalto/ataque	**11** assault	tráfico de drogas	**22** drug dealing

[1–13]
A. I want to report a/an _____.
B. What's your location?
A. ....

[14–18]
A. Why is this street closed?
B. It's closed because of a _____.

[19–22]
A. I'm very concerned about the amount of _____ in our community.
B. I agree. _____ is a very serious problem.

Is there much crime in your community? Tell about it.

Have you ever experienced a crime or emergency? What happened?

EL CUERPO HUMANO

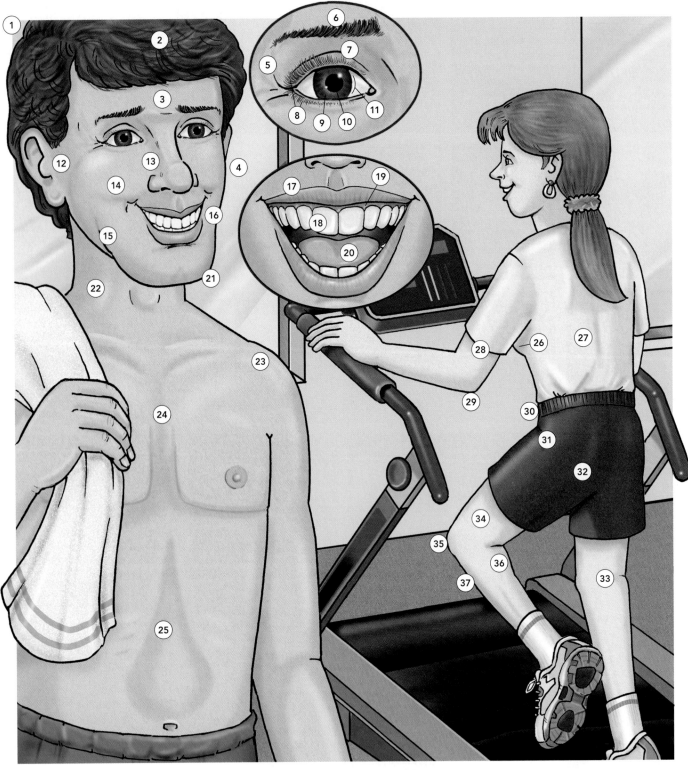

cabeza	**1**	head	pupila	**10**	pupil	diente(s)	**18**	tooth–teeth	brazo	**28**	arm
cabello/	**2**	hair	córnea	**11**	cornea	encías	**19**	gums	codo	**29**	elbow
pelo			oreja	**12**	ear	lengua	**20**	tongue	cintura	**30**	waist
frente	**3**	forehead	nariz	**13**	nose	mentón/barbilla	**21**	chin	cadera	**31**	hip
cara	**4**	face	mejilla/	**14**	cheek	cuello	**22**	neck	nalgas	**32**	buttocks
ojo	**5**	eye	pómulo			hombro	**23**	shoulder	pierna	**33**	leg
ceja	**6**	eyebrow	mandíbula/	**15**	jaw	pecho	**24**	chest	muslo	**34**	thigh
párpado	**7**	eyelid	quijada			abdomen/vientre	**25**	abdomen	rodilla	**35**	knee
pestañas	**8**	eyelashes	boca	**16**	mouth	seno/busto/pecho	**26**	breast	pantorrilla	**36**	calf
iris	**9**	iris	labio	**17**	lip	espalda	**27**	back	espinilla	**37**	shin

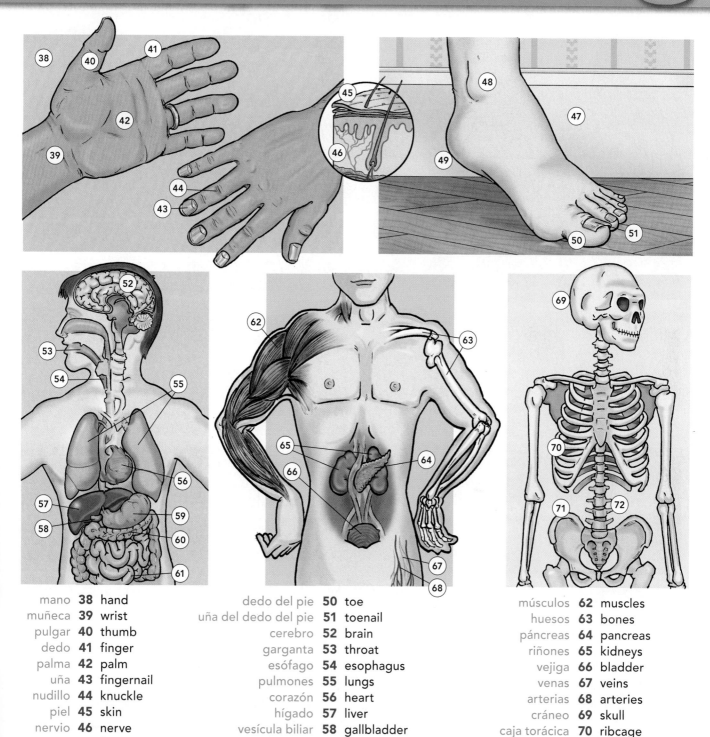

mano	**38**	hand	dedo del pie	**50**	toe	músculos	**62**	muscles
muñeca	**39**	wrist	uña del dedo del pie	**51**	toenail	huesos	**63**	bones
pulgar	**40**	thumb	cerebro	**52**	brain	páncreas	**64**	pancreas
dedo	**41**	finger	garganta	**53**	throat	riñones	**65**	kidneys
palma	**42**	palm	esófago	**54**	esophagus	vejiga	**66**	bladder
uña	**43**	fingernail	pulmones	**55**	lungs	venas	**67**	veins
nudillo	**44**	knuckle	corazón	**56**	heart	arterias	**68**	arteries
piel	**45**	skin	hígado	**57**	liver	cráneo	**69**	skull
nervio	**46**	nerve	vesícula biliar	**58**	gallbladder	caja torácica	**70**	ribcage
pie	**47**	foot	estómago	**59**	stomach	pelvis	**71**	pelvis
tobillo	**48**	ankle	intestino grueso	**60**	large intestine	columna vertebral/	**72**	spinal column/
talón	**49**	heel	intestino delgado	**61**	small intestine	espina dorsal		spinal cord

A. My doctor checked my **head** and said everything is okay.
B. I'm glad to hear that.

[1, 3–7, 12–29, 31–51]
A. Ooh!
B. What's the matter?
{ My _____ hurts!
{ My _____s hurt!

[52–72]
A. My doctor wants me to have some tests.
B. Why?
A. She's concerned about my _____.

Describe yourself as completely as you can.

Which parts of the body are most important at school? at work? when you play your favorite sport?

MALESTARES, SÍNTOMAS Y LESIONES

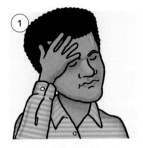  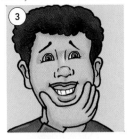  

   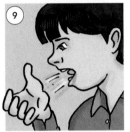 

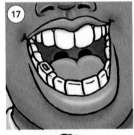 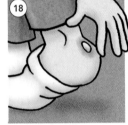 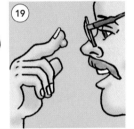  

dolor de cabeza	1	headache	infección	10	infection	verruga	19	wart
dolor de oído	2	earache	sarpullido/salpullido	11	rash	hipo	20	(the) hiccups
dolor de muelas/dientes	3	toothache	picadura/picada	12	insect bite	escalofrío	21	(the) chills
dolor de estómago	4	stomachache	quemadura de sol	13	sunburn	calambre/retortijón	22	cramps
dolor de espalda	5	backache	tortícolis	14	stiff neck	diarrea	23	diarrhea
dolor de garganta	6	sore throat	moquear	15	runny nose	dolor en el pecho	24	chest pain
fiebre/calentura	7	fever/temperature	hemorragia nasal	16	bloody nose	jadeo	25	shortness of breath
catarro/resfriado	8	cold	caries	17	cavity	laringitis	26	laryngitis
tos	9	cough	ampolla	18	blister			

A. What's the matter?
B. I have a/an _____[1–19]_____.

A. What's the matter?
B. I have _____[20–26]____.

desmayo **27** faint	respiración sibilante **35** wheeze	quemadura **43** burn
(tener) mareo **28** dizzy	eructo **36** burp	lesionarse **44** hurt–hurt
tener náuseas **29** nauseous	vómito **37** vomit/throw up	cortarse **45** cut–cut
hinchazón del **30** bloated	sangrado **38** bleed	torcedura **46** sprain
abdomen/gases	torcedura de pie **39** twist	dislocación **47** dislocate
congestionado(a) **31** congested	arañazo **40** scratch	fracturarse **48** break–broke
agotado(a) **32** exhausted	raspadura/rasguño **41** scrape	hinchazón **49** swollen
tos **33** cough	moretón/magulladura/ **42** bruise	comezón/picazón **50** itchy
estornudo **34** sneeze	cardenal	

A. What's the problem?
B. { I feel [27–30] .
{ I'm [31–32] .
{ I've been [33–38] ing a lot.

A. What happened?
B. { I [39–45] ed my ....
{ I think I [46–48] ed my ....
{ My .... is/are [49–50] .

A. How do you feel?
B. Not so good. / Not very well. / Terrible!
A. What's the matter?
B. .... / .... , and ....
A. I'm sorry to hear that.

Tell about the last time you didn't feel well. What was the matter?

Tell about a time you hurt yourself. What happened? How? What did you do about it?

What do you do when you have a cold? a stomachache? an insect bite? the hiccups?

PRIMEROS AUXILIOS

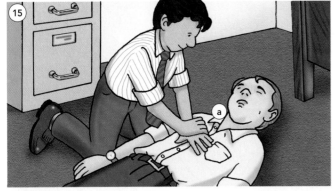 

  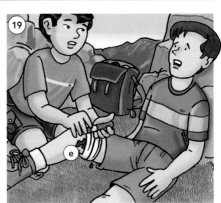

manual de primeros auxilios	**1** first-aid manual		venda elástica	**12** elastic bandage/ Ace™ bandage
maletín/botiquín de primeros auxilios	**2** first-aid kit		aspirina	**13** aspirin
tirita/curita	**3** (adhesive) bandage/ Band-Aid™		analgésico sin aspirina	**14** non-aspirin pain reliever
toallita antiséptica	**4** antiseptic cleansing wipe		respiración artificial/ resucitación cardiopulmonar	**15** CPR (cardiopulmonary resuscitation)
almohadilla estéril	**5** sterile (dressing) pad		no tiene pulso	**a** has no pulse
agua oxigenada	**6** hydrogen peroxide		respiración artificial/asistida	**16** rescue breathing
ungüento antibiótico	**7** antibiotic ointment		no está respirando	**b** isn't breathing
gasa	**8** gauze		la maniobra de Heimlich	**17** the Heimlich maneuver
esparadrapo/ cinta adhesiva	**9** adhesive tape		está atorado/se está asfixiando	**c** is choking
			entablillar	**18** splint
pinzas	**10** tweezers		se rompió un dedo	**d** broke a finger
crema antihistamínica	**11** antihistamine cream		torniquete	**19** tourniquet
			está sangrando	**e** is bleeding

A. Do we have any _____[3–5, 12]_____s/ _____[6–11, 13, 14]_____ ?
B. Yes. Look in the first-aid kit.

A. Help! My friend _____[a–e]_____ !
B. I can help!
{ I know how to do _____[15–17]_____ .
{ I can make a _____[18, 19]_____ .

Do you have a first-aid kit? If you do, what's in it? If you don't, where can you buy one?

Tell about a time when you gave or received first aid.

Where can a person learn first aid in your community?

herido(a)/lastimado(a)	1	hurt/injured
en estado de choque	2	in shock
inconsciente	3	unconscious
insolación	4	heatstroke
congelado(a)/daño en el cuerpo por el frío	5	frostbite
ataque al corazón	6	heart attack
reacción alérgica	7	allergic reaction
tragar veneno	8	swallow poison
sobredosis de medicinas/drogas	9	overdose on drugs
caerse	10	fall–fell
sufrir un choque eléctrico	11	get–got an electric shock
influenza/gripe	12	the flu/influenza
infección de oído	13	an ear infection
infección (de estreptococos) en la garganta	14	strep throat
sarampión	15	measles
paperas	16	mumps
varicela/viruela loca	17	chicken pox
asma	18	asthma
cáncer	19	cancer
depresión	20	depression
diabetes	21	diabetes
afección del corazón	22	heart disease
presión alta/hipertensión	23	high blood pressure/hypertension
tuberculosis	24	TB/tuberculosis
SIDA*	25	AIDS*
* Síndrome de Inmunodeficiencia Adquirida		* Acquired Immune Deficiency Syndrome

A. What happened?
B. My .... {
  is _____[1–3]_____ .
  has _____[4–5]_____ .
  is having a/an _____[6–7]_____ .
  _____[8–11]_____ ed.
}
A. What's your location?
B. ....(address)..........

A. My .... is sick.
B. What's the matter?
A. He/She has _____[12–25]_____ .
B. I'm sorry to hear that.

Tell about a medical emergency that happened to you or someone you know.

Which illnesses in this lesson are you familiar with?

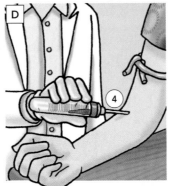

medir*le* y pesar*le*	**A** measure *your* height and weight	báscula/balanza	**1** scale
tomar*le* la temperatura	**B** take *your* temperature	termómetro	**2** thermometer
tomar*le* la presión arterial	**C** check *your* blood pressure	manómetro	**3** blood pressure gauge
sacar*le* sangre	**D** draw some blood	aguja/jeringa/jeringuilla	**4** needle/syringe
hacer*le* algunas preguntas sobre *su* salud	**E** ask *you* some questions about *your* health	consultorio	**5** examination room
examinar*le* los ojos, oídos, nariz y garganta	**F** examine *your* eyes, ears, nose, and throat	camilla de examen/ mesa de reconocimiento	**6** examination table
escuchar*le* el corazón	**G** listen to *your* heart	cartilla para medir la vista	**7** eye chart
tomar*le* una radiografía del pecho	**H** take a chest X-ray	estetoscopio	**8** stethoscope
		máquina de rayos X/ radiografías	**9** X-ray machine

[A–H]
A. Now I'm going to **measure your height and weight**.
B. All right.

[A–H]
A. What did the doctor/nurse do during the examination?
B. She/He **measured my height and weight**.

[1–3, 5–9]
A. So, how do you like our new **scale?**
B. It's very nice, doctor.

How often do you have a medical exam? What does the doctor/nurse do?

PROCEDIMIENTOS MÉDICOS Y DENTALES

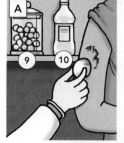

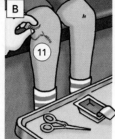

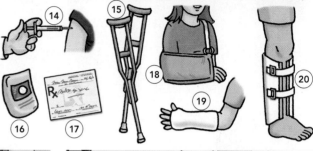

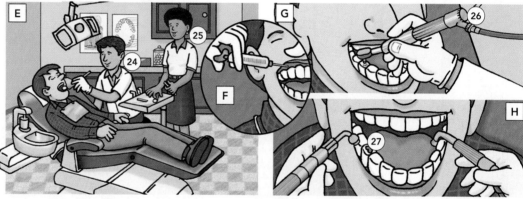

limpiar la herida	**A** clean the wound	consultorio	**5** examination room	bolsa de hielo	**16** ice pack
coser/suturar la herida	**B** close the wound	médico/doctor	**6** doctor/physician	receta médica	**17** prescription
vendar la herida	**C** dress the wound			cabestrillo	**18** sling
limpiar*le* los dientes	**D** clean *your* teeth	paciente	**7** patient	yeso/enyesado/escayola	**19** cast
examinar*le* los dientes	**E** examine *your* teeth	enfermero(a)	**8** nurse	férula/entablillado	**20** brace
poner*le* una inyección con anestesia/Novocaína™	**F** give *you* a shot of anesthetic/Novocaine™	motas/bolas de algodón	**9** cotton balls	higienista dental	**21** dental hygienist
taladrar el diente/la caries	**G** drill the cavity	alcohol	**10** alcohol	mascarilla/máscara	**22** mask
rellenar la cavidad/el diente	**H** fill the tooth	sutura/puntos	**11** stitches	guantes	**23** gloves
sala de espera	**1** waiting room	gasa	**12** gauze	dentista	**24** dentist
recepcionista	**2** receptionist	esparadrapo	**13** tape	asistente (del dentista)	**25** dental assistant
tarjeta de seguro médico	**3** insurance card	inyección	**14** injection/shot	fresa/taladro	**26** drill
formulario para la historia/el historial clínico(a)	**4** medical history form	muletas	**15** crutches	empaste/relleno	**27** filling

A. Now I'm going to {
 ___[A–H]___.
 give you (a/an) ___[14–17]___.
 put your .... in a ___[18–20]___.

B. Okay.

A. I need {
 ___[9, 10, 12, 13, 23]___.
 a ___[22, 26]___.

B. Here you are.

Tell about a personal experience you had with a medical or dental procedure.

RECOMENDACIONES MÉDICAS

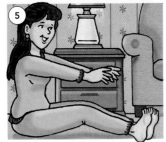

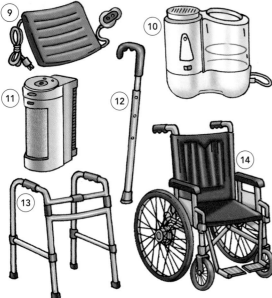

guardar cama	**1**	rest in bed	purificador de aire	**11**	air purifier
tomar líquidos	**2**	drink fluids	bastón	**12**	cane
hacer gárgaras	**3**	gargle	andadera	**13**	walker
ponerse a dieta	**4**	go on a diet	silla de ruedas	**14**	wheelchair
hacer ejercicio	**5**	exercise	análisis/pruebas de sangre	**15**	blood work/blood tests
tomar vitaminas	**6**	take vitamins	exámenes médicos/análisis	**16**	tests
ver a un especialista	**7**	see a specialist	fisioterapia	**17**	physical therapy
recibir tratamiento de acupuntura	**8**	get acupuncture	operación/cirugía	**18**	surgery
bolsa caliente/almohadilla eléctrica	**9**	heating pad	consejo personal/psicoterapia	**19**	counseling
humidificador	**10**	humidifier	frenos	**20**	braces

A. I think { you should _____ [1–8].
you should use a/an _____ [9–14].
you need _____ [15–20].

B. I see.

A. What did the doctor say?

B. The doctor thinks { I should _____ [1–8].
I should use a/an _____ [9–14].
I need _____ [15–20].

Tell about medical advice a doctor gave you. What did the doctor say? Did you follow the advice?

REMEDIOS/MEDICINAS

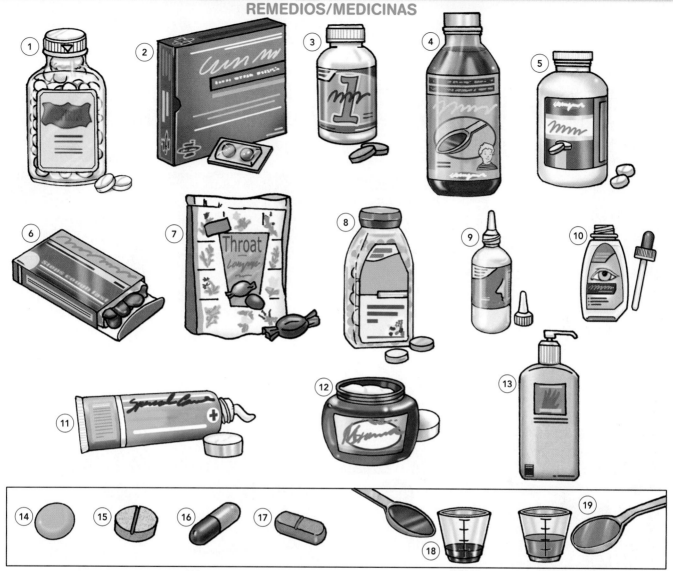

aspirina **1** aspirin	gotas para los ojos **10** eye drops
píldoras para el resfriado/catarro **2** cold tablets	ungüento/pomada **11** ointment
vitaminas **3** vitamins	pomada/crema **12** cream/creme
jarabe para la tos **4** cough syrup	loción **13** lotion
analgésico sin aspirina **5** non-aspirin pain reliever	píldora **14** pill
pastillas para la tos **6** cough drops	tableta/pastilla **15** tablet
pastillas para la garganta **7** throat lozenges	cápsula **16** capsule
antiácido en tabletas **8** antacid tablets	cápsula comprimida **17** caplet
descongestionante nasal (en **9** decongestant spray/	cucharadita/cuchara de té **18** teaspoon
atomizador/spray) nasal spray	cucharada/cuchara sopera **19** tablespoon

[1–13]

A. What did the doctor say?

B. { She / He told me to take _____[1–4]_____ / a ___[5]___.
{ She / He told me to use _____[6–13]_____.

[14–19]

A. What's the dosage?

B. One _____ every four hours.

What medicines in this lesson do you have at home? What other medicines do you have?

What do you take or use for a fever? a headache? a stomachache? a sore throat? a cold? a cough?

Tell about any medicines in your country that are different from the ones in this lesson.

MÉDICOS ESPECIALISTAS

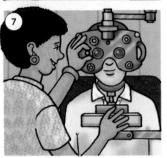
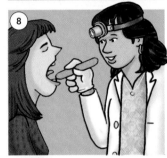

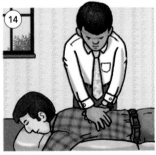
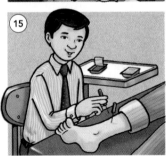
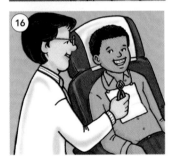

cardiólogo(a)	**1**	cardiologist
ginecólogo(a)	**2**	gynecologist
pediatra	**3**	pediatrician
geriatra	**4**	gerontologist
alergista/alergólogo(a)	**5**	allergist
ortopeda/ortopedista	**6**	orthopedist
oftalmólogo(a)	**7**	ophthalmologist
otorrinolaringólogo(a)	**8**	ear, nose, and throat (ENT) specialist

audiólogo(a)	**9**	audiologist
fisioterapeuta	**10**	physical therapist
psicoterapeuta/terapeuta	**11**	counselor/therapist
psiquiatra	**12**	psychiatrist
gastroenterólogo(a)	**13**	gastroenterologist
quiropráctico(a)	**14**	chiropractor
acupuntor(a)/acupunturista	**15**	acupuncturist
ortodoncista	**16**	orthodontist

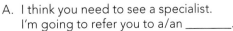

A. I think you need to see a specialist. I'm going to refer you to a/an _____.
B. A/An _____?
A. Yes.

A. When is your next appointment with the _____?
B. It's at ...... (time) ...... on ...... (date) ......

Do you or members of your family see any of these medical specialists? Which ones?

EL HOSPITAL

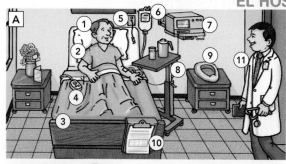

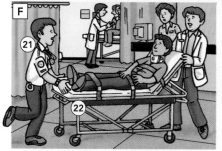

cuarto del/de la paciente	**A patient's room**
paciente	1 patient
bata de hospital	2 hospital gown
cama de hospital	3 hospital bed
control de la cama	4 bed control
timbre	5 call button
venoclisis/intravenosa	6 I.V.
monitor/pantalla con control de signos vitales	7 vital signs monitor
mesa de cama	8 bed table
cuña/paleta/bacín/cómodo/silleta	9 bed pan
cuadrícula/hoja clínica	10 medical chart
médico(a)/doctor(a)	11 doctor/physician
estación de enfermeros(as)	**B nurse's station**
enfermero(a)	12 nurse
especialista en dietética	13 dietitian
asistente de enfermero(a)	14 orderly

sala de operaciones/quirófano	**C operating room**
cirujano(a)	15 surgeon
enfermero(a)/quirúrgico(a)	16 surgical nurse
anestesiólogo(a)/anestesista	17 anesthesiologist
sala de espera	**D waiting room**
voluntario(a)	18 volunteer
sala de partos	**E birthing room/delivery room**
ginecólogo(a)/obstetra	19 obstetrician
enfermera comadrona/partera	20 midwife/nurse-midwife
sala de emergencias	**F emergency room/ER**
paramédico(a)	21 emergency medical technician/EMT
camilla	22 gurney
departamento de radiología	**G radiology department**
técnico(a) radiólogo(a)	23 X-ray technician
radiólogo	24 radiologist
laboratorio	**H laboratory/lab**
técnico de laboratorio	25 lab technician

A. This is your ____[2–10]____.
B. I see.

A. Do you work here?
B. Yes. I'm a/an ____[11–21, 23–25]____.

A. Where's the ____[11–21, 23–25]____?
B. She's/He's { in the ____[A, C–H]____.
            at the ____[B]____.

Tell about an experience you or a family member had in the hospital.

PERSONAL HYGIENE

HIGIENE PERSONAL

me estoy cepillando los dientes	**A brush *my* teeth**
cepillo de dientes	**1** toothbrush
pasta de dientes/crema dental	**2** toothpaste
estoy usando el hilo dental	**B floss *my* teeth**
seda/hilo dental/hilo de dientes	**3** dental floss
estoy haciendo gárgaras	**C gargle**
antiséptico/enjuague bucal	**4** mouthwash
me estoy blanqueando los dientes	**D whiten *my* teeth**
blanqueador de dientes	**5** teeth whitener
me estoy bañando en la tina	**E bathe/take a bath**
jabón	**6** soap
baño de burbujas/espuma	**7** bubble bath
me estoy bañando/duchando	**F take a shower**
gorra(o) de baño	**8** shower cap
me estoy lavando el pelo/cabello	**G wash *my* hair**
champú	**9** shampoo
acondicionador/enjuague	**10** conditioner/rinse

me estoy secando el pelo/cabello	**H dry *my* hair**
secador(a) de pelo/cabello	**11** hair dryer/ blow dryer
me estoy peinando	**I comb *my* hair**
peine/peinilla	**12** comb
me estoy cepillando el pelo/cabello	**J brush *my* hair**
cepillo para el pelo/cabello	**13** (hair) brush
me estoy arreglando el pelo/ cabello	**K style *my* hair**
peinilla caliente/alisadora/ tenazas eléctricas/moldeador/ rizador de pelo/cabello	**14** hot comb/ curling iron
fijador/spray para el pelo/cabello	**15** hairspray
fijador/gel para el pelo/cabello	**16** hair gel
gancho/horquilla/pasador	**17** bobby pin
pasador/hebilla/barra para el pelo/ cabello	**18** barrette
pinza/sujetador de pelo/cabello	**19** hairclip

me estoy afeitando/rasurando	L	shave
crema para afeitarse/rasurarse	20	shaving cream
maquinilla de afeitar/rastrillo	21	razor
hoja de navaja	22	razor blade
máquina de afeitar eléctrica	23	electric shaver
astringente	24	styptic pencil
loción para después de afeitar	25	aftershave (lotion)

me estoy arreglando las uñas	M	do my nails
lima de metal para las uñas	26	nail file
lima de cartón para las uñas	27	emery board
cortaúñas	28	nail clipper
cepillo de uñas	29	nail brush
tijeras	30	scissors
esmalte de uñas/barniz	31	nail polish
acetona/quitaesmalte de uñas	32	nail polish remover

me estoy poniendo . . .	N	put on . . .
desodorante	33	deodorant
crema/loción para las manos	34	hand lotion

crema/loción para el cuerpo	35	body lotion
talco/polvo	36	powder
colonia/perfume	37	cologne/perfume
bloqueador solar/loción protectora	38	sunscreen

me estoy maquillando	O	put on makeup
colorete	39	blush/rouge
base para el maquillaje	40	foundation/base
crema/loción humectante	41	moisturizer
polvo para la cara	42	face powder
delineador de ojos	43	eyeliner
sombra para los ojos	44	eye shadow
rímel/pintador de pestañas	45	mascara
lápiz de cejas	46	eyebrow pencil
pintalabios/lápiz de labios/	47	lipstick
carmín/bilé		

me estoy lustrando los zapatos	P	polish my shoes
betún/cera para zapatos	48	shoe polish
cordones de zapatos/agujetas	49	shoelaces

[A–M, N (33–38), O, P]
A. What are you doing?
B. I'm _____ing.

[1, 8, 11–14, 17–19, 21–24, 26–30, 46, 49]
A. Excuse me. Where can I find
   _____(s)?
B. They're in the next aisle.

[2–7, 9, 10, 15, 16, 20, 25, 31–45, 47, 48]
A. Excuse me. Where can I find
   _____?
B. It's in the next aisle.

Which of these personal care products do you use?

You're going on a trip. Make a list of the personal care products you need to take with you.

EL CUIDADO DEL BEBÉ

darle la comida	**A feed**	palillo de algodón/hisopo	**15** cotton swab
papillas/comidas de bebé	**1** baby food	loción para niños	**16** baby lotion
en frasquitos o tarritos/colados			
babero	**2** bib	cargar	**D hold**
biberón/mamadera/tetero/mamila	**3** bottle	chupete/consuelo/chupón	**17** pacifier
chupón/chupete/tetina/tetilla/mamadera	**4** nipple	chupador/chupón/mordedera	**18** teething ring
fórmula/leche en polvo	**5** formula	amamantar	**E nurse**
vitaminas en líquido/en gotas	**6** (liquid) vitamins	vestir	**F dress**
cambiarle el pañal	**B change the baby's diaper**	mecer/arrullar	**G rock**
pañal desechable	**7** disposable diaper	guardería infantil	**19** child-care center
pañal de tela/algodón	**8** cloth diaper	trabajador(a) de guardería infantil	**20** child-care worker
imperdible/alfiler de gancho/seguridad	**9** diaper pin	mecedora	**21** rocking chair
toallitas húmedas desechables	**10** (baby) wipes	leerle a	**H read to**
polvo/talco para niños	**11** baby powder	armario	**22** cubby
pañal entrenador/pull up	**12** training pants	jugar con	**I play with**
pomada/ungüento	**13** ointment	juguetes	**23** toys
bañar	**C bathe**		
champú para niños	**14** baby shampoo		

A. What are you doing?
B. { I'm _____[A, C–I]_____ ing the baby.
    { I'm _____[B]_____ ing.

A. Do we need anything from the store?
B. Yes. We need some more { _____[2–4, 7–9, 15, 17, 18]_____ s
                            { _____[1, 5, 6, 10–14, 16]_____ .

In your opinion, which are better: cloth diapers or disposable diapers? Why? Tell about baby products in your country.

TIPOS DE ESCUELA

jardín de la infancia/preescolar/kínder	**1**	preschool/nursery school	institución que imparte los	**7**	community college
escuela primaria	**2**	elementary school	dos primeros años de una		
primer ciclo de escuela secundaria/	**3**	middle school/	carrera y educación para adultos		
liceo (grados séptimo a noveno)		junior high school	universidad	**8**	college
segundo ciclo de escuela	**4**	high school	universidad	**9**	university
secundaria/instituto/bachillerato			escuela de postgrado/posgrado	**10**	graduate school
escuela para adultos	**5**	adult school	facultad de leyes	**11**	law school
escuela de artes y oficios/vocacional	**6**	vocational school/trade school	facultad de medicina	**12**	medical school

A. Are you a student?
B. Yes. I'm in _____ [1–4, 8, 10–12] _____.

A. Are you a student?
B. Yes. I go to a/an _____ [5–7, 9] _____.

A. Is this apartment building near a/an _____?

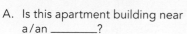

B. Yes. _____ *(name of school)* _____ is nearby.

A. Tell me about your previous education.
B. I went to _____ *(name of school)* _____.
A. Did you like it there?
B. Yes. It was an excellent _____.

What types of schools are there in your community? What are their names, and where are they located?

What types of schools have you gone to?

Where? When? What did you study?

LA ESCUELA

oficina/administración	**A**	(main) office
dirección/rectoría	**B**	principal's office
enfermería	**C**	nurse's office
consejería	**D**	guidance office
salón/sala de clases/aula	**E**	classroom
pasillo/corredor	**F**	hallway
casillero	**a**	locker
laboratorio de ciencias	**G**	science lab
gimnasio	**H**	gym/gymnasium
vestidor	**a**	locker room
pista	**I**	track
gradería/gradas	**a**	bleachers
campo de juego	**J**	field
auditorio	**K**	auditorium
cafetería	**L**	cafeteria
biblioteca	**M**	library

secretario(a) de la escuela	**1**	clerk/(school) secretary
director(a)	**2**	principal
enfermero(a)	**3**	(school) nurse
consejero(a)	**4**	(guidance) counselor
maestro(a)/profesor(a)	**5**	teacher
subdirector(a)	**6**	assistant principal/vice-principal
guardia de seguridad	**7**	security officer
maestro(a) de ciencias	**8**	science teacher
maestro(a) de educación física	**9**	P.E. teacher
entrenador(a)	**10**	coach
portero(a)/afanador(a)	**11**	custodian
empleado(a) de la cafetería	**12**	cafeteria worker
supervisor(a) de la cafetería	**13**	lunchroom monitor
bibliotecario(a)	**14**	(school) librarian

A. Where are you going?
B. I'm going to the ___[A–D, G–M]___ .
A. Do you have a hall pass?
B. Yes. Here it is.

A. Where's the ___[1–14]___ ?
B. He's/She's in the ___[A–M]___ .

Describe the school where you study English.
Tell about the rooms, offices, and people.

Tell about differences between the school
in this lesson and schools in your country.

CURSOS/MATERIAS

   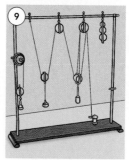 

matemáticas	1	math/mathematics	informática/computación	11	computer science
inglés	2	English	español	12	Spanish
historia	3	history	francés	13	French
geografía	4	geography	economía doméstica	14	home economics
gobierno/civismo	5	government	artes industriales/taller	15	industrial arts/shop
ciencias	6	science	comercio/negocios	16	business education
biología	7	biology	educación física	17	physical education/P.E.
química	8	chemistry	curso para aprender a manejar/conducir	18	driver's education/driver's ed
física	9	physics	arte	19	art
salud/higiene	10	health	música	20	music

A. What do you have next period?
B. **Math**. How about you?
A. **English**.
B. There's the bell. I've got to go.

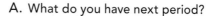

What is/was your favorite subject? Why?

In your opinion, what's the most interesting subject? the most difficult subject? Why do you think so?

ACTIVIDADES EXTRACURRICULARES

banda	**1**	band
orquesta	**2**	orchestra
coro	**3**	choir/chorus
drama/teatro	**4**	drama
fútbol americano	**5**	football
animadores(as)	**6**	cheerleading/pep squad
asociación de estudiantes	**7**	student government
servicio comunitario	**8**	community service
periódico estudiantil	**9**	school newspaper
anuario	**10**	yearbook
revista literaria	**11**	literary magazine
equipo/cuadrilla de luces y sonido	**12**	A.V. crew
club de oratoria	**13**	debate club
club de informática/computación	**14**	computer club
club de relaciones internacionales	**15**	international club
club de ajedrez	**16**	chess club

A. Are you going home right after school?

B. { No. I have ____[1–6]____ practice.
{ No. I have a ____[7–16]____ meeting.

What extracurricular activities do/did you participate in?

Which extracurricular activities in this lesson are there in schools in your country? What other activities are there?

Arithmetic   Aritmética

$$2+1=3 \qquad 8-3=5 \qquad 4\times2=8 \qquad 10\div2=5$$

suma addition	resta subtraction	multiplicación multiplication	división division
2 **plus** 1 **equals*** 3.	8 **minus** 3 **equals*** 5.	4 **times** 2 **equals*** 8.	10 **divided by** 2 **equals*** 5.

*You can also say: **is**

A. How much is *two plus one*?
B. *Two plus one* equals / is *three.*

Make conversations for the arithmetic problems above and others.

Fractions   Fracciones

one quarter/ one fourth	one third	one half/ half	two thirds	three quarters/ three fourths

A. Is this on sale?
B. Yes. It's _____ off the regular price.

A. Is the gas tank almost empty?
B. It's about _____ full.

Percents   Porcentajes

   10% ten percent

   50% fifty percent

   75% seventy-five percent

   100% one-hundred percent

A. How did you do on the test?
B. I got _____ percent of the answers right.

A. What's the weather forecast?
B. There's a _____ percent chance of rain.

Types of Math   Tipos de matemáticas

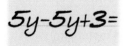   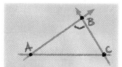   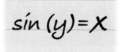   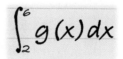   

algebra	geometry	trigonometry	calculus	statistics
álgebra	geometría	trigonometría	cálculo	estadística

A. What math course are you taking this year?
B. I'm taking _____.

Are you good at math?

What math courses do/did you take in school?

Tell about something you bought on sale. How much off the regular price was it?

Research and discuss: What percentage of people in your country live in cities? live on farms? work in factories? vote in general elections?

MEDIDAS Y FORMAS GEOMÉTRICAS

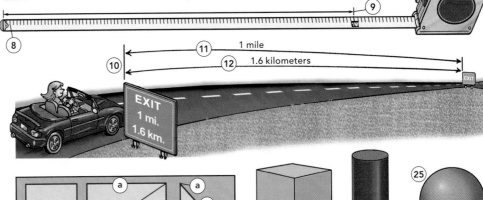
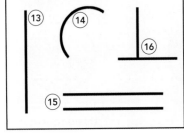

1 mile
1.6 kilometers

EXIT
1 mi.
1.6 km.

Medidas	Measurements
altura	**1** height
ancho/anchura	**2** width
profundidad	**3** depth
largo/longitud	**4** length
pulgada	**5** inch
pie-pies	**6** foot–feet
yarda	**7** yard
centímetro	**8** centimeter
metro	**9** meter
distancia	**10** distance
milla	**11** mile
kilómetro	**12** kilometer

Líneas	Lines
línea recta	**13** straight line
línea curva	**14** curved line

líneas paralelas	**15** parallel lines
líneas perpendiculares	**16** perpendicular lines

Formas geométricas	Geometric Shapes
cuadrado	**17** square
lado	**a** side
rectángulo	**18** rectangle
base	**a** length
altura	**b** width
diagonal	**c** diagonal
triángulo rectángulo	**19** right triangle
vértice	**a** apex
ángulo recto	**b** right angle
base	**c** base
hipotenusa	**d** hypotenuse

triángulo isósceles	**20** isosceles triangle
ángulo agudo	**a** acute angle
ángulo obtuso	**b** obtuse angle
círculo	**21** circle
centro	**a** center
radio	**b** radius
diámetro	**c** diameter
circunferencia	**d** circumference
elipse	**22** ellipse/oval

Sólidos/Figuras tridimensionales	Solid Figures
cubo	**23** cube
cilindro	**24** cylinder
esfera	**25** sphere
cono	**26** cone
pirámide	**27** pyramid

1 inch (1")	= 2.54 centimeters (cm)
1 foot (1')	= 0.305 meters (m)
1 yard (1 yd.)	= 0.914 meters (m)
1 mile (mi.)	= 1.6 kilometers (km)

[1–9]
A. What's the ___[1–4]___?
B. .... ___[5–9]___ (s).

[11–12]
A. What's the distance?
B. .... _____(s).

[17–22]
A. Who can tell me what shape this is?
B. I can. It's a/an _____.

[23–27]
A. Who knows what figure this is?
B. I do. It's a/an _____.

[13–27]
A. This painting is magnificent!
B. Hmm. I don't think so. It just looks like a lot of _____s and _____s to me!

EL IDIOMA INGLÉS: LENGUAJE Y REDACCIÓN

Types of Sentences & Parts of Speech   Tipos de oraciones y elementos del habla

A Students study in the new library.   **C** Read page nine.
   1   2   3   4   5

B Do they study hard?   **D** This cake is fantastic!
   6   7

declarativo	**A** declarative	sustantivo	**1** noun	
interrogativo	**B** interrogative	verbo	**2** verb	
imperativo	**C** imperative	preposición	**3** preposition	
exclamativo	**D** exclamatory	artículo	**4** article	

adjetivo	**5** adjective
pronombre	**6** pronoun
adverbio	**7** adverb

We study English every day.

A. What type of sentence is this?
B. It's a/an ___[A–D]___ sentence.

The student is tired.

A. What part of speech is this?
B. It's a/an ___[1–7]___.

Punctuation Marks & the Writing Process   Signos de puntuación y el proceso de la escritura

punto	**8** period	recolectar y asociar ideas	**16** brainstorm ideas
signo de interrogación	**9** question mark	organizar *mis* ideas	**17** organize *my* ideas
signo de exclamación	**10** exclamation point	escribir un borrador	**18** write a first draft
coma	**11** comma	título	**a** title
apóstrofe	**12** apostrophe	párrafo	**b** paragraph
comillas	**13** quotation marks	corregir/revisar/editar	**19** make corrections/revise/edit
dos puntos	**14** colon	recibir reacciones/comentarios	**20** get feedback
punto y coma	**15** semi-colon	pasar en limpio/escribir la copia final	**21** write a final copy/rewrite

A. Did you find any mistakes?
B. Yes. You forgot to put a/an ___[8–15]___ in this sentence.

A. Are you working on your composition?
B. Yes. I'm ___[16–21]___ ing.

LA LITERATURA Y LA ESCRITURA

ficción	**1**	fiction
novela	**2**	novel
cuento	**3**	short story
poesía/poemas	**4**	poetry/poems
no ficción	**5**	non-fiction
biografía	**6**	biography
autobiografía	**7**	autobiography
ensayo	**8**	essay
trabajo/reporte/ informe escolar	**9**	report
artículo de revista	**10**	magazine article

artículo periodístico	**11**	newspaper article
editorial	**12**	editorial
carta	**13**	letter
tarjeta postal	**14**	postcard
nota	**15**	note
invitación	**16**	invitation
nota de agradecimiento	**17**	thank-you note
memorándum/memoranda	**18**	memo
mensaje por correo electrónico/e-mail	**19**	e-mail
mensaje instantáneo	**20**	instant message

A. What are you doing?
B. I'm writing { [1, 4, 5] .
a/an _____ [2, 3, 6–20] .

What kind of literature do you like to read?
What are some of your favorite books?
Who is your favorite author?

Do you like to read newspapers and magazines? Which ones do you read?

Do you sometimes send or receive letters, postcards, notes, e-mail, or instant messages? Tell about the people you communicate with, and how.

GEOGRAFÍA

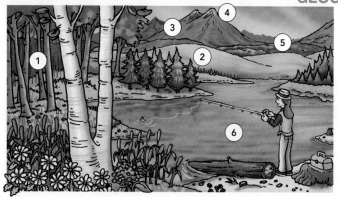

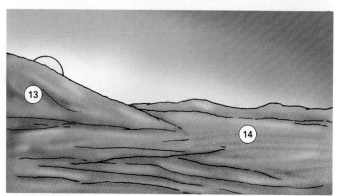

bosque	**1**	forest/woods
colina	**2**	hill
cordillera/sierra	**3**	mountain range
cumbre	**4**	mountain peak
valle	**5**	valley
lago	**6**	lake
llanuras	**7**	plains
pradera	**8**	meadow
arroyo/quebrada/riachuelo	**9**	stream/brook
laguna/charca/estanque	**10**	pond
meseta	**11**	plateau
cañón	**12**	canyon

duna	**13**	dune/sand dune
desierto	**14**	desert
selva tropical/jungla	**15**	jungle
playa/costa	**16**	seashore/shore
bahía	**17**	bay
océano	**18**	ocean
isla	**19**	island
península	**20**	peninsula
selva húmeda/tropical	**21**	rainforest
río	**22**	river
cascada (pequeña)/ catarata (grande)	**23**	waterfall

A. { Isn't this a beautiful _____?!
{ Aren't these beautiful _____s?!

B. Yes. It's / They're magnificent!

Tell about the geography of your country.
Describe the different geographic features.

Have you seen some of the geographic
features in this lesson? Which ones? Where?

CIENCIAS

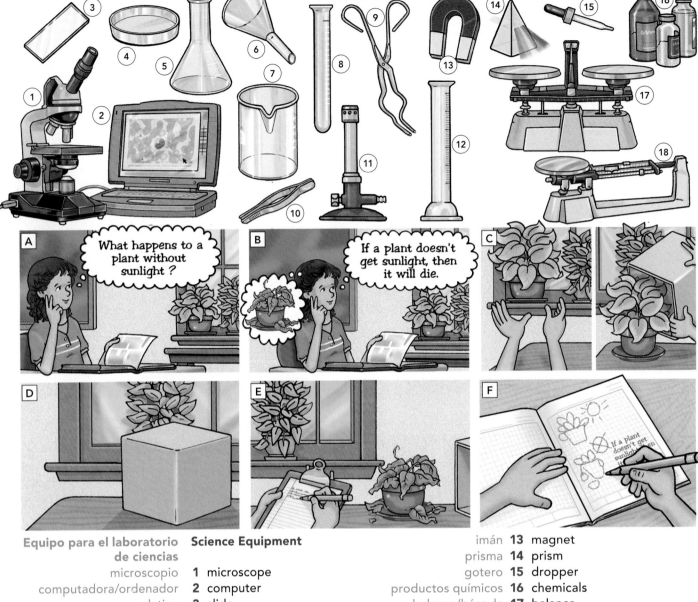

Equipo para el laboratorio de ciencias		Science Equipment
microscopio	**1**	microscope
computadora/ordenador	**2**	computer
platina	**3**	slide
caja de Petri/de cultivos	**4**	Petri dish
matraz	**5**	flask
embudo	**6**	funnel
vaso de precipitados	**7**	beaker
tubo de ensayo/probeta	**8**	test tube
fórceps/tenazas	**9**	forceps
pinzas para crisol	**10**	crucible tongs
mechero de Bunsen	**11**	Bunsen burner
probeta graduada	**12**	graduated cylinder

imán	**13**	magnet
prisma	**14**	prism
gotero	**15**	dropper
productos químicos	**16**	chemicals
balanza/báscula	**17**	balance
balanza/báscula	**18**	scale

El método científico		The Scientific Method
presentar el problema	**A**	state the problem
formular una hipótesis	**B**	form a hypothesis
planear un procedimiento	**C**	plan a procedure
realizar el procedimiento	**D**	do a procedure
anotar las observaciones	**E**	make/record observations
sacar conclusiones	**F**	draw conclusions

A. What do we need to do this procedure?
B. We need a/an/the _____[1–18]_____.

A. How is your experiment coming along?
B. I'm getting ready to _____[A–F]_____.

Do you have experience with the scientific equipment in this lesson? Tell about it.

What science courses do/did you take in school?

Think of an idea for a science experiment.
What question about science do you want to answer? State the problem.
What do you think will happen in the experiment? Form a hypothesis.
How can you test your hypothesis? Plan a procedure.

EL UNIVERSO

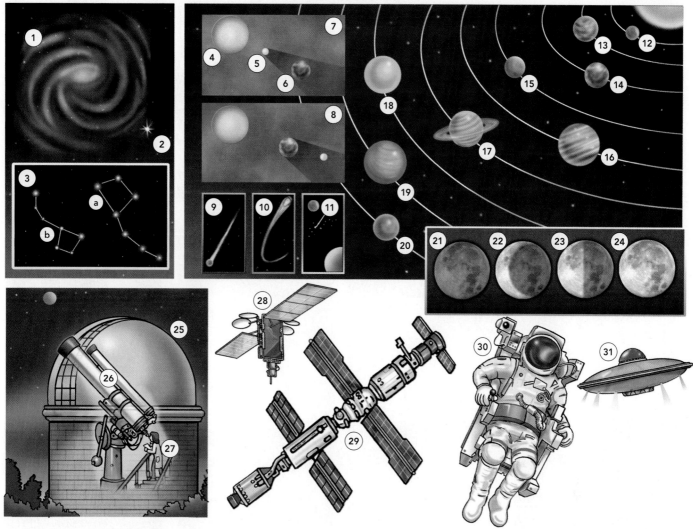

El universo		The Universe
galaxia	**1**	galaxy
estrella	**2**	star
constelación	**3**	constellation
La Osa Mayor	**a**	The Big Dipper
La Osa Menor	**b**	The Little Dipper

El sistema solar		The Solar System
sol	**4**	sun
luna	**5**	moon
planeta	**6**	planet
eclipse solar	**7**	solar eclipse
eclipse lunar	**8**	lunar eclipse
meteoro/bólido/ estrella fugaz	**9**	meteor

cometa/bólido/ estrella fugaz	**10**	comet
asteroide	**11**	asteroid
Mercurio	**12**	Mercury
Venus	**13**	Venus
La Tierra	**14**	Earth
Marte	**15**	Mars
Júpiter	**16**	Jupiter
Saturno	**17**	Saturn
Urano	**18**	Uranus
Neptuno	**19**	Neptune
Plutón	**20**	Pluto
luna nueva	**21**	new moon
cuarto creciente	**22**	crescent moon

media luna	**23**	quarter moon
luna llena	**24**	full moon

Astronomía		Astronomy
observatorio	**25**	observatory
telescopio	**26**	telescope
astrónomo(a)	**27**	astronomer

La exploración espacial		Space Exploration
satélite	**28**	satellite
estación espacial	**29**	space station
astronauta/cosmonauta	**30**	astronaut
platillo volador/ volante/ OVNI/UFO	**31**	U.F.O./ Unidentified Flying Object/ flying saucer

[1–24]
A. Is that (a/an/the) _____?
B. I'm not sure. I think it might be (a/an/the) _____.

[28–30]
A. Is the _____ ready for tomorrow's launch?
B. Yes. "All systems are go!"

Pretend you are an astronaut traveling in space. What do you see?

Draw and name a constellation you are familiar with.

Do you think space exploration is important? Why?

Have you ever seen a U.F.O.? Do you believe there is life in outer space? Why?

OCCUPATIONS I
PROFESIONES Y OFICIOS I

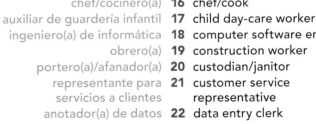

What's the problem?

contador/contable	1	accountant
actor	2	actor
actriz	3	actress
arquitecto(a)	4	architect
pintor(a)	5	artist
montador(a)/ensamblador(a)/armador(a)	6	assembler
niñero(a)/canguro	7	babysitter
panadero(a)	8	baker
peluquero(a)/barbero(a)	9	barber
albañil	10	bricklayer/mason
hombre de negocios	11	businessman
mujer de negocios	12	businesswoman
carnicero(a)	13	butcher
carpintero(a)	14	carpenter
cajero(a)	15	cashier
chef/cocinero(a)	16	chef/cook
auxiliar de guardería infantil	17	child day-care worker
ingeniero(a) de informática	18	computer software engineer
obrero(a)	19	construction worker
portero(a)/afanador(a)	20	custodian/janitor
representante para servicios a clientes	21	customer service representative
anotador(a) de datos	22	data entry clerk

repartidor(a)	**23** delivery person	jardinero(a)/paisajista	**32** gardener/landscaper
estibador(a)	**24** dockworker	costurero(a)	**33** garment worker
ingeniero(a)	**25** engineer	peluquero(a)	**34** hairdresser
obrero(a)	**26** factory worker	ayudante/asistente de salud	**35** health-care aide/attendant
granjero(a)/agricultor(a)	**27** farmer	ayudante/asistente	**36** home health aide/
bombero(a)	**28** firefighter	de salud en casa	home attendant
pescador(a)	**29** fisher	encargado(a) de la casa/amo(a) de casa	**37** homemaker
empleado(a) de cafetería	**30** food-service worker	sirviente(a)/criado(a)/	**38** housekeeper
maestro(a) de obras/capataz	**31** foreman	empleado(a) de servicio doméstico	

A. What do you do?
B. I'm an **accountant**. How about you?
A. I'm a **carpenter**.

[At a job interview]

A. Are you an experienced _____?
B. Yes. I'm a very experienced _____.

A. How long have you been a/an _____?
B. I've been a/an _____ for
.... months / years.

Which of these occupations do you think are the most interesting? the most difficult? Why?

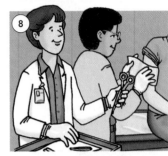

periodista/reportero(a)	**1**	journalist/reporter
abogado(a)	**2**	lawyer
maquinista	**3**	machine operator
cartero(a)	**4**	mail carrier/letter carrier
director(a)/gerente/ administrador(a)	**5**	manager
manicurista	**6**	manicurist
mecánico(a)	**7**	mechanic
técnico(a) sanitario(a)/ asistente médico(a)	**8**	medical assistant/ physician assistant
mensajero(a)	**9**	messenger/courier

mozo(a) de mudanzas	**10**	mover
músico	**11**	musician
pintor(a)	**12**	painter
boticario(a)/farmacéutico(a)/farmacista	**13**	pharmacist
fotógrafo(a)	**14**	photographer
piloto	**15**	pilot
policía	**16**	police officer
empleado(a) de correos	**17**	postal worker
recepcionista/recepcionista-telefonista	**18**	receptionist
reparador(a)/mecánico(a)	**19**	repairperson
vendedor(a)	**20**	salesperson

basurero(a)/recolector(a) de basura	**21**	sanitation worker/ trash collector	maestro(a)/profesor(a)	**30** teacher/instructor
secretario(a)	**22**	secretary	agente de ventas por teléfono	**31** telemarketer
guardia de seguridad	**23**	security guard	traductor(a)/intérprete	**32** translator/interpreter
soldado	**24**	serviceman	agente de viajes	**33** travel agent
soldada	**25**	servicewoman	camionero(a)	**34** truck driver
empleado(a) de almacén	**26**	stock clerk	veterinario(a)	**35** veterinarian/vet
tendero(a)/comerciante	**27**	store owner/shopkeeper	mesero/camarero	**36** waiter/server
supervisor(a)	**28**	supervisor	mesera/camarera	**37** waitress/server
sastre(a)	**29**	tailor	soldador(a)	**38** welder

A. What's your occupation?
B. I'm a **journalist**.
A. A **journalist**?
B. Yes. That's right.

A. Are you still a _____?
B. No. I'm a _____.
A. Oh. That's interesting.

A. What kind of job would you like in the future?
B. I'd like to be a _____.

Do you work? What's your occupation?

What are the occupations of people in your family?

JOB SKILLS AND ACTIVITIES

ACTIVIDADES RELACIONADAS CON EL TRABAJO

actuar	**1** act	manejar/conducir *un camión*	**11** drive *a truck*
armar/montar *componentes*	**2** assemble *components*	archivar	**12** file
ayudar a *pacientes*	**3** assist *patients*	pilotear *un avión*	**13** fly *an airplane*
hornear	**4** bake	cultivar *vegetales*	**14** grow *vegetables*
hacer/construir *cosas*	**5** build *things*/construct *things*	vigilar/cuidar *edificios*	**15** guard *buildings*
limpiar	**6** clean	administrar *un restaurante*	**16** manage *a restaurant*
cocinar	**7** cook	cortar *el césped*	**17** mow *lawns*
repartir *pizzas*	**8** deliver *pizzas*	manejar *herramientas/máquinas*	**18** operate *equipment*
diseñar *edificios*	**9** design *buildings*	pintar	**19** paint
dibujar/trazar	**10** draw	tocar *el piano*	**20** play the *piano*

preparar *la comida*	**21**	prepare *food*	supervisar *empleados*	**28**	supervise *people*
reparar/componer/ arreglar *cosas*	**22**	repair *things*/ fix *things*	cuidar a *gente mayor*	**29**	take care of *elderly people*
vender *autos*/ carros/coches	**23**	sell *cars*	hacer inventario	**30**	take inventory
			enseñar	**31**	teach
servir *comida*	**24**	serve *food*	traducir	**32**	translate
coser	**25**	sew	mecanografiar/teclear	**33**	type
cantar	**26**	sing	usar *una caja registradora*	**34**	use *a cash register*
hablar *español*	**27**	speak *Spanish*	lavar *platos*	**35**	wash *dishes*
			escribir	**36**	write

A. Can you **act**?
B. Yes, I can.

A. Do you know how to _____?
B. Yes. I've been _____ing for years.

A. Tell me about your skills.
B. I can _____, and I can _____.

Tell about your job skills.
What can you do?

EN BUSCA DE EMPLEO

CASHIERS

FT & PT positions avail. $11/hr.

M-F. Days & eves. Prev. exper. req.

Excel. salary. Save-Mart, 2540 Central Ave.

Tipos de anuncios	Types of Job Ads
letrero de se busca ayuda	**1** help wanted sign
tablero de anuncios	**2** job notice/announcement
anuncio/clasificado/ de empleo	**3** classified ad/want ad

Abreviaturas en los anuncios	Job Ad Abbreviations
tiempo completo	**4** full-time
tiempo parcial/medio tiempo	**5** part-time
disponible	**6** available
por hora	**7** hour
de lunes a viernes	**8** Monday through Friday
por las tardes	**9** evenings
previo(a)	**10** previous
experiencia	**11** experience
se requiere	**12** required
excelente	**13** excellent

En busca de empleo	Job Search
responder a un anuncio	**A** respond to an ad
solicitar información	**B** request information
solicitar una entrevista	**C** request an interview
preparar el currículum vítae	**D** prepare a resume
vestirse de manera apropiada	**E** dress appropriately
llenar una solicitud	**F** fill out an application (form)
ir a una entrevista	**G** go to an interview
hablar sobre sus aptitudes y habilidades	**H** talk about your skills and qualifications
hablar sobre suexperiencia laboral	**I** talk about your experience
pedir información acerca del sueldo	**J** ask about the salary
pedir información acerca de los subsidios y prestaciones laborales	**K** ask about the benefits
escribir una nota de agradecimiento	**L** write a thank-you note
ser contratado(a)/nombrado(a)	**M** get hired

A. How did you find your job?
B. I found it through a ___[1–3]___.

A. How was your job interview?
B. It went very well.
A. Did you ___[D–F, H–M]___?
B. Yes, I did.

Tell about a job you are familiar with. What are the skills and qualifications required for the job? What are the hours? What is the salary?

Tell about how people you know found their jobs.

Tell about your own experience with a job search or a job interview.

EL SITIO DE TRABAJO

recepción **A** reception area	báscula de cartas **6** postal scale	gerente **23** office manager
sala de **B** conference room	máquina para sellos **7** postage meter	estante/armario de **24** supply cabinet
conferencias	ayudante de oficina **8** office assistant	artículos de oficina
cuarto del correo **C** mailroom	buzón **9** mailbox	estante/armario de **25** storage cabinet
área de trabajo **D** work area	cubículo **10** cubicle	almacenaje
oficina **E** office	silla giratoria **11** swivel chair	vendedora **26** vending machine
cuarto de artículos **F** supply room	máquina de escribir **12** typewriter	automática
de oficina	calculadora/sumadora **13** adding machine	fuente **27** water cooler
cuarto de **G** storage room	fotocopiadora **14** copier/photocopier	cafetera eléctrica **28** coffee machine
almacenaje	trituradora de papel **15** paper shredder	tablero **29** message board
salón de **H** employee lounge	guillotina **16** paper cutter	(de anuncios)
empleados	archivista **17** file clerk	tomar un mensaje **a** take a message
perchero **1** coat rack	archivador/archivero **18** file cabinet	hacer una **b** give a presentation
ropero **2** coat closet	secretario(a) **19** secretary	presentación
recepcionista **3** receptionist	estación/módulo **20** computer workstation	clasificar el correo **c** sort the mail
mesa de reuniones/ **4** conference table	de computadora	fotocopiar/copiar **d** make copies
conferencias	jefe(a)/empleador(a) **21** employer/boss	archivar **e** file
tablero para **5** presentation board	asistente **22** administrative assistant	escribir **f** type a letter
presentaciones	administrativo(a)	una carta

[A–H]
A. Where's .....(name).....?
B. He's / She's in the _____.

[1–29]
A. What do you think of the new _____?
B. He's / She's / It's very nice.

[a–f]
A. What's .....(name)..... doing?
B. He's / She's _____ing.

Describe a workplace you are familiar with. Tell about the rooms, the areas, and the employees.

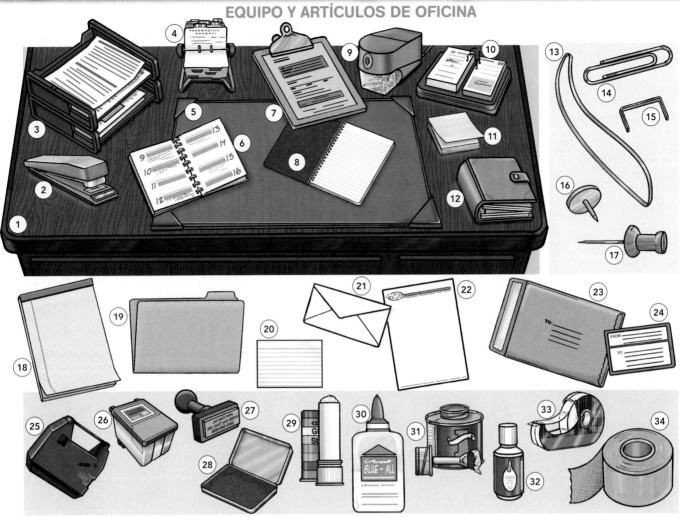

escritorio	**1** desk
engrapadora/	**2** stapler
presilladora/	
grapadora	
bandeja tamaño	**3** letter tray/
carta/apilable	stacking tray
agenda rotatoria	**4** rotary card file
carpeta de felpa	**5** desk pad
agenda	**6** appointment book
tablilla con sujetapapeles	**7** clipboard
libreta de notas/ memorandas	**8** note pad/ memo pad
sacapuntas eléctrico	**9** electric pencil sharpener
calendario de escritorio	**10** desk calendar

libretita de notas autoadhesivas	**11** Post-It note pad
agenda personal	**12** organizer/ personal planner
liga/goma	**13** rubber band
clip/sujetador	**14** paper clip
grapa	**15** staple
tachuela	**16** thumbtack
chinche/chincheta	**17** pushpin
libreta tamaño legal	**18** legal pad
carpeta/fólder	**19** file folder
ficha	**20** index card
sobre	**21** envelope
papel para escribir cartas/ con membrete	**22** stationery/ letterhead (paper)
sobre paquete/ acolchado	**23** mailer

etiqueta postal	**24** mailing label
cartucho de tinta para máquina de escribir	**25** typewriter cartridge
cartucho de tinta para impresora	**26** ink cartridge
sello de goma	**27** rubber stamp
almohadilla de tinta/ tampón	**28** ink pad
lápiz adhesivo	**29** glue stick
goma/pegamento	**30** glue
pegalotodo/ goma sintética	**31** rubber cement
líquido corrector	**32** correction fluid
cinta pegante de celofán	**33** cellophane tape/ clear tape
cinta pegante canela para empacar	**34** packing tape/ sealing tape

A. My desk is a mess! I can't find my __[2–12]__ !
B. Here it is next to your __[2–12]__ .

A. Could you get some more __[13–21, 23–29]__ s / __[22, 30–34]__ from the supply room?
B. Some more __[13–21, 23–29]__ s / __[22, 30–34]__ ? Sure. I'd be happy to.

Which supplies and equipment do you use? What do you use them for?

Which supplies in this lesson do you have at home? at school?

LA FÁBRICA

reloj marcador/checador	**1**	time clock	embalador(a)/empacador(a)	**12** packer
tarjetas de asistencia	**2**	time cards	portacarga/montacarga	**13** forklift
vestidor	**3**	locker room	ascensor de carga	**14** freight elevator
cadena/línea de montaje	**4**	(assembly) line	circular del sindicato	**15** union notice
obrero(a)/operario(a)	**5**	(factory) worker	buzón de sugerencias	**16** suggestion box
estación de trabajo	**6**	work station	sección/departamento de envíos	**17** shipping department
supervisor(a) de cadena de montaje	**7**	line supervisor	encargado(a) de envíos	**18** shipping clerk
supervisor(a) de control de calidad	**8**	quality control supervisor	carrito manual/diablito	**19** hand truck/dolly
máquina	**9**	machine	muelle de carga	**20** loading dock
cinta transportadora	**10**	conveyor belt	oficina de pagos/de nómina	**21** payroll office
almacén/depósito	**11**	warehouse	oficina de personal	**22** personnel office

A. Excuse me. I'm a new employee.
Where's / Where are the _____?
B. Next to / Near / In / On the _____.

A. Have you seen *Tony*?
B. Yes. *He's* in / on / at / next to / near
the _____.

Are there any factories where you live? What kind?
What are the working conditions there?

What products do factories in your country produce?

UN SITIO DE CONSTRUCCIÓN

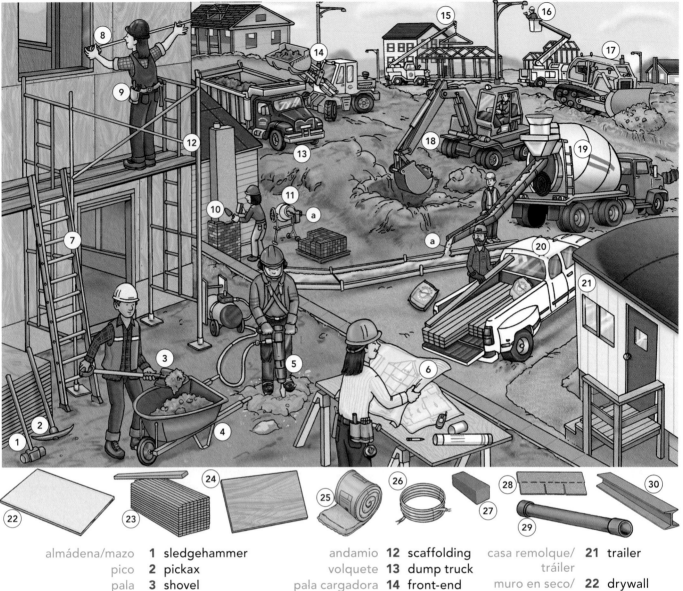

almádena/mazo	**1**	sledgehammer	andamio	**12**	scaffolding	casa remolque/	**21** trailer
pico	**2**	pickax	volquete	**13**	dump truck	tráiler	
pala	**3**	shovel	pala cargadora	**14**	front-end	muro en seco/	**22** drywall
carretilla	**4**	wheelbarrow	mecánica		loader	muro ensamblable	
taladro/	**5**	jackhammer/	grúa	**15**	crane	madera	**23** wood/lumber
neumático perforador		pneumatic drill	grúa (con plataforma	**16**	cherry	madera	**24** plywood
planos	**6**	blueprints	movible)		picker	contrachapada	
escalera	**7**	ladder	bulldozer/tractor	**17**	bulldozer	fibra aislante	**25** insulation
cinta métrica	**8**	tape measure	tractor excavador(a)	**18**	backhoe	alambre	**26** wire
cinturón para herramientas	**9**	toolbelt	revolvedora de	**19**	concrete	ladrillo	**27** brick
palustre/paleta/llana	**10**	trowel	concreto/hormigonera		mixer truck	teja	**28** shingle
mezcladora de cemento/	**11**	cement	concreto/hormigón	**a**	concrete	tubo	**29** pipe
mortero		mixer	camioneta de carga/	**20**	pickup truck	viga/trabe	**30** girder/beam
cemento		**a** cement	pickup				

A. Could you get me that/those ___[1–10]___?
B. Sure.

A. Watch out for that ___[11–21]___!
B. Oh! Thanks for the warning!

A. Do we have enough
___[22–26]___ / ___[27–30]___ s?
B. I think so.

What building materials is your home made of?
When was it built?

Describe a construction site near your home or school.
Tell about the construction equipment and the materials.

SEGURIDAD LABORAL

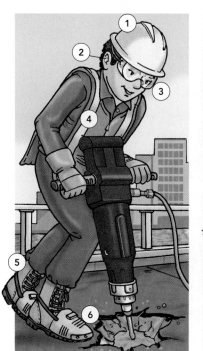

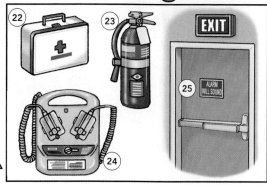

casco de construcción	1	hard hat/helmet
tapones para oídos	2	earplugs
anteojos protectores/gafas protectoras	3	goggles
chaleco de seguridad	4	safety vest
botas protectoras	5	safety boots
protector para los dedos de los pies	6	toe guard
faja/arnés de soporte	7	back support
orejeras protectoras	8	safety earmuffs
redecilla	9	hairnet
mascarilla/máscara	10	mask
guantes de látex	11	latex gloves
mascarilla filtrante	12	respirator
visor para soldar/gafas de seguridad	13	safety glasses
inflamable	14	flammable
venenoso(a)	15	poisonous
corrosivo(a)	16	corrosive
radioactivo(a)	17	radioactive
peligroso(a)	18	dangerous
peligroso(a)	19	hazardous
peligro de agente biológico infeccioso/patógeno tóxico	20	biohazard
peligro de electrocución	21	electrical hazard
botiquín/maletín de primeros auxilios	22	first-aid kit
extinguidor/extintor de incendios	23	fire extinguisher
desfibrilador	24	defibrillator
salida de emergencia	25	emergency exit

A. Don't forget to wear your ___[1–13]___ !
B. Thanks for reminding me.

A. Be careful!
- That material is ___[14–17]___ !
- That machine is ___[18]___ !
- That work area is ___[19]___ !
- That's a ___[20]___ !/That's an ___[21]___ !

B. Thanks for the warning.

A. Where's the ___[22–25]___ ?
B. It's over there.

Have you ever used any of the safety equipment in this lesson?
What have you used? When? Where?

Where do you see people using safety equipment in your community?

EL TRANSPORTE PÚBLICO

autobús/bus/ guagua/camión	**A**	**bus**
parada/paradero	1	bus stop
ruta	2	bus route
pasajero(a)	3	passenger/rider
tarifa	4	(bus) fare
billete de trasbordo	5	transfer
conductor(a)/chofer de autobús/busero(a)	6	bus driver
estación de autobuses	7	bus station
boletería/taquilla	8	ticket counter
billete/pasaje/boleto	9	ticket
maletero	10	baggage compartment/ luggage compartment
tren	**B**	**train**
estación del tren	11	train station
taquilla/ ventanilla	12	ticket window
tablero de llegadas y salidas	13	arrival and departure board
mostrador de información	14	information booth
horarios	15	schedule/ timetable
andén	16	platform
riel/vía	17	track
cobrador(a)	18	conductor
metro/ subterráneo	**C**	**subway**
estación del metro	19	subway station
ficha	20	(subway) token
torniquete/contador de entrada	21	turnstile
tarjeta de pasaje/ boleto prepagado	22	fare card
máquina expendedora de pasajes/boletos	23	fare card machine
taxi	**D**	**taxi**
parada de taxis/ piquera	24	taxi stand
taxi	25	taxi/cab/ taxicab
taxímetro	26	meter
taxista/ chofer de taxi	27	cab driver/ taxi driver
transbordador/ ferry	**E**	**ferry**

[A–E]
A. How are you going to get there?
B. { I'm going to take the __[A–C, E]__.
{ I'm going to take a __[D]__.

[1, 7, 8, 10–19, 21, 23–25]
A. Excuse me. Where's the _____?
B. Over there.

How do you get to different places in your community? Describe public transportation where you live.

In your country, can you travel far by train or by bus? Where can you go? How much do tickets cost? Describe the buses and trains.

TIPOS DE VEHÍCULOS

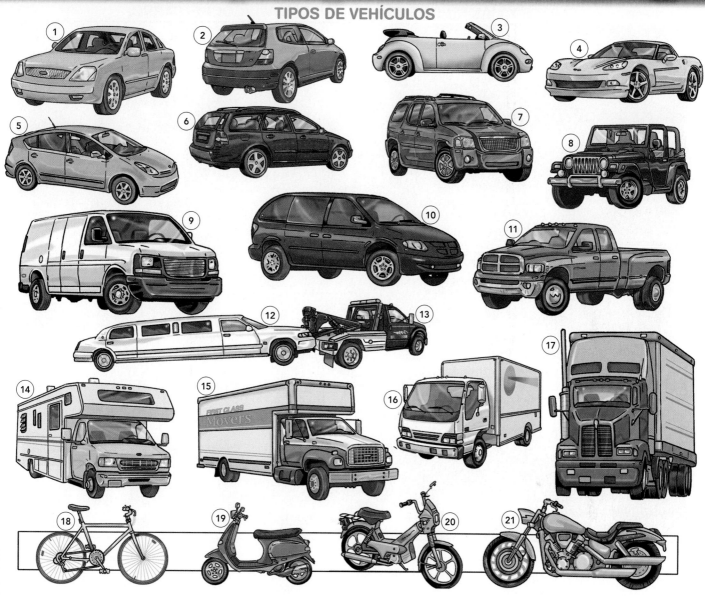

sedán	**1** sedan	limusina	**12** limousine
cupé/carro de tres puertas/hatchback	**2** hatchback	camión remolque/grúa	**13** tow truck
convertible/descapotable	**3** convertible	camper(o)/caravana/remolque	**14** R.V. (recreational vehicle)/camper
carro/coche deportivo	**4** sports car	camión de mudanzas	**15** moving van
carro/coche híbrido	**5** hybrid	camión	**16** truck
camioneta/vagoneta	**6** station wagon	tráiler/camión con remolque/acoplado	**17** tractor trailer/semi
camioneta todoterreno/cuatro por cuatro/utilitaria	**7** S.U.V. (sport utility vehicle)	bicicleta	**18** bicycle/bike
todoterreno/jeep	**8** jeep	ciclomotor/bicimoto	**19** motor scooter
furgoneta/van/camioneta repartidora	**9** van	scooter/motoneta/vespa	**20** moped
miniván/minibús/microbús	**10** minivan	motocicleta	**21** motorcycle
camioneta de carga/pickup	**11** pickup truck		

A. What kind of vehicle are you looking for?
B. I'm looking for a **sedan**.

A. Do you drive a/an _____?
B. No. I drive a/an _____.

A. I just saw an accident between a/an _____ and a/an _____!
B. Was anybody hurt?
A. No. Fortunately, nobody was hurt.

What are the most common types of vehicles in your country?

What's your favorite type of vehicle? Why? In your opinion, which company makes the best one?

PARTES Y MANTENIMIENTO DEL AUTOMÓVIL/COCHE/CARRO

parachoques/paragolpes	1	bumper
luces delanteras/faros	2	headlight
luz direccional/intermitente	3	turn signal
señal de estacionamiento/luz de aparcamiento/posición	4	parking light
guardafango/guardabarros/salpicadera	5	fender
llanta/neumático/goma	6	tire
tapacubos/embellecedor/pollera/copa	7	hubcap
capó del motor/cofre	8	hood
parabrisas/cristal delantero	9	windshield
limpiaparabrisas/cepillo/limpiadores	10	windshield wipers
espejo lateral/retrovisor exterior	11	side mirror
portaequipaje/parrilla	12	roof rack
media luna/tragaluz/quemacocos/claraboya	13	sunroof
antena	14	antenna
ventana trasera	15	rear window
descongelador/desempañador trasero	16	rear defroster
maletero/cajuela	17	trunk
luz trasera/calavera	18	taillight
luz del freno/indicadora de frenado	19	brake light
luz de retroceso/reverso	20	backup light
placa/chapa de matrícula/tablilla	21	license plate
tubo de escape	22	tailpipe/exhaust pipe
silenciador/mofle(r)	23	muffler
transmisión	24	transmission
tanque de gasolina	25	gas tank
gato	26	jack
llanta de repuesto/refacción	27	spare tire
llave de cruz/cruceta	28	lug wrench
señales de peligro/bengala	29	flare
cables de conexión/reactivadores/pasacorriente	30	jumper cables
bujías	31	spark plugs
filtro	32	air filter
motor	33	engine
sistema de inyección de combustible	34	fuel injection system
radiador	35	radiator
manguera/manga del radiador	36	radiator hose
banda/correa del ventilador	37	fan belt
alternador	38	alternator
indicador de aceite/varilla del aceite	39	dipstick
batería	40	battery
bomba de aire	41	air pump
surtidor/bomba de gasolina	42	gas pump
boca/boquilla	43	nozzle
tapón de gasolina	44	gas cap
gasolina	45	gas
aceite	46	oil
refrigerante	47	coolant
aire	48	air

bolsa de aire	**49**	air bag	ventila/rejilla	**62**	vent	transmisión	**76**	manual transmission
visera	**50**	visor	sistema de navegación	**63**	navigation system	manual		
espejo retrovisor	**51**	rearview mirror	radio	**64**	radio	palanca de cambios	**77**	stickshift
tablero/panel de instrumentos/ mandos	**52**	dashboard/ instrument panel	reproductor de CD	**65**	CD player	embrague/ clutch	**78**	clutch
indicador de temperatur	**53**	temperature gauge	calefacción	**66**	heater	seguro	**79**	door lock
medidor/ indicador de gasolina	**54**	gas gauge/ fuel gauge	aire acondicionado	**67**	air conditioning	manija/manilla/ manigueta	**80**	door handle
velocímetro	**55**	speedometer	descongelador/ desempañador	**68**	defroster	cinturón de seguridad	**81**	shoulder harness
odómetro	**56**	odometer	tomacorriente	**69**	power outlet	apoyabrazos	**82**	armrest
señal de alarma/luz (indicadora) de alarma	**57**	warning lights	guantera/gaveta	**70**	glove compartment	cabezal/ protector de cabeza	**83**	headrest
palanca de direccionales	**58**	turn signal	freno de emergencia	**71**	emergency brake	asiento	**84**	seat
volante/guía	**59**	steering wheel	freno/pedal de freno	**72**	brake (pedal)	cinturón de seguridad	**85**	seat belt
claxon/bocina/pito	**60**	horn	acelerador	**73**	accelerator/ gas pedal			
encendido	**61**	ignition	transmisión automática	**74**	automatic transmission			
			palanca de cambios	**75**	gearshift			

[2, 3, 9–16, 24, 35–39, 49–85]
A. What's the matter with your car?
B. The _____(s) is/are broken.

[45–48]
A. Can I help you?
B. { Yes. My car needs ___[45–47]___ .
     Yes. My tires need ___[48]___ .

[1, 2, 4–15, 17–23, 25]
A. I was just in a car accident!
B. Oh, no! Were you hurt?
A. No. But my _____(s) was/were damaged.

In your opinion, what are the most important features to look for when you buy a car?

Do you own a car? What kind? Tell about any repairs your car has needed.

HIGHWAYS AND STREETS

CARRETERAS/AUTOPISTAS Y CALLES

túnel	**1**	tunnel	jardín divisor/ vereda/camellón	**12**	median	carril/rampa de salida	**20** exit (ramp)
puente	**2**	bridge	carril izquierdo	**13**	left lane	letrero de salida	**21** exit sign
garita/caseta de peaje	**3**	tollbooth	carril central	**14**	middle lane/ center lane	calle	**22** street
letrero/indicador de rutas	**4**	route sign	carril derecho	**15**	right lane	calle de un solo sentido	**23** one-way street
autopista	**5**	highway	borde/orilla/	**16**	shoulder	línea amarilla doble/ de ''no doblar''	**24** double yellow line
carretera	**6**	road	acotamiento/margen/ de la carretera			vía /paso/ cruce de peatones/ línea de seguridad	**25** crosswalk
muro de contención/ divisor central	**7**	divider/ barrier	línea discontinua/ de ''se puede pasar''	**17**	broken line		
paso elevado/a desnivel	**8**	overpass	línea continua/ de ''no pasar''	**18**	solid line	cruce	**26** intersectio
paso inferior	**9**	underpass				semáforo	**27** traffic light traffic sign
carril/ rampa de entrada	**10**	entrance ramp/ on ramp	letrero de límite de velocidad	**19**	speed limit sign	esquina	**28** corner
autopista interestatal	**11**	interstate (highway)				cuadra/manzana	**29** block

[1–28]
A. Where's the accident?
B. It's on/in/at/near the _____.

Describe a highway you travel on.

Describe an intersection near where you live.

In your area, on which highways and streets do most accidents occur? Why are these places dangerous?

PREPOSICIONES PARA DAR DIRECCIONES

(manejar) sobre/por	**1**	over
(manejar) por debajo/bajo	**2**	under
(manejar) por/a través de	**3**	through
(caminar) alrededor de	**4**	around

(ir) hacia arriba	**5**	up
(ir) hacia abajo	**6**	down
(cruzar) del otro lado	**7**	across
(ir) más allá de	**8**	past

(subir) al (autobús)	**9**	on
(bajar) del (autobús)	**10**	off
(entrar) a	**11**	into
(salir) de	**12**	out of
(entrar) a/en (la autopista)	**13**	onto

[1–8]
A. Go **over** the bridge.
B. **Over** the bridge?
A. Yes.

[9–13]
A. I can't talk right now. I'm getting **on** a train.
B. You're getting **on** a train?
A. Yes. I'll call you later.

What places do you go past on your way to school?   Tell how to get to different places from your home or your school.

SEÑALES E INDICACIONES/INSTRUCCIONES DE TRÁNSITO

Señales de tránsito	Traffic Signs			Instrucciones para el examen de conducir/manejar	Road Test Instructions
alto/stop	**1** stop	unión de carriles **12** merging traffic		Doble a la izquierda.	**21** Turn left.
no doble a la izquierda	**2** no left turn	ceda el paso **13** yield		Doble a la derecha.	**22** Turn right.
no doble a la derecha	**3** no right turn	desvío **14** detour		Siga derecho/recto.	**23** Go straight.
no doble en U	**4** no U-turn	resbaladizo(a) **15** slippery		Estaciónese paralelo a la acera.	**24** Parallel park.
doble sólo a la derecha	**5** right turn only	si está mojado(a) when wet		Dé un viraje de tres puntos.	**25** Make a 3-point turn.
prohibido el paso	**6** do not enter	estacionamiento para **16** handicapped discapacitados(as) parking only		Use señales de mano.	**26** Use hand signals.
un solo sentido	**7** one way	**Direcciones** **Compass**			
calle sin salida	**8** dead end/no outlet	**de la brújula** **Directions**			
cruce de peatones	**9** pedestrian crossing	norte **17** north			
cruce de rieles/ de ferrocarril	**10** railroad crossing	sur **18** south			
cruce escolar	**11** school crossing	oeste/poniente **19** west			
		este/oriente **20** east			

[1–16]
A. Careful! That sign says "**stop**"!
B. Oh. Thanks.

[17–20]
A. Which way should I go?
B. Go **north**.

[21–26]
A. Turn **right**.
B. Turn **right**?
A. Yes.

Which of these traffic signs are in your neighborhood? What other traffic signs do you usually see?

Describe any differences between traffic signs in different countries you know.

EL AEROPUERTO

Registro de pasajeros		A Check-In
pasaje/boleto/billete	**1**	ticket
mostrador de pasajes	**2**	ticket counter
expendedor(a) de pasajes	**3**	ticket agent
maleta/valija/petaca	**4**	suitcase
monitor de llegadas y salidas	**5**	arrival and departure monitor

Seguridad		B Security
control de seguridad	**6**	security checkpoint
detector de metales	**7**	metal detector
guardia de seguridad	**8**	security officer
máquina de rayos X	**9**	X-ray machine
equipaje de mano	**10**	carry-on bag

La puerta/sala (de embarque y desembarque)		C The Gate
mostrador de factura/ registro/chequeo	**11**	check-in counter
tarjeta de abordaje	**12**	boarding pass
puerta/sala	**13**	gate
área de abordaje	**14**	boarding area

Reclamo/Retiro de equipaje		D Baggage Claim
área de reclamo/retiro de equipaje	**15**	baggage claim (area)
carrusel de equipaje	**16**	baggage carousel
equipaje	**17**	baggage
carreta/carrito para equipaje	**18**	baggage cart/ luggage cart
carretilla/carrito para equipaje	**19**	luggage carrier
bolsa para trajes/vestidos/ sacos y abrigos	**20**	garment bag
etiqueta/boleto de factura del equipaje	**21**	baggage claim check

Inmigración y aduana		E Customs and Immigration
aduana	**22**	customs
empleado(a) de aduana	**23**	customs officer
tarjeta/formulario de declaración de aduana	**24**	customs declaration form
inmigración	**25**	immigration
oficial de inmigración	**26**	immigration officer
pasaporte	**27**	passport
visa	**28**	visa

[2, 3, 5–9, 11, 13–16, 22, 23, 25, 26]
A. Excuse me. Where's the _____?*
B. Right over there.

*With 22 and 25 use: Excuse me. Where's _____?

[1, 4, 10, 12, 17–21, 24, 27, 28]
A. Oh, no! I think I've lost my _____!
B. I'll help you look for it.

Describe an airport you are familiar with. Tell about the check-in area, the security area, the gates, and the baggage claim area.

Have you ever gone through Customs and Immigration? Tell about your experience.

EL VIAJE EN AVIÓN

cabina (de mando)	**1**	cockpit
piloto/capitán	**2**	pilot/captain
copiloto	**3**	co-pilot
baño	**4**	lavatory/bathroom
aeromozo(a)/azafata/sobrecargo	**5**	flight attendant
compartimiento superior	**6**	overhead compartment
pasillo	**7**	aisle
asiento con ventanilla	**8**	window seat
asiento central	**9**	middle seat
asiento de pasillo	**10**	aisle seat
señal de "abrocharse los cinturones"	**11**	Fasten Seat Belt sign
señal de "no fumar"	**12**	No Smoking sign
botón de llamada para servicio	**13**	call button
mascarilla de oxígeno	**14**	oxygen mask
puerta de emergencia	**15**	emergency exit
mesa abatible	**16**	tray (table)
tarjeta de instrucciones de emergencia	**17**	emergency instruction card
bolsa para mareos	**18**	air sickness bag

chaleco salvavidas	**19**	life vest/life jacket
pista	**20**	runway
terminal (edificio)	**21**	terminal (building)
torre de control	**22**	control tower
avión/jet	**23**	airplane/plane/jet

quítese los zapatos	**A**	take off your shoes
vacíese los bolsillos	**B**	empty your pockets
ponga el equipaje en la cinta/banda transportadora	**C**	put your bag on the conveyor belt
ponga la computadora en una bandeja	**D**	put your computer in a tray
camine a través del detector de metales	**E**	walk through the metal detector
preséntese en la entrada	**F**	check in at the gate
obtenga su tarjeta de abordaje	**G**	get your boarding pass
aborde el avión	**H**	board the plane
guarde su equipaje de mano	**I**	stow your carry-on bag
encuentre su asiento	**J**	find your seat
abróchese el cinturón de seguridad	**K**	fasten your seat belt

[1–23]
A. Where's the _____?
B. In/On/Next to/Behind/In front of/ Above/Below the _____.

[A–K]
A. Please _____.
B. All right. Certainly.

Have you ever flown in an airplane? Tell about a flight you took.

Be an airport security officer! Give passengers instructions as they go through the security area. Now, be a flight attendant! Give passengers instructions before take-off.

EL HOTEL

portero(a)	**1**	doorman	recepcionista	**9**	desk clerk	elevador/ascensor **18** elevator
servicio de estacionamiento a cargo del hotel	**2**	valet parking	huésped(a)	**10**	guest	máquina **19** ice machine de hacer hielo
encargado(a) de estacionamiento/ guardacoches	**3**	parking attendant	escritorio del conserje	**11**	concierge desk	pasillo/corredor **20** hall/hallway
botones	**4**	bellhop	conserje	**12**	concierge	llave **21** room key
carreta/carrito para equipaje	**5**	luggage cart	restaurante	**13**	restaurant	carrito de camarero(a)/ **22** housekeeping recamarero(a) cart
supervisor de botones	**6**	bell captain	sala para reuniones	**14**	meeting room	camarero(a)/ **23** housekeeper recamarero(a)
vestíbulo/lobby	**7**	lobby	tienda para regalos	**15**	gift shop	habitación **24** guest room
recepción	**8**	front desk	piscina/alberca	**16**	pool	servicio de restaurante **25** room service a la habitación
			gimnasio	**17**	exercise room	

A. Where do you work?
B. I work at the *Grand* Hotel.
A. What do you do there?
B. I'm a/an _____[1, 3, 4, 6, 9, 12, 23]_____ .

A. Excuse me. Where's the _____[1–19, 22, 23]_____ ?
B. Right over there.
A. Thanks.

Tell about a hotel you are familiar with. Describe the place and the people.

In your opinion, which hotel employee has the most interesting job? the most difficult job? Why?

ACTIVIDADES MANUALES, PASATIEMPOS Y JUEGOS

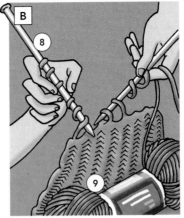

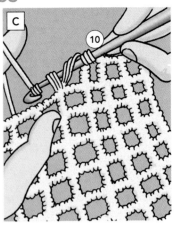

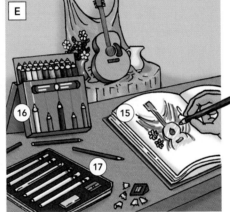

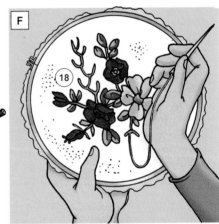

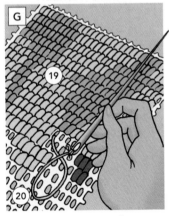

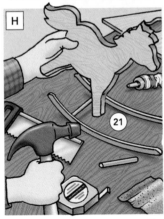

coser	**A**	**sew**
máquina de coser	**1**	sewing machine
alfiler	**2**	pin
alfiletero	**3**	pin cushion
(carrete de) hilo	**4**	(spool of) thread
aguja (de coser)	**5**	(sewing) needle
dedal	**6**	thimble
imperdible/	**7**	safety pin
alfiler de gancho		
tejer	**B**	**knit**
aguja de tejer	**8**	knitting needle
estambre/	**9**	yarn
hilo para tejer		
tejer a ganchillo/	**C**	**crochet**
gancho/crochet		
aguja de gancho/	**10**	crochet hook
gancho para tejer		

pintar	**D**	**paint**
pincel	**11**	paintbrush
caballete	**12**	easel
lienzo	**13**	canvas
pintura	**14**	paint
óleo		**a** oil paint
acuarela		**b** watercolor
dibujar	**E**	**draw**
cuaderno de	**15**	sketch book
bocetos		
(juego de)	**16**	(set of)
lápices de		colored
colores		pencils
lápiz de	**17**	drawing
dibujo		pencil
bordar	**F**	**do embroidery**
bordado	**18**	embroidery

bordar sobre	**G**	**do needlepoint**
cañamazo		
bordado sobre	**19**	needlepoint
cañamazo		
patrón	**20**	pattern
tallar madera	**H**	**do woodworking**
juego para	**21**	woodworking kit
tallar madera		
hacer origami	**I**	**do origami**
papel de origami	**22**	origami paper
hacer alfarería/	**J**	**make pottery**
cerámica		
arcilla/barro	**23**	clay
torno (de alfarero)	**24**	potter's wheel

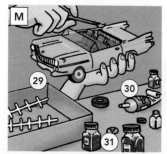

coleccionar estampillas/ sellos/timbres	**K**	**collect stamps**
álbum para estampillas/ sellos/timbres	25	stamp album
lupa	26	magnifying glass
coleccionar monedas	**L**	**collect coins**
catálogo de monedas	27	coin catalog
colección de monedas	28	coin collection
armar modelos	**M**	**build models**
juego de modelo	29	model kit
goma para armar modelos/pegamento	30	glue
pintura acrílica	31	acrylic paint

observar pájaros	**N**	**go bird-watching**
binoculares	32	binoculars
guía	33	field guide
jugar a los naipes/ las barajas/ cartas	**O**	**play cards**
juego de naipes barajas/cartas	34	(deck of) cards
trébol	**a**	club
diamante	**b**	diamond
corazón	**c**	heart
espada	**d**	spade
jugar a juegos de tablero	**P**	**play board games**
ajedrez	35	chess
damas/tablero	36	checkers

chaquete/tablas reales/negritas	37	backgammon
monopolio	38	Monopoly
dado	**a**	dice
sopa de letras/scrabble	39	Scrabble
navegar la red/ usar el/la Internet	**Q**	**go online/ browse the Web/ "surf" the net**
navegador de Internet	40	web browser
dirección en Internet/URL	41	web address/ URL
fotografía	**R**	**photography**
cámara	42	camera
astronomía	**S**	**astronomy**
telescopio	43	telescope

A. What do you like to do in your free time?
B. { I like to ____[A–Q]____ .
{ I enjoy ____[R, S]____ .

A. May I help you?
B. Yes, please. I'd like to buy (a/an) ____[1–34, 42, 43]____ .

A. What do you want to do?
B. Let's play ____[35–39]____ .
A. Good idea!

Do you like to do any of these activities in your free time? Which ones?

What games are popular in your country? Describe how to play one.

PLACES TO GO

LUGARES DE DIVERSIÓN

museo	**1**	museum
galería de arte	**2**	art gallery
concierto	**3**	concert
obra de teatro	**4**	play
parque de	**5**	amusement
diversiones		park
sitio histórico	**6**	historic site
parque nacional	**7**	national park

feria de artesanías	**8**	craft fair
venta de patio	**9**	yard sale
mercado de pulgas/	**10**	swap meet/
mercadillo/tianguis		flea market
parque	**11**	park
playa	**12**	beach
montañas	**13**	mountains

acuario	**14**	aquarium
jardín botánico	**15**	botanical gardens
planetario	**16**	planetarium
zoológico	**17**	zoo
cine	**18**	movies
feria ambulante	**19**	carnival
exposición/feria	**20**	fair

A. What do you want to do today?

B. Let's go to { a/an _____[1–9]_. / the _____[10–20]_. }

A. What did you do over the weekend?

B. I went to { a/an _____[1–9]_. / the _____[10–20]_ }

A. What are you going to do on your day off?

B. I'm going to go to { a/an _____[1–9]_. / the _____[10–20]_. }

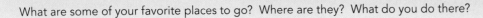

What are some of your favorite places to go? Where are they? What do you do there?

pista/camino	**1**	bicycle path/	banca	**9**	bench	pared para	**17** climbing
para bicicletas/		bike path/	cancha de tenis	**10**	tennis court	alpinismo	wall
ciclovía		bikeway	campo de béisbol	**11**	ballfield	columpios	**18** swings
estanque para patos	**2**	duck pond	fuente/bebedero	**12**	fountain	trepador	**19** climber
merendero/área para	**3**	picnic area	soporte para bicicletas	**13**	bike rack	deslizadero/	**20** slide
comer al aire libre/de picnic			caballitos	**14**	merry-go-round/	resbaladero/	
basurero/zafacón	**4**	trash can			carousel	tobogán	
parrilla	**5**	grill	rampa para	**15**	skateboard	balancín/sube y	**21** seesaw
mesa para merendar	**6**	picnic table	patinetas		ramp	baja/tintibajo	
fuente para beber agua	**7**	water fountain	área de juegos	**16**	playground	caja de arena	**22** sandbox
pista para trotar/correr	**8**	jogging path	para niños(as)			arena	**23** sand

[1–22]
A. Excuse me. Does this park
    have (a) _____?
B. Yes. Right over there.

[17–23]
A. { Be careful on the _____[17–21]_____!
   { Be careful in the _____[22, 23]_____!
B. I will, Dad/Mom.

Describe a park and playground you are familiar with.

salvavidas	**1**	lifeguard	sombrilla de playa/	**11**	beach	concha	**19**	seashell/shell
silla de salvavidas	**2**	lifeguard stand	parasol		umbrella	piedra	**20**	rock
salvavidas/flotador	**3**	life preserver	castillo de arena	**12**	sand castle	hielera/	**21**	cooler
puesto de	**4**	snack bar/	tabla/balsa para	**13**	boogie	nevera de playa		
refrescos		refreshment	girar con la ola		board	sombrero de sol	**22**	sun hat
		stand	amante de asolearse/	**14**	sunbather	loción protectora	**23**	sunscreen/
vendedor(a)	**5**	vendor	broncearse			contra el sol/		sunblock/
nadador(a)/bañista	**6**	swimmer	lentes/gafas de sol	**15**	sunglasses	bronceadora		suntan lotion
ola	**7**	wave	toalla de playa	**16**	(beach) towel	manta/	**24**	(beach)
surfista	**8**	surfer	pelota/balón/	**17**	beach ball	frisa		blanket
cometa/papalote/	**9**	kite	bola de playa			palita	**25**	shovel
chiringa			tabla de surf/deslizador/	**18**	surfboard	cubito	**26**	pail
silla de playa	**10**	beach chair	tabla hawaiana					

[1–26]
A. What a nice beach!
B. It is. Look at all the _____s!

[9–11, 13, 15–18, 21–26]
A. Are you ready for the beach?
B. Almost. I just have to get my _____.

Do you like to go to the beach? Describe your favorite beach. What do you take when you go there?

ACTIVIDADES AL AIRE LIBRE

acampar	**A camping**
tienda de campaña/carpa	**1** tent
bolsa/saco de dormir	**2** sleeping bag
estacas	**3** tent stakes
lámpara de gas	**4** lantern
hacha	**5** hatchet
hornillo/hornillar	**6** camping stove
navaja tipo ejército suizo	**7** Swiss army knife
repelente de insectos	**8** insect repellent
cerillas(os)/fósforos	**9** matches

ir de excursión	**B hiking**
mochila de excursión	**10** backpack
cantimplora	**11** canteen
brújula/compás	**12** compass
mapa	**13** trail map
aparato de GPS (Sistema de Posición Global)	**14** GPS device
botas de excursión	**15** hiking boots

escalar rocas	**C rock climbing/technical climbing**
aparejo/arnés	**16** harness
cuerda (de nudos para trepar)	**17** rope

hacer ciclismo de montaña	**D mountain biking**
bicicleta de montaña	**18** mountain bike
casco	**19** (bike) helmet

merendar/comer al aire libre/ir de picnic	**E picnic**
manta/frisa	**20** (picnic) blanket
termo	**21** thermos
canasta/cesto de picnic	**22** picnic basket

A. Let's go __[A–E]__* this weekend.
B. Good idea! We haven't gone __[A–E]__* in a long time.

*With E, say: on a picnic.

A. Did you bring
 { the __[1–9, 11–14, 16, 17, 20–22]__ ?
 { your __[10, 15, 18, 19]__ ?
B. Yes, I did.
A. Oh, good.

Have you ever gone camping, hiking, rock climbing, or mountain biking? Tell about it: What did you do? Where? What equipment did you use?

Do you like to go on picnics? Where? What picnic supplies and food do you take with you?

DEPORTES Y ACTIVIDADES INDIVIDUALES

footing/correr al trote/trotar	**A**	**jogging**
traje para correr/chándal	**1**	jogging suit
zapatillas para correr	**2**	jogging shoes
correr	**B**	**running**
shorts para correr	**3**	running shorts
zapatillas para correr	**4**	running shoes
caminar	**C**	**walking**
zapatillas para caminar	**5**	walking shoes
patinaje/patinar	**D**	**inline skating/rollerblading**
patines	**6**	inline skates/rollerblades
rodilleras	**7**	knee pads
ciclismo	**E**	**cycling/biking**
bicicleta	**8**	bicycle/bike
casco	**9**	(bicycle/bike) helmet
andar en patineta/ monopatín	**F**	**skateboarding**
patineta/monopatín/patín	**10**	skateboard
coderas/codales	**11**	elbow pads
jugar a los bolos/al boliche	**G**	**bowling**
bola para jugar a los bolos/ de bolera/boliche	**12**	bowling ball
zapatos para jugar a los bolos	**13**	bowling shoes

montar a caballo	**H**	**horseback riding**
silla de montar/montura	**14**	saddle
riendas	**15**	reins
estribos	**16**	stirrups
tenis	**I**	**tennis**
raqueta de tenis	**17**	tennis racket
pelota/bola de tenis	**18**	tennis ball
shorts para tenis	**19**	tennis shorts
bádminton	**J**	**badminton**
raqueta de bádminton	**20**	badminton racket
gallito de bádminton	**21**	birdie/shuttlecock
pelota vasca/ frontón con raqueta	**K**	**racquetball**
gafas/lentes protectores(as)	**22**	safety goggles
pelota	**23**	racquetball
raqueta	**24**	racquet
tenis de mesa/pimpón/ ping-pong	**L**	**table tennis/ ping pong**
raqueta/paleta	**25**	paddle
mesa para jugar pimpón/ping-pong	**26**	ping pong table
malla/red	**27**	net
pelota/bola de pimpón/ping-pong	**28**	ping pong ball

golf	**M**	**golf**		gimnasia	**Q**	**gymnastics**		boxear	**T**	**box**
palos de golf	**29**	golf clubs		potro	**36**	horse		guantes de boxeo	**45**	boxing gloves
pelota/bola de golf	**30**	golf ball		barras paralelas	**37**	parallel bars		shorts de boxeo	**46**	(boxing) trunks

golf **M** golf
palos de golf **29** golf clubs
pelota/bola **30** golf ball
de golf

lanzar el disco/ **N** **Frisbee**
platillo volador/
Frisbee
disco/platillo **31** Frisbee/
volador/Frisbee flying disc

billar **O** **billiards/pool**
mesa de billar **32** pool table
taco/palo de billar **33** pool stick
bolas de billar **34** billiard balls

artes marciales **P** **martial arts**
cinta/cinturón **35** black belt
negro(a)

gimnasia **Q** **gymnastics**
potro **36** horse
barras paralelas **37** parallel bars
colchoneta/estera **38** mat
barra/viga de **39** balance
equilibrio/ beam
balance
trampolín **40** trampoline

levantar pesas **R** **weightlifting**
barra con pesas **41** barbell
pesas/ **42** weights
mancuernas

arco **S** **archery**
arco y **43** bow and
flecha arrow
diana/blanco **44** target

boxear **T** **box**
guantes de boxeo **45** boxing gloves
shorts de boxeo **46** (boxing) trunks

practicar lucha libre **U** **wrestle**
uniforme de lucha libre **47** wrestling uniform
lona/estera/ **48** (wrestling) mat
cuadrilátero

hacer ejercicio(s) **V** **work out/exercise**
caminadora **49** treadmill
estacionaria
remadora **50** rowing machine
estacionaria
bicicleta estacionaria **51** exercise bike
equipo de ejercicios **52** universal/
para estar en forma/ exercise
máquina universal equipment

[A–V]
A. What do you like to do in your free time?
B. { I like to go ___[A–H]___ .
   { I like to play ___[I–O]___ .
   { I like to do ___[P–S]___ .
   { I like to ___[T–V]___ .

[1–52]
A. I really like this/these new _____.
B. It's/They're very nice.

Do you do any of these activities? Which ones? Which are popular in your country?

DEPORTES EN EQUIPO

béisbol	**A baseball**	**lacrosse/cross**	**D lacrosse**	**voleibol/ balonvolea**	**G volleyball**
jugador(a) de béisbol	**1** baseball player	jugador(a) de lacrosse	**7** lacrosse player	jugador(a) de voleibol	**13** volleyball player
campo de juego/ diamante de béisbol	**2** baseball field/ ballfield	campo de lacrosse	**8** lacrosse field	cancha de voleibol	**14** volleyball court
softball/sófbol	**B softball**	**hockey sobre hielo**	**E (ice) hockey**	**fútbol/ balompié/ sóquer**	**H soccer**
jugador(a) de sófbol	**3** softball player	jugador(a) de hockey	**9** hockey player	jugador(a) de fútbol	**15** soccer player
campo de sófbol	**4** ballfield	pista de hielo	**10** hockey rink	campo de fútbol	**16** soccer field
fútbol americano	**C football**	**baloncesto/básquetbol**	**F basketball**		
jugador(a) de fútbol americano	**5** football player	jugador(a) de baloncesto/básquetbol	**11** basketball player		
campo de fútbol americano	**6** football field	cancha/pista de baloncesto/básquetbol	**12** basketball court		

[A–H]
A. Do you like to play **baseball**?
B. Yes. **Baseball** is one of my favorite sports.

A. .... plays __[A–H]__ very well.
B. You're right. I think he's/she's one of the best _____s* on the team.

*Use 1, 3, 5, 7, 9, 11, 13, 15.

A. Now listen, team! I want all of you to go out on that _____† and play the best game of __[A–H]__ you've ever played!
B. All right, Coach!

† Use 2, 4, 6, 8, 10, 12, 14, 16.

Which sports in this lesson do you like to play? Which do you like to watch?

What are your favorite teams?

Name some famous players of these sports.

EQUIPO PARA DEPORTES EN EQUIPO

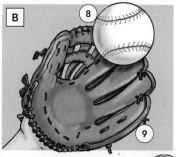

béisbol	**A**	**baseball**
pelota de béisbol	1	baseball
bate	2	bat
casco de béisbol	3	batting helmet
uniforme	4	(baseball) uniform
máscara/protector	5	catcher's mask
guante	6	(baseball) glove
guante de receptor	7	catcher's mitt
softball/sófbol	**B**	**softball**
pelota de sófbol	8	softball
guante	9	softball glove
fútbol americano	**C**	**football**
pelota de fútbol americano	10	football
casco protector	11	football helmet
protector de hombros	12	shoulder pads
lacrosse/cross	**D**	**lacrosse**
pelota de lacrosse	13	lacrosse ball
careta/máscara	14	face guard
raqueta de lacrosse	15	lacrosse stick
hockey sobre hielo	**E**	**(ice) hockey**
disco	16	hockey puck
palo/bastón de hockey	17	hockey stick
máscara/careta	18	hockey mask
guante de hockey	19	hockey glove
patines de hockey	20	hockey skates
básquetbol/baloncesto	**F**	**basketball**
balón de básquetbol/baloncesto	21	basketball
tablero	22	backboard
canasta	23	basketball hoop
voleibol/balonvolea	**G**	**volleyball**
balón de voleibol	24	volleyball
red	25	volleyball net
fútbol/sóquer/balompié	**H**	**soccer**
balón de fútbol	26	soccer ball
espinillera/polaina	27	shinguards

[1–27]
A. I can't find my **baseball**!
B. Look in the closet.*

*closet, basement, garage

[In a store]
A. Excuse me. I'm looking for (a) __[1–27]__ .
B. All our __[A–H]__ equipment is over there.
A. Thanks.

[At home]
A. I'm going to play __[A–H]__ after school today.
B. Don't forget your __[1–21, 24, 26, 27]__ !

Which sports in this lesson are popular in your country? Which sports do students play in high school?

ACTIVIDADES Y DEPORTES DE INVIERNO

esquiar/practicar esquí alpino	**A**	**(downhill) skiing**
esquís	1	skis
botas de esquí/esquiar	2	ski boots
ataduras/cogederas	3	bindings
bastones/palos de esquí	4	(ski) poles
practicar esquí de campo traviesa/fondo	**B**	**cross-country skiing**
esquís de campo traviesa/fondo	5	cross-country skis
patinar sobre hielo	**C**	**(ice) skating**
patines de hielo	6	(ice) skates
cuchilla	7	blade
protector de la cuchilla	8	skate guard

practicar patinaje artístico	**D**	**figure skating**
patines de hielo	9	figure skates
practicar snowboarding	**E**	**snowboarding**
tabla de snowboard/para nieve	10	snowboard
deslizarse en trineo/plato	**F**	**sledding**
trineo	11	sled
plato	12	sledding dish/ saucer
practicar el bobsleigh/ bambolearse sobre hielo	**G**	**bobsledding**
bobsleigh/bobsled/bamboleador	13	bobsled
ir de travesía/en moto de nieve	**H**	**snowmobiling**
moto de nieve	14	snowmobile

[A–H]
A. What's your favorite winter sport?
B. **Skiing**.

[A–H]
　[At work or at school on Friday]
A. What are you going to do this weekend?
B. I'm going to go _____.

[1–14]
　[On the telephone]
A. Hello. *Sally's* Sporting Goods.
B. Hello. Do you sell _____(s)?
A. Yes, we do. / No, we don't.

Have you ever done any of these activities? Which ones?

Have you ever watched the Winter Olympics? Which event do you think is the most exciting? the most dangerous?

ACTIVIDADES Y DEPORTES ACUÁTICOS

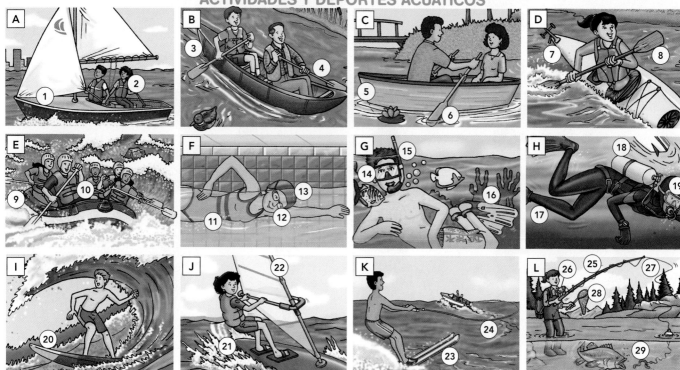

ir de vela/velear	**A**	**sailing**
velero/bote/barco de vela	**1**	sailboat
chaleco salvavidas/flotador	**2**	life jacket/life vest
navegar en canoa	**B**	**canoeing**
canoa	**3**	canoe
pala/remo	**4**	paddles
remar	**C**	**rowing**
bote de remos	**5**	rowboat
remos	**6**	oars
navegar en kayak	**D**	**kayaking**
kayak	**7**	kayak
pala/remo	**8**	paddles
descender en balsa	**E**	**(white-water) rafting**
balsa	**9**	raft
chaleco salvavidas/flotador	**10**	life jacket/life vest
nadar	**F**	**swimming**
traje/vestido de baño/bañador	**11**	swimsuit/bathing suit
gafas/gafas saltonas/gogles	**12**	goggles
gorra de baño	**13**	bathing cap
nadar con tubo de respiración/ con esnórquel	**G**	**snorkeling**
visor/máscara	**14**	mask
tubo de respiración/esnórquel	**15**	snorkel

aletas/chapaletas	**16**	fins
bucear	**H**	**scuba diving**
traje de buceo	**17**	wet suit
tanque de aire	**18**	(air) tank
visor/máscara	**19**	(diving) mask
practicar surf/surfear	**I**	**surfing**
tabla de surf/ tabla hawaiana/ deslizador	**20**	surfboard
practicar windsurfing/ surfear con vela	**J**	**windsurfing**
tabla de vela	**21**	sailboard
vela	**22**	sail
practicar esquí acuático	**K**	**waterskiing**
esquís acuáticos	**23**	water skis
cable/cuerda de remolque	**24**	towrope
pescar	**L**	**fishing**
caña de pescar	**25**	(fishing) rod/ pole
carrete/bobina	**26**	reel
sedal/cuerda	**27**	(fishing) line
red	**28**	(fishing) net
cebo/carnada	**29**	bait

[A–L]
A. Would you like to go **sailing** tomorrow?
B. Sure. I'd love to.

A. Have you ever gone ___[A–L]___ ?
B. Yes, I have. / No, I haven't.

A. Do you have everything you need to go ___[A–L]___ ?
B. Yes. I have my ___[1–29]___ (and my ___[1–29]___).
A. Have a good time!

Which sports in this lesson have you tried? Which sports would you like to try?

Are any of these sports popular in your country? Which ones?

ACCIONES AL HACER DEPORTES Y EJERCICIOS

pégue(n)le	**1**	hit	dóble(n)se/ haga(n) flexiones	**12**	bend
lance(n)	**2**	pitch	camine(n)	**13**	walk
tire(n)	**3**	throw	corra(n)	**14**	run
coja(n)/agarre(n)	**4**	catch	salte(n) con un pie	**15**	hop
pase(n)	**5**	pass	dé(n) saltos	**16**	skip
patee(n)	**6**	kick	brinque(n)/salte(n)	**17**	jump
sirva(n)	**7**	serve	alcance(n)	**18**	reach
rebote(n)	**8**	bounce	balancée(n)se	**19**	swing
haga(n) una finta	**9**	dribble	levante(n)	**20**	lift
dispare(n)/tire(n)	**10**	shoot	nade(n)	**21**	swim
estíre(n)se	**11**	stretch			

zambúlla(n)se/tíre(n)se de cabeza/haga(n) clavados	**22**	dive
dispare(n)	**23**	shoot
pechadas/flexiones/lagartijas	**24**	push-up
abdominales	**25**	sit-up
sentadillas	**26**	deep knee bend
saltos de buscapié	**27**	jumping jack
volteretas/vueltas de carnero/maromas	**28**	somersault
volteretas laterales/mediaslunas	**29**	cartwheel
pinos/paradas de cabeza	**30**	handstand

[1–10]
A. _____ the ball!
B. Okay, Coach!

[11–23]
A. Now _____!
B. Like this?
A. Yes.

[24–30]
A. Okay, everybody. I want you to do twenty _____s!
B. Twenty _____s?!
A. That's right.

Do you exercise regularly?
Which exercises do you do?

Be an exercise instructor! Lead your friends in an exercise routine using the actions in this lesson.

DIVERSIONES

obra de teatro	**A**	**play**
teatro	**1**	theater
actor	**2**	actor
actriz	**3**	actress
concierto	**B**	**concert**
sala de conciertos/ auditorio	**4**	concert hall
orquesta	**5**	orchestra
músico	**6**	musician
director(a) de orquesta	**7**	conductor

banda/conjunto musical	**8**	band
ópera	**C**	**opera**
cantante de ópera	**9**	opera singer
ballet	**D**	**ballet**
bailarín de ballet	**10**	ballet dancer
bailarina de ballet	**11**	ballerina
club nocturno/cabaré con música viva	**E**	**music club**
cantante	**12**	singer

películas	**F**	**movies**
sala de cine/cine	**13**	(movie) theater
pantalla	**14**	(movie) screen
actriz	**15**	actress
actor	**16**	actor
club nocturno/ cabaré con programa de cómicos	**G**	**comedy club**
cómico(a)/humorista	**17**	comedian

[A–G]
A. What are you doing this evening?
B. I'm going to { a _____ [A, B, E, G] .
the _____ [C, D, F] .

[1–17]
A. What a magnificent _____!
B. I agree.

What kinds of entertainment in this lesson do you like?
What kinds of entertainment are popular in your country?

Who are some of your favorite actors? actresses?
musicians? singers? comedians?

TIPOS DE DIVERSIÓN

A

B

tipos de música	**A**	**music**
música clásica	**1**	classical music
música popular	**2**	popular music
música country	**3**	country music
música rock	**4**	rock music
música folklórica	**5**	folk music
música rap (de denuncia)	**6**	rap music
gospel	**7**	gospel music
jazz	**8**	jazz
blues	**9**	blues
bluegrass	**10**	bluegrass
hip hop	**11**	hip hop
reggae/regue/reguetón	**12**	reggae
tipos de obras de teatro	**B**	**plays**
dramas	**13**	drama
comedias	**14**	comedy
tragedias	**15**	tragedy
comedias musicales	**16**	musical (comedy)

tipos de películas	C	movies/films
dramas	17	drama
comedias	18	comedy
películas del oeste	19	western
películas de misterio	20	mystery
comedias musicales	21	musical
dibujos/viñetas/ caricaturas animados(as)	22	cartoon
documentales	23	documentary
películas de aventuras/ de acción	24	action movie/ adventure movie
películas de guerra	25	war movie
películas de horror	26	horror movie

películas de ciencia ficción	27	science fiction movie
películas extranjeras	28	foreign film

tipos de programas de televisión	D	TV programs
dramas	29	drama
comedias	30	(situation) comedy/sitcom
programas de entrevistas/ opinión	31	talk show
programas concurso/ de juegos	32	game show/ quiz show

programas sobre la vida real/reality show	33	reality show
telenovelas	34	soap opera
caricaturas/dibujos/ viñetas animadas(os)	35	cartoon
programas infantiles	36	children's program
noticieros/ telediarios	37	news program
teledeportes	38	sports program
programas sobre la naturaleza	39	nature program
tevemall/ programas de ventas	40	shopping program

A. What kind of _____[A–D]_____ do you like?

B. { I like _____[1–12]_____.
{ I like _____[13–40]_____ s.

What's your favorite type of music?
Who is your favorite singer? musician? musical group?

What kind of movies do you like?
Who are your favorite movie stars?
What are the titles of your favorite movies?

What kind of TV programs do you like?
What are your favorite shows?

MUSICAL INSTRUMENTS
INSTRUMENTOS MUSICALES

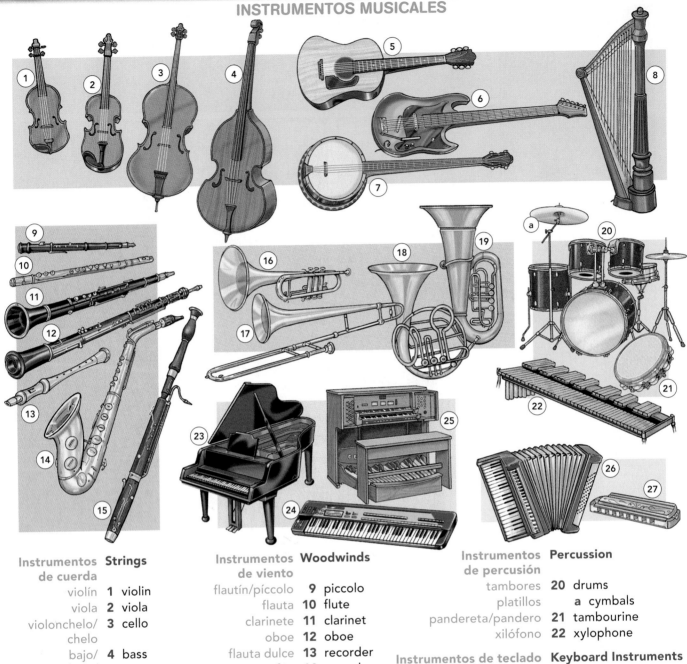

Instrumentos de cuerda	Strings		Instrumentos de viento	Woodwinds		Instrumentos de percusión	Percussion	
violín	1	violin	flautín/píccolo	9	piccolo	tambores	20	drums
viola	2	viola	flauta	10	flute	platillos		a cymbals
violonchelo/chelo	3	cello	clarinete	11	clarinet	pandereta/pandero	21	tambourine
bajo/contrabajo/violón	4	bass	oboe	12	oboe	xilófono	22	xylophone
			flauta dulce	13	recorder			
guitarra (acústica)	5	(acoustic) guitar	saxofón	14	saxophone	**Instrumentos de teclado**	**Keyboard Instruments**	
guitarra eléctrica	6	electric guitar	fagot	15	bassoon	piano	23	piano
banjo	7	banjo				teclado eléctrico	24	electric keyboard
arpa	8	harp	**Los metales**	**Brass**		órgano	25	organ
			trompeta	16	trumpet			
			trombón	17	trombone	**Otros instrumentos**	**Other Instruments**	
			corno francés/trompa	18	French horn	acordeón	26	accordion
			tuba	19	tuba	armónica	27	harmonica

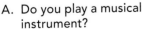

A. Do you play a musical instrument?
B. Yes. I play the **violin**.

A. You play the **trumpet** very well.
B. Thank you.

A. What's that noise?!
B. That's my son/daughter practicing the **drums**.

Do you play a musical instrument? Which one?

Which instruments are usually in an orchestra? a marching band? a rock group?

Name and describe typical musical instruments in your country.

LA GRANJA Y LOS ANIMALES DOMÉSTICOS

finca/casa	**1**	farmhouse	gallo	**14**	rooster	vaca	**26**	cow
granjero(a)/	**2**	farmer	pocilga/chiquero/	**15**	pig pen	carnero/oveja/	**27**	sheep
agricultor(a)			porqueriza			borrego		
huerta/huerto	**3**	(vegetable) garden	cerdo/puerco/	**16**	pig	huerto de árboles	**28**	orchard
espantapájaros	**4**	scarecrow	marrano/cochino			frutales		
heno	**5**	hay	gallinero	**17**	chicken coop	árbol de fruta	**29**	fruit tree
peón	**6**	hired hand	gallina	**18**	chicken	labrador(a)/	**30**	farm worker
granero	**7**	barn	gallinero	**19**	hen house	mozo(a) de labranza		
establo	**8**	stable	gallina ponedora	**20**	hen	alfalfa	**31**	alfalfa
caballo	**9**	horse	campo de cultivos	**21**	crop	maíz	**32**	corn
corral	**10**	barnyard	sistema de irrigación	**22**	irrigation system	algodón	**33**	cotton
pavo/guajolote	**11**	turkey	tractor	**23**	tractor	arroz	**34**	rice
cabra/chivo	**12**	goat	campo	**24**	field	soja/soya	**35**	soybeans
cordero	**13**	lamb	dehesa/pasto/potrero	**25**	pasture	trigo	**36**	wheat

[1–30]
A. Where's the _____?
B. In / Next to the _____.

A. The __[9, 11–14, 16, 18, 20, 26]__ s / __[27]__ are loose again!
B. Oh, no! Where are they?
A. They're in the __[1, 3, 7, 8, 10, 15, 17, 19, 24, 25, 28]__.

[31–36]
A. Do you grow _____ on your farm?
B. No. We grow _____.

Tell about farms in your country. What crops and animals are common on these farms?

ANIMALES Y MASCOTAS

alce	**1**	moose	castor	**14**	beaver	rata	**29** rat
cuerno/asta	**a**	antler	mapache	**15**	raccoon	ardilla listada/rayada	**30** chipmunk
oso polar	**2**	polar bear	zarigüeya/	**16**	possum/	ardilla	**31** squirrel
venado/ciervo	**3**	deer	tlacuache		opossum	topo/ardilla de tierra/	**32** gopher
pezuña-pezuñas	**a**	hoof-hooves	caballo	**17**	horse	taltuza/tuza	
lobo-lobos	**4**	wolf-wolves	cola	**a**	tail	perrito de las praderas	**33** prairie dog
pelaje	**a**	coat/fur	poni	**18**	pony	gato	**34** cat
oso negro	**5**	(black) bear	burro	**19**	donkey	bigotes	**a** whiskers
garra	**a**	claw	armadillo	**20**	armadillo	gatito	**35** kitten
puma	**6**	mountain lion	murciélago	**21**	bat	perro	**36** dog
oso pardo	**7**	(grizzly) bear	lombriz	**22**	worm	perrito/cachorro	**37** puppy
búfalo/bisonte	**8**	buffalo/bison	babosa	**23**	slug	hámster	**38** hamster
coyote	**9**	coyote	mono	**24**	monkey	jerbo	**39** gerbil
zorro	**10**	fox	oso hormiguero	**25**	anteater	conejillo de indias/	**40** guinea pig
mofeta/zorrillo	**11**	skunk	llama	**26**	llama	cuis/cobayo	
puercoespín	**12**	porcupine	jaguar	**27**	jaguar	carpa dorada	**41** goldfish
púa	**a**	quill	manchas	**a**	spots	canario	**42** canary
conejo	**13**	rabbit	ratón-ratones	**28**	mouse-mice	perico	**43** parakeet

Spanish	#	English	Spanish	#	English	Spanish	#	English	Spanish	#	English
antílope	44	antelope	tigre	51	tiger	hiena	54	hyena	hipopótamo	59	hippopotamus
mandril	45	baboon	garra		**a** paw	león	55	lion	leopardo	60	leopard
rinoceronte	46	rhinoceros	camello	52	camel	melena		**a** mane	gorila	61	gorilla
cuerno		**a** horn	joroba		**a** hump	jirafa	56	giraffe	canguro	62	kangaroo
panda	47	panda	elefante	53	elephant	zebra	57	zebra	bolsa		**a** pouch
orangután	48	orangutan	colmillo		**a** tusk	rayas		**a** stripes	koala	63	koala (bear)
pantera	49	panther	trompa		**b** trunk	chimpancé	58	chimpanzee	ornitorrinco	64	platypus
gibón	50	gibbon									

[1–33, 44–64]
A. Look at that _____!
B. Wow! That's the biggest _____ I've ever seen!

[34–43]
A. Do you have a pet?
B. Yes. I have a _____.
A. What's your _____'s name?
B. ....

What animals are there where you live?

Is there a zoo near where you live? What animals does it have?

What are some common pets in your country?

If you could be an animal, which animal would you like to be? Why?

Does your culture have any popular folk tales or children's stories about animals? Tell a story you know.

Pájaros	Birds		halcón/falcón	9	hawk
petirrojo/	1	robin	águila	10	eagle
pechirrojo			garra		**a** claw
nido	**a** nest		cisne	11	swan
huevo	**b** egg		colibrí/visitaflor/	12	hummingbird
urraca azul/	2	blue jay	picaflor		
arrendajo			pato	13	duck
ala	**a** wing		pico		**a** bill
cola	**b** tail		gorrión/	14	sparrow
pluma	**c** feather		tierrerita		
cardenal	3	cardinal	ganso-	15	goose-
cuervo	4	crow	gansos		geese
gaviota	5	seagull	pingüino	16	penguin
pájaro	6	woodpecker	flamenco	17	flamingo
carpintero			grulla	18	crane
pico	**a** beak		cigüeña	19	stork
paloma/	7	pigeon	pelícano	20	pelican
pichón/			pavo real	21	peacock
tórtola			papagayo/	22	parrot
búho/lechuza	8	owl	loro/cotorra		

avestruz	23	ostrich
Insectos	**Insects**	
mosca	24	fly
mariquita/	25	ladybug
catarina/		
catarinita		
luciérnaga/	26	firefly/
cocuyo/cucuyo/		lightning
cucubano		bug
polilla	27	moth
oruga	28	caterpillar
capullo		**a** cocoon
mariposa	29	butterfly
garrapata	30	tick
mosquito	31	mosquito
libélula/	32	dragonfly
caballito del		
diablo/caballito		
de San Pedro		

araña	33	spider
telaraña		**a** web
mantis/	34	praying
mariapalito/		mantis
santateresa		
religiosa		
avispa	35	wasp
abeja	36	bee
panal		**a** beehive
saltamontes/	37	grasshopper
grillo/		
chapulín		
escarabajo/	38	beetle
cocorrón		
escorpión/	39	scorpion
alacrán		
ciempiés	40	centipede
grillo/	41	cricket
cigarra/		
chicharra		

[1–41]
A. Is that a/an _____?
B. No. I think it's a/an _____.

[24–41]
A. Hold still! There's a _____ on your shirt!
B. Oh! Can you get it off me?
A. There! It's gone!

What birds and insects are there where you live?

Does your culture have any popular folk tales or children's stories about birds or insects? Tell a story you know.

PECES, ANIMALES MARINOS Y REPTILES

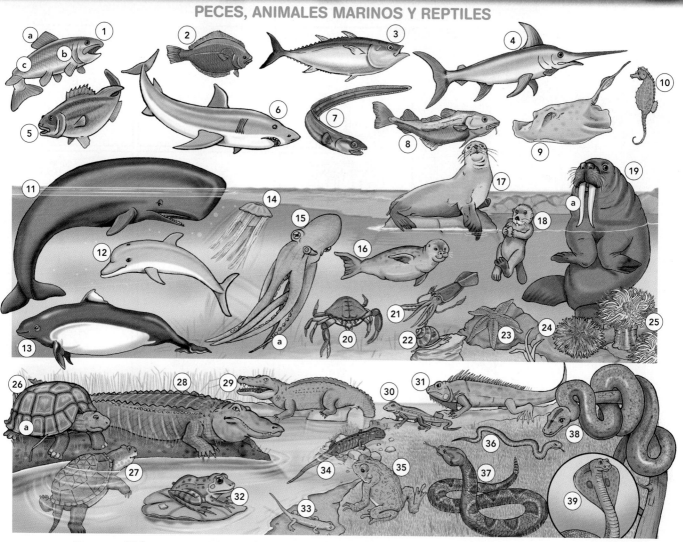

Peces	Fish				
trucha	**1** trout				
aleta	**a** fin				
agalla/branquia	**b** gill				
escamas	**c** scales				
lenguado	**2** flounder				
atún	**3** tuna				
pez espada	**4** swordfish				
róbalo	**5** bass				
tiburón	**6** shark				
anguila	**7** eel				
bacalao	**8** cod				
raya/mantarraya	**9** ray/stingray				
caballito de mar	**10** sea horse				

Animales marinos	Sea Animals
ballena	**11** whale
delfín	**12** dolphin

marsopa/marsopla	**13**	porpoise
aguamala/ medusa/aguaviva	**14**	jellyfish
pulpo	**15**	octopus
tentáculo		**a** tentacle
foca	**16**	seal
león marino/ vaquita de mar	**17**	sea lion
nutria	**18**	otter
morsa	**19**	walrus
colmillo		**a** tusk
cangrejo	**20**	crab
calamar	**21**	squid
caracol	**22**	snail
estrella de mar	**23**	starfish
erizo de mar	**24**	sea urchin
anémona de mar	**25**	sea anemone

Anfibios y reptiles	Amphibians and Reptiles
tortuga	**26** tortoise
caparazón/carapacho	**a** shell
tortuga de mar	**27** turtle
caimán/lagarto	**28** alligator
cocodrilo	**29** crocodile
lagartija	**30** lizard
iguana	**31** iguana
rana	**32** frog
tritón	**33** newt
salamandra	**34** salamander
sapo	**35** toad
culebra/serpiente	**36** snake
serpiente/víbora de cascabel	**37** rattlesnake
boa	**38** boa constrictor
cobra/serpiente de anteojos	**39** cobra

[1–39]
A. Is that a/an _____?
B. No. I think it's a/an _____.

[26–39]
A. Are there any _____s around here?
B. No. But there are lots of _____!

What fish, sea animals, and reptiles can be found in your country?
Which ones are endangered and need to be protected? Why?

In your opinion, which ones are the most interesting?
the most beautiful? the most dangerous?

TREES, PLANTS, AND FLOWERS

ÁRBOLES, PLANTAS Y FLORES

árbol	**1** tree	cono/piña	**10** pine cone	arce	**18** maple	bayas/cerecitas	**25** berries
hoja-hojas	**2** leaf-leaves	cornejo/	**11** dogwood	roble	**19** oak	arbusto	**26** shrub
ramita/	**3** twig	sanguiñuelo		pino	**20** pine	helecho	**27** fern
bejuco		aquifolio/	**12** holly	secuoya/secoya	**21** redwood	mata/planta	**28** plant
rama	**4** branch	acebo (árbol)		sauce llorón	**22** (weeping)	cactus	**29** cactus-cacti
brazo	**5** limb	magnolia	**13** magnolia		willow	enredadera	**30** vine
tronco	**6** trunk	olmo	**14** elm	arbusto	**23** bush	ortiga/hiedra/	**31** poison
corteza	**7** bark	cerezo	**15** cherry	acebo/flor del	**24** holly	yedra venenosa	ivy
raíz	**8** root	palmera/palma	**16** palm	amor/laurel de		zumaque venenoso	**32** poison sumac
aguja/hoja	**9** needle	abedul	**17** birch	Navidad		roble venenoso	**33** poison oak

flor	**34**	flower	caléndula/maravilla/	**43**	marigold	
pétalo	**35**	petal	cempasúchil			
tallo	**36**	stem	clavel	**44**	carnation	
botón/capullo	**37**	bud	gardenia	**45**	gardenia	
espina	**38**	thorn	lirio	**46**	lily	
bulbo/cebolleta	**39**	bulb	azucena	**47**	iris	
crisantemo	**40**	chrysanthemum	pensamiento	**48**	pansy	
narciso	**41**	daffodil	petunia	**49**	petunia	
margarita	**42**	daisy	orquídea	**50**	orchid	

rosa	**51**	rose
girasol	**52**	sunflower
azafrán	**53**	crocus
tulipán	**54**	tulip
geranio	**55**	geranium
violeta	**56**	violet
flor de Navidad/Nochebuena	**57**	poinsettia
jazmín	**58**	jasmine
hibisco/papo	**59**	hibiscus

[11–22]
A. What kind of tree is that?
B. I think it's a/an _____ tree.

[31–33]
A. Watch out for the _____ over there!
B. Oh. Thanks for the warning.

[40–57]
A. Look at all the _____s!*
B. They're beautiful!

*With 58 and 59, use: Look at all the ___!

Describe your favorite tree and your favorite flower.

What kinds of trees and flowers grow where you live?

In your country, what flowers do you see at weddings? at funerals? during holidays? in hospital rooms? Tell which flowers people use for different occasions.

LA ENERGÍA, EL MEDIO AMBIENTE Y LA PROTECCIÓN DE LOS RECURSOS NATURALES

Fuentes de energía	Sources of Energy
petróleo	**1** oil/petroleum
gas	**2** (natural) gas
carbón	**3** coal
energía nuclear	**4** nuclear energy
energía solar	**5** solar energy
energía hidroeléctrica	**6** hydroelectric power
viento	**7** wind
energía geotérmica	**8** geothermal energy

Protección de recursos naturales	Conservation
reciclar/reutilizar	**9** recycle
ahorrar energía	**10** save energy/ conserve energy
ahorrar agua	**11** save water/ conserve water
compartir el automóvil	**12** carpool

Problemas ambientales	Environmental Problems
contaminación del aire	**13** air pollution
contaminación del agua	**14** water pollution
residuos tóxicos	**15** hazardous waste/ toxic waste
lluvia ácida	**16** acid rain
radiación	**17** radiation
calentamiento de la Tierra	**18** global warming

[1–8]
A. In my opinion, _____ will be our best source of energy in the future.
B. I disagree. I think our best source of energy will be _____.

[9–12]
A. Do you _____?
B. Yes. I'm very concerned about the environment.

[13–18]
A. Do you worry about the environment?
B. Yes. I'm very concerned about _____.

What kind of energy do you use to heat your home? to cook? In your opinion, which will be the best source of energy in the future?

Do you practice conservation? What do you do to help the environment?

In your opinion, what is the most serious environmental problem in the world today? Why?

DESASTRES NATURALES

terremoto/temblor **1** earthquake	inundación **6** flood	avalancha/ **11** landslide
huracán **2** hurricane	maremoto/tsunami **7** tsunami	derrumbe de tierra
tifón **3** typhoon	sequía **8** drought	avalancha de lodo **12** mudslide
ventisca/ **4** blizzard	incendio forestal **9** forest fire	alud/avalancha **13** avalanche
tormenta de nieve	fuego arrasador **10** wildfire	erupción volcánica **14** volcanic eruption
tornado/torbellino **5** tornado		

A. Did you hear about the _____ in ....(country)........ ?
B. Yes, I did. I saw it on the news.

Have you or someone you know ever experienced a natural disaster? Tell about it.

Which natural disasters sometimes happen where you live? How do people prepare for them?

TIPOS DE VIAJE

Tipos de viaje	Types of Travel
viaje de negocios	**1** business trip
viaje con la familia	**2** family trip
crucero	**3** cruise
viaje guiado/tour	**4** (guided) tour
excursión/tour en autobús/guagua	**5** bus tour

viaje en tren	**6** train trip
viaje en lancha/barco/paseo en bote	**7** boat trip
viaje para esquiar	**8** ski trip
viaje de estudios	**9** study tour
tour ecológico	**10** eco-tour
safari	**11** safari

expedición	**12** expedition
Reservar un viaje	**Booking a Trip**
agencia de viajes	**13** travel agency
agencia/empresa de turismo guiado	**14** tour company
en Internet/en línea	**15** online
por teléfono	**16** over the phone

[1–12]
A. Are you planning to travel soon?
B. Yes. I'm going on a _____ to ...(country)...
A. A _____ to ...(country)...? That's wonderful!

[13–16]
A. How did you make the arrangements for your trip?
B. I booked it { through a _____ [13, 14].
_____ [15, 16].

Tell about a trip you took: Where did you travel? What kind of trip was it? How did you book the trip?

inmigración/ control de pasaportes	**1**	**immigration/ passport control**
área de reclamo de equipaje	**2**	**baggage claim area**
aduana	**3**	**customs**
mostrador/puesto de cambio de divisas/dinero	**4**	**money exchange counter**
parada de taxi	**5**	**taxi stand**
autobús de enlace/transferencia	**6**	**shuttle bus**

mostradores/ventanillas de alquiler/renta de coches/carros	**7**	**car rental counters**
vehículos de cortesía del hotel	**8**	**hotel courtesy vehicles**
baños	**9**	**restrooms**
pasaporte	**10**	**passport**
visa	**11**	**visa**
comprobante/boleto de factura de equipaje	**12**	**baggage claim check**
formulario/forma de declaración de aduana	**13**	**customs declaration form**

[1–9]

A. Excuse me.
- Where's ___[1, 3]___?
- Where's the ___[2, 4–6]___?
- Where are the ___[7–9]___?

B. Over there.

[10–13]

A. May I see your _____?
B. My _____? Yes. Here you are.
A. Thank you.

[At immigration/passport control]

A. What is the purpose of your trip—business or pleasure?

B. ....

A. How long do you plan to stay?

B. ....

[At customs]

A. How many bags do you have?

B. ....

A. Can you open them, please? I need to inspect them.

B. Certainly.

Tell about your arrival at a destination:

Where did you arrive?
What happened after you arrived?
Where did you go?
What did you do?

HOTEL COMMUNICATION
COMUNICACIÓN DENTRO DEL HOTEL

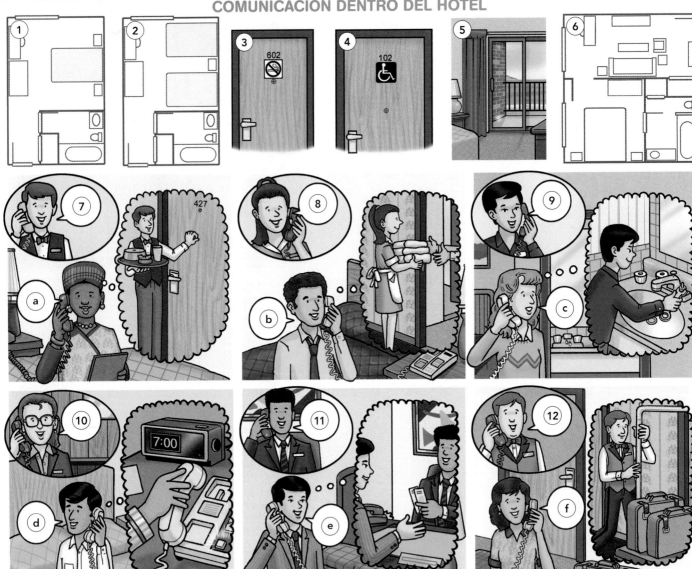

habitación/cuarto individual	**1** single room	Recepción	**10** Front Desk
habitación/cuarto doble	**2** room with double beds	Conserje	**11** Concierge
habitación/cuarto para no fumadores(as)	**3** non-smoking room	Servicio de botones	**12** Bell Desk
		Quisiera ordenar *una cena.*	**a** I'd like to order *dinner.*
habitación/cuarto accesible para discapacitados(as)	**4** handicapped-accessible room	Necesitamos *toallas.*	**b** We need some *towels.*
		El lavabo/lavamanos de nuestro cuarto no funciona.	**c** The *sink* in our room is broken.
habitación/cuarto con vista	**5** room with a view	Por favor, quisiera que me despertaran a las 7 A.M.	**d** I'd like a wake-up call at 7 A.M., please.
suite	**6** suite		
Servicio de restaurante a la habitación/cuarto	**7** Room Service	Quisiera boletos para una *función/un show.*	**e** I'd like to get tickets for a *show.*
Limpieza/Servicio de camarero(a)/recamarero(a)	**8** Housekeeping	Voy a desocupar la habitación. ¿Podría enviar a alguien a recoger mis bolsas/maletas, por favor?	**f** I'm checking out. Can you please send someone to get my bags?
Mantenimiento	**9** Maintenance		

[1–6]
A. I'd like a _____, please.
B. Let me see if that's available.
A. Thank you.

A. _____[7–12]_____.
B. _____[a–f]_____.
A. Certainly.

Tell about a hotel you stayed in: What type of room did you have? What hotel services did you use?

ACTIVIDADES TURÍSTICAS

visitar lugares de interés	**1** go sightseeing	comprar boletos para un *show*/ un *concierto*	**9** get tickets for a *show/concert*
ir de paseo/gira a pie	**2** take a walking tour	visitar un sitio histórico	**10** visit an historic site
ir de paseo/gira en autobús/guagua	**3** take a bus tour	ir de compras	**11** go shopping
cambiar divisas/dinero	**4** exchange money	ir al parque	**12** go to a park
comprar recuerdos/regalos	**5** buy souvenirs	ir al museo	**13** go to a museum
enviar/mandar postales por correo	**6** mail some postcards	ir a un gimnasio/club de acondicionamiento físico	**14** go to a health club/ fitness club
hacer una reservación en un restaurante	**7** make a restaurant reservation	ir a un café Internet/ciber café	**15** go to an Internet cafe
alquilar/rentar un coche/carro	**8** rent a car	ir a un club/una discoteca	**16** go to a club

A. May I help you?
B. Yes, please. I'd like to _____.

A. What did you do today?
B. We _____ed.

Tell about a tourist experience you had: Where did you go? What did you do there?

TOURIST COMMUNICATION
CONVERSACIONES TURÍSTICAS

Tourist Requests   Gestiones del/de la turista

Asking Permission   Pedir permiso

Talking with Local People   Hablar con los/las residentes

cambiar divisas/dinero	**1** exchange money	usar un teléfono celular/móvil aquí	**9** use a cell phone here
cambiar un cheque de viajero	**2** cash a traveler's check	pagar con tarjeta de crédito	**10** pay with a credit card
comprar esto	**3** buy this	Soy de ....(país)..........	**11** I'm from ..(country)..
comprar *dos* boletos	**4** buy *two* tickets	Estaré aquí *cinco* días.	**12** I'm here for *five* days.
enviar/mandar esto a mi país por correo	**5** mail this to my country	He visto .... y	**13** I've seen .... and ....
tomar fotografías aquí	**6** take photographs here	Me gusta mucho su ciudad. Es muy	**14** I like your city very much. It's very ....
comer aquí	**7** eat here		
entrar	**8** go in		

[1–5]
A. May I help you?
B. Yes, please. I'd like to _____.

[6–10]
A. Can I _____?
B. { Yes, you can.
    { No, you can't.

[11–14]
A. __[a–d]__ ?
B. __[11–14]__ .

Emergency Expressions   Expresiones en caso de emergencia

Useful Expressions   Expresiones útiles

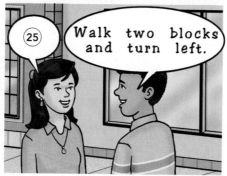

¡Socorro!/¡Auxilio!/¡Ayuda!	**15**	Help!
¡Policía!	**16**	Police!
¡No me moleste!/	**17**	Please don't bother
¡Déjeme en paz!/		me!/Please go away!/
¡Déjeme tranquilo(a)!		Get away from me!
¡Incendio!/¡Fuego!	**18**	Fire!
¡Cuidado!	**19**	Look out!
¡Quieto(a)!/¡Alto!/¡Pare!/	**20**	Freeze!/Stop!/
¡No se mueva!/¡Deténgase!		Don't move!

¿Habla usted ....(idioma)....?	**21**	Do you speak .....(language).....?
Por favor, escríbamelo.	**22**	Please write that down for me.
¿Cómo se dice/se llama eso en inglés?	**23**	What do you call that in English?
Repita, por favor.	**24**	Please repeat that.
Más despacio, por favor.	**25**	Please speak slowly.
Perdone/Disculpe. ¿Qué dijo?	**26**	I'm sorry. What did you say?

Be a tourist! Practice conversations with other students. Use all the expressions on pages 164 and 165.

EL MUNDO

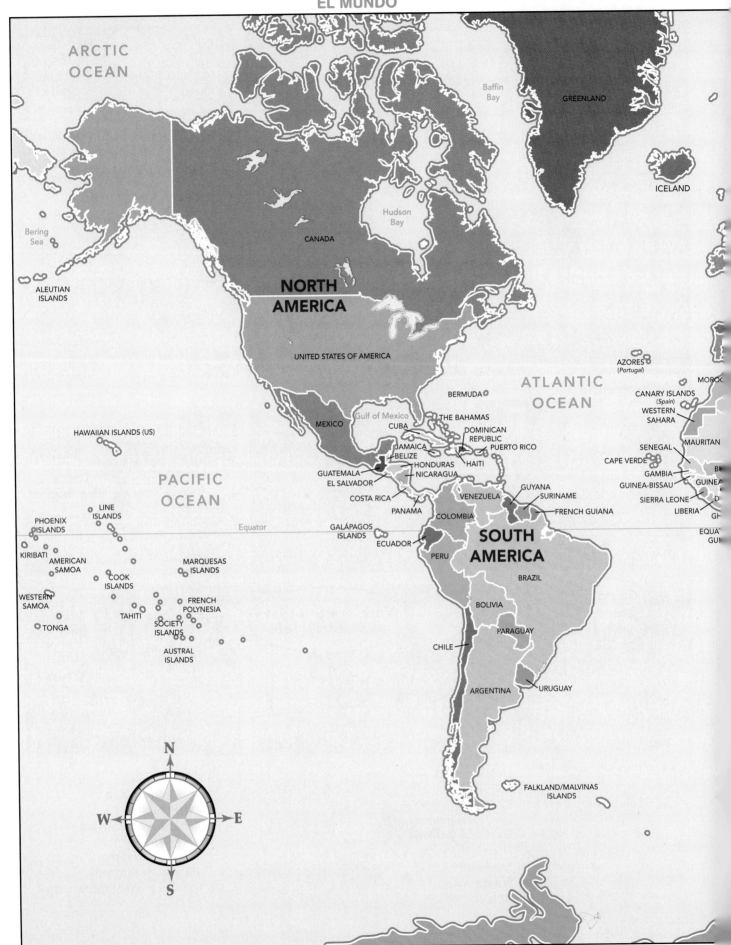

ARCTIC OCEAN

Baffin Bay

GREENLAND

ICELAND

Hudson Bay

CANADA

Bering Sea

ALEUTIAN ISLANDS

NORTH AMERICA

UNITED STATES OF AMERICA

ATLANTIC OCEAN

AZORES (Portugal)

MOROC

BERMUDA

CANARY ISLANDS (Spain)

WESTERN SAHARA

HAWAIIAN ISLANDS (US)

MEXICO

Gulf of Mexico

THE BAHAMAS

CUBA

DOMINICAN REPUBLIC

PUERTO RICO

SENEGAL

MAURITAN

CAPE VERDE

JAMAICA

HAITI

BELIZE

HONDURAS

GUATEMALA

NICARAGUA

EL SALVADOR

GAMBIA

GUINEA-BISSAU

GUINEA

B

PACIFIC OCEAN

COSTA RICA

VENEZUELA

GUYANA

SURINAME

SIERRA LEONE

D

PANAMA

COLOMBIA

FRENCH GUIANA

LIBERIA

GH

LINE ISLANDS

Equator

GALÁPAGOS ISLANDS

ECUADOR

SOUTH AMERICA

EQUA GU

PHOENIX ISLANDS

KIRIBATI

PERU

BRAZIL

AMERICAN SAMOA

MARQUESAS ISLANDS

COOK ISLANDS

BOLIVIA

WESTERN SAMOA

FRENCH POLYNESIA

TAHITI

PARAGUAY

TONGA

SOCIETY ISLANDS

CHILE

AUSTRAL ISLANDS

ARGENTINA

URUGUAY

N

W   E

S

FALKLAND/MALVINAS ISLANDS

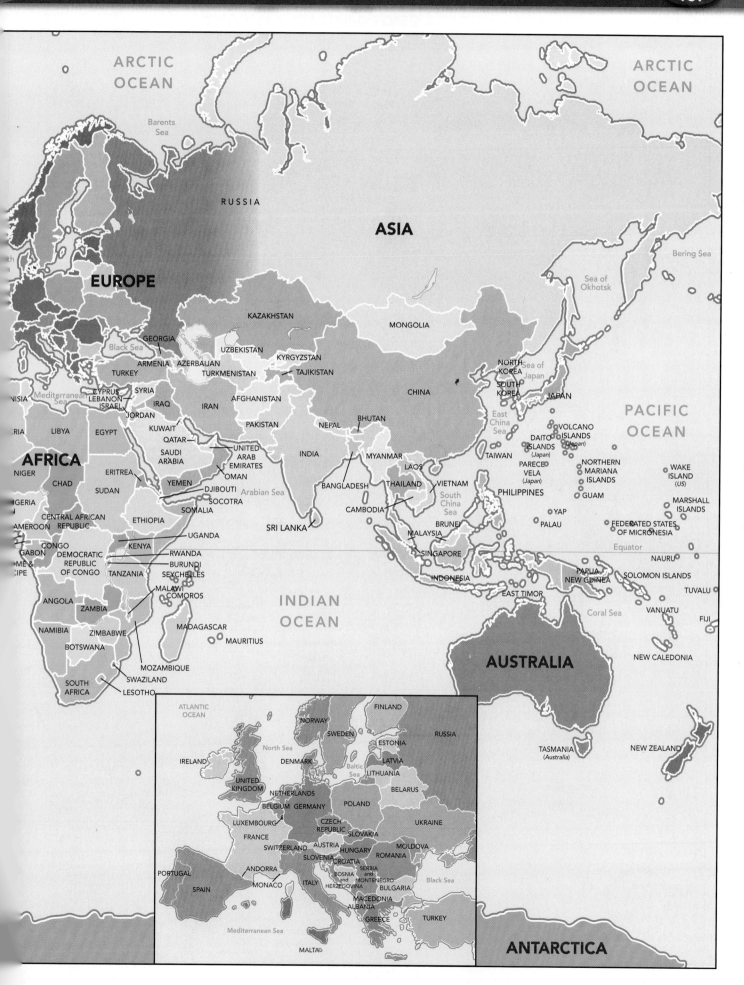

NORTEAMÉRICA, CENTROAMÉRICA Y EL CARIBE

SUDAMÉRICA

Caribbean Sea

Barranquilla
Cartagena
Maracaibo
Valencia
Barquisimeto
Caracas

ATLANTIC
OCEAN

VENEZUELA

Medellín

Georgetown
Paramaribo

GUYANA
Cayenne

Bogotá

SURINAME **FRENCH
GUIANA**

Cali

COLOMBIA

Equator
Quito

Equator

ECUADOR

Belém

Gulf of
Guayaquil
Guayaquil

Manaus

Fortaleza

Teresina

PERU

BRAZIL

Recife

Lima

Salvador

La Paz

Brasília

Goiânia

BOLIVIA

Sucre

Belo Horizonte

Rio de Janeiro
Campinas
São Paulo

PARAGUAY

CHILE

Curitiba

PACIFIC
OCEAN

Asuncion

Pôrto Alegre

ARGENTINA

Córdoba

Rosario

URUGUAY

Santiago

Buenos Aires
Montevideo

Gulf of San Matías

ATLANTIC
OCEAN

N

W   E

Gulf of
San Jorge

S

Strait of Magellan

**FALKLAND
ISLANDS**

Port Stanley

**SOUTH GEORGIA
ISLAND**

0   500 Miles

0   500 KM

EUROPA

Denmark Strait

Reykjavik ★ **ICELAND**

Norwegian Sea

White Sea

SWEDEN

FINLAND

NORWAY

Helsinki ★

Oslo ★

RUSSIA

Stockholm ★

Baltic Sea

★ Tallinn

ESTONIA

North Sea

Moscow ★

Riga ★

LATVIA

CopenHagen ★

LITHUANIA

Vilnius ★

★ Minsk

DENMARK

Dublin ★

BELARUS

IRELAND

UNITED KINGDOM

NETHERLANDS

★ Amsterdam

Berlin ★

Warsaw ★

London ★

The Hague

POLAND

★ Kiev

ATLANTIC OCEAN

★ Brussels

GERMANY

BELGIUM

LUXEMBOURG

★ Prague

UKRAINE

English Channel

Luxembourg

CZECH REPUBLIC

SLOVAKIA

Paris ★

Vienna ★ ★ Bratislava

MOLDOVA

★ Chisinau

Sea of Azov

LIECHTENSTEIN

AUSTRIA

★ Budapest

Bay of Biscay

FRANCE

Bern ★

HUNGARY

SWITZERLAND

SLOVENIA

ROMANIA

Ljubljana ★

★ Zagreb

Belgrade ★

★ Bucharest

Black Sea

CROATIA

MONACO

SAN MARINO

BOSNIA and HERZEGOVINA

★ Sarajevo

SERBIA and MONTENEGRO

SPAIN

ANDORRA

ITALY

BULGARIA

Sofia ★

CORSICA (France)

Rome ★

Skopje ★

Ankara ★

PORTUGAL

★ Madrid

MACEDONIA

Tirana ★

★ Lisbon

Adriatic Sea

SARDINIA (Italy)

ALBANIA

TURKEY

BALEARIC ISLANDS (Spain)

Tyrrhenian Sea

GREECE

Aegean Sea

Mediterranean Sea

Ionian Sea

★ Athens

Strait of Gibraltar

GIBRALTAR

SICILY (Italy)

Nicosia ★

★ Valletta

CRETE (Greece)

CYPRUS

MALTA

Mediterranean Sea

N

W ★ E

S

0

500 Miles

0

500KM

ÁFRICA Y MEDIO ORIENTE

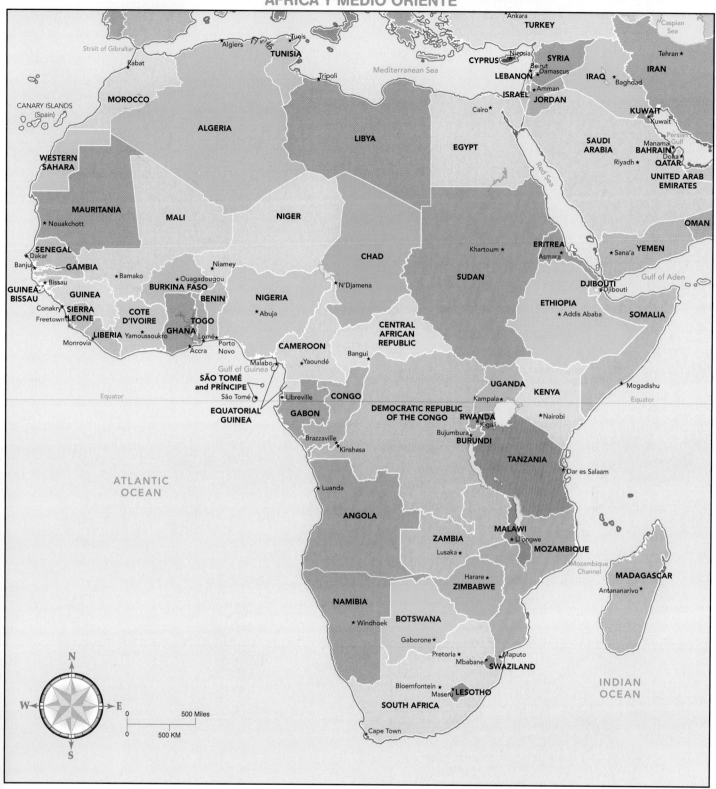

TURKEY
*Ankara

Caspian
Sea

Strait of Gibraltar
Algiers ★ *Tunis

TUNISIA

Mediterranean Sea

CYPRUS
Nicosia*

SYRIA

Tehran ★

IRAN

Rabat ★

Tripoli

Beirut ★ ★Damascus

LEBANON

*Baghdad

Baghdad

MOROCCO

CANARY ISLANDS
(Spain)

ALGERIA

LIBYA

EGYPT

Cairo ★

ISRAEL
Amman ★
JORDAN

IRAQ

KUWAIT
*Kuwait

SAUDI
ARABIA

Manama

Persian
Gulf

BAHRAIN
Doha

WESTERN
SAHARA

Riyadh ★

QATAR

UNITED ARAB
EMIRATES

MAURITANIA

MALI

NIGER

CHAD

Khartoum ★

ERITREA
Asmara ★

OMAN

Sana'a ★

YEMEN

Nouakchott ★

SENEGAL
★Dakar
Banjul
GAMBIA

Bamako ★

Niamey ★

Ouagadougou ★

BURKINA FASO

N'Djamena ★

SUDAN

Gulf of Aden

DJIBOUTI
Djibouti

Bissau ★
GUINEA
BISSAU
Conakry ★
Freetown ★

GUINEA
SIERRA
LEONE

LIBERIA
Monrovia ★

COTE
D'IVOIRE
Yamoussoukro

BENIN
TOGO
GHANA
Lomé ★
Accra ★

NIGERIA
★Abuja

Porto
Novo

CAMEROON

Yaoundé ★

CENTRAL
AFRICAN
REPUBLIC
Bangui ★

ETHIOPIA
★ Addis Ababa

SOMALIA

Malabo ★

Gulf of Guinea

SÃO TOMÉ
and PRÍNCIPE
São Tomé ★

Libreville ★

EQUATORIAL
GUINEA

CONGO

GABON

Brazzaville ★

DEMOCRATIC REPUBLIC
OF THE CONGO

UGANDA

Kampala ★

KENYA

Mogadishu ★

Equator

RWANDA
Kigali ★

Bujumbura ★
BURUNDI

★Nairobi

Equator

Kinshasa ★

ATLANTIC
OCEAN

Luanda ★

ANGOLA

TANZANIA

Dar es Salaam

ZAMBIA

Lusaka ★

MALAWI
Lilongwe ★

MOZAMBIQUE

Mozambique
Channel

MADAGASCAR

Harare ★

ZIMBABWE

Antananarivo ★

NAMIBIA

★ Windhoek

BOTSWANA

Gaborone ★

Pretoria ★

Mbabane

Maputo ★

SWAZILAND

INDIAN
OCEAN

Bloemfontein ★

Maseru
LESOTHO

N

SOUTH AFRICA

W   E

Cape Town

S

0   500 Miles

0   500 KM

ASIA AND AUSTRALIA

ASIA Y AUSTRALIA

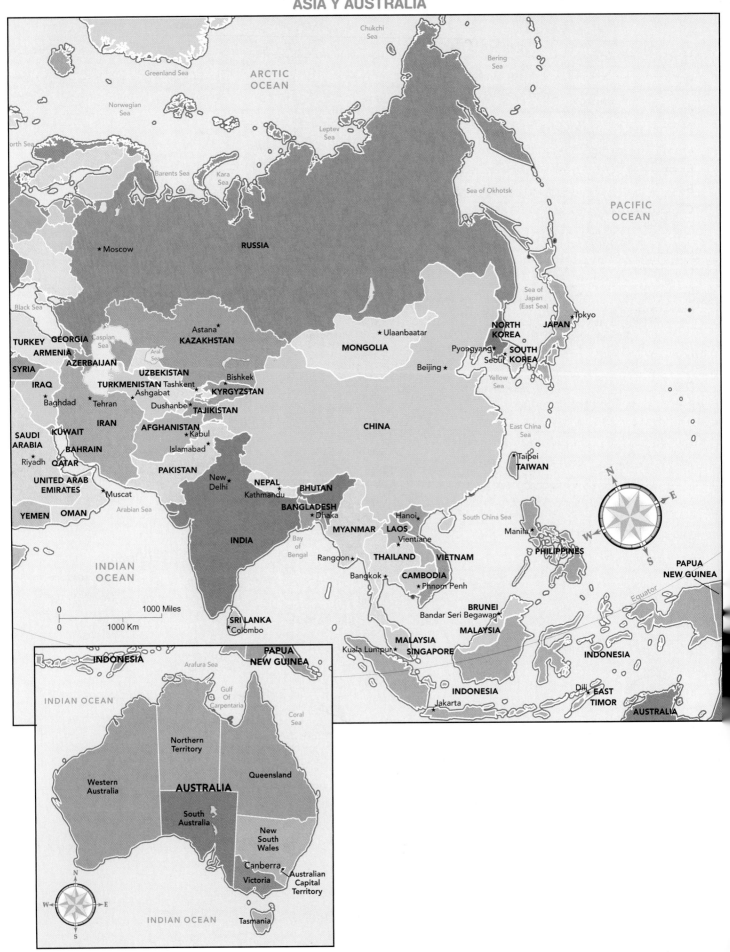

ARCTIC OCEAN

Chukchi Sea

Greenland Sea

Norwegian Sea

Leptev Sea

Bering Sea

Barents Sea

Kara Sea

North Sea

Sea of Okhotsk

PACIFIC OCEAN

★ Moscow

RUSSIA

Black Sea

Sea of Japan (East Sea)

★ Ulaanbaatar

NORTH KOREA

JAPAN ★ Tokyo

TURKEY
GEORGIA
ARMENIA

Caspian Sea

Astana ★

KAZAKHSTAN

MONGOLIA

Pyongyang ★
SOUTH KOREA

AZERBAIJAN

Aral Sea

UZBEKISTAN

Seoul

SYRIA

Bishkek ★

Beijing ★

Yellow Sea

IRAQ

TURKMENISTAN Tashkent
Ashgabat ★

KYRGYZSTAN

Baghdad ★ ★ Tehran

Dushanbe ★

TAJIKISTAN

CHINA

East China Sea

IRAN

AFGHANISTAN ★ Kabul

SAUDI
ARABIA
KUWAIT

Islamabad ★

★ Taipei

BAHRAIN

TAIWAN

Riyadh ★
QATAR

PAKISTAN

New Delhi ★

UNITED ARAB
EMIRATES

NEPAL

★ Muscat

Kathmandu ★

BHUTAN

YEMEN OMAN

BANGLADESH

Arabian Sea

★ Dhaka

Hanoi ★

South China Sea

INDIAN OCEAN

MYANMAR
LAOS

Manila ★

INDIA

Vientiane ★

PHILIPPINES

Bay of Bengal

Rangoon ★

THAILAND
VIETNAM

N

0   1000 Miles

Bangkok ★

CAMBODIA

W   E

0   1000 Km

★ Phnom Penh

S

SRI LANKA
★ Colombo

BRUNEI

PAPUA
NEW GUINEA

Bandar Seri Begawan ★

MALAYSIA

Equator

INDONESIA

Kuala Lumpur ★
MALAYSIA

PAPUA
NEW GUINEA

SINGAPORE

INDONESIA

Arafura Sea

Dili ★ EAST
TIMOR

INDIAN OCEAN

Gulf
Of
Carpentaria

INDONESIA

Jakarta ★

AUSTRALIA

Coral Sea

Northern
Territory

Queensland

Western
Australia

AUSTRALIA

South
Australia

New
South
Wales

Canberra
Victoria

Australian
Capital
Territory

N

W   E

S

INDIAN OCEAN

Tasmania

PAÍSES, NACIONALIDADES E IDIOMAS

Country	Nationality	Language
Afghanistan	Afghan	Afghan
Argentina	Argentine	Spanish
Australia	Australian	English
Bolivia	Bolivian	Spanish
Brazil	Brazilian	Portuguese
Bulgaria	Bulgarian	Bulgarian
Cambodia	Cambodian	Cambodian
Canada	Canadian	English/French
Chile	Chilean	Spanish
China	Chinese	Chinese
Colombia	Colombian	Spanish
Costa Rica	Costa Rican	Spanish
Cuba	Cuban	Spanish
(The) Czech Republic	Czech	Czech
Denmark	Danish	Danish
(The) Dominican Republic	Dominican	Spanish
Ecuador	Ecuadorian	Spanish
Egypt	Egyptian	Arabic
El Salvador	Salvadorean	Spanish
England	English	English
Estonia	Estonian	Estonian
Ethiopia	Ethiopian	Amharic
Finland	Finnish	Finnish
France	French	French
Germany	German	German
Greece	Greek	Greek
Guatemala	Guatemalan	Spanish
Haiti	Haitian	Haitian Kreyol
Honduras	Honduran	Spanish
Hungary	Hungarian	Hungarian
India	Indian	Hindi
Indonesia	Indonesian	Indonesian
Israel	Israeli	Hebrew

Country	Nationality	Language
Italy	Italian	Italian
Japan	Japanese	Japanese
Jordan	Jordanian	Arabic
Korea	Korean	Korean
Laos	Laotian	Laotian
Latvia	Latvian	Latvian
Lebanon	Lebanese	Arabic
Lithuania	Lithuanian	Lithuanian
Malaysia	Malaysian	Malay
Mexico	Mexican	Spanish
New Zealand	New Zealander	English
Nicaragua	Nicaraguan	Spanish
Norway	Norwegian	Norwegian
Pakistan	Pakistani	Urdu
Panama	Panamanian	Spanish
Peru	Peruvian	Spanish
(The) Philippines	Filipino	Tagalog
Poland	Polish	Polish
Portugal	Portuguese	Portuguese
Puerto Rico	Puerto Rican	Spanish
Romania	Romanian	Romanian
Russia	Russian	Russian
Saudi Arabia	Saudi	Arabic
Slovakia	Slovak	Slovak
Spain	Spanish	Spanish
Sweden	Swedish	Swedish
Switzerland	Swiss	German/French/Italian
Taiwan	Taiwanese	Chinese
Thailand	Thai	Thai
Turkey	Turkish	Turkish
Ukraine	Ukrainian	Ukrainian
(The) United States	American	English
Venezuela	Venezuelan	Spanish
Vietnam	Vietnamese	Vietnamese

A. Where are you from?
B. I'm from **Mexico**.

A. What's your nationality?
B. I'm **Mexican**.

A. What language do you speak?
B. I speak **Spanish**.

Tell about yourself: Where are you from? What's your nationality? What languages do you speak?

Now interview and tell about a friend.

LISTAS DE VERBOS

Verbos regulares

Los verbos regulares tienen cuatro patrones de deletreo diferentes para el pasado y el participio.

1 Hay que añadir **–ed** al final del verbo. Por ejemplo:

act → act**ed**

act	cook	grill	pass	simmer
add	correct	guard	peel	sort
answer	cough	hand (in)	plant	spell
appear	cover	help	play	sprain
ask	crash	insert	polish	steam
assist	cross (out)	invent	pour	stow
attack	deliver	iron	print	stretch
attend	deposit	kick	reach	surf
bank	design	land	record	swallow
board	discuss	leak	register	talk
boil	dress	learn	relax	turn
box	drill	lengthen	repair	twist
brainstorm	dust	lift	repeat	unload
broil	edit	listen	request	vacuum
brush	end	load	respond	vomit
burn	enter	look	rest	walk
burp	establish	lower	return	wash
carpool	explain	mark	roast	watch
cash	faint	match	rock	wax
check	fasten	mix	saute	weed
clean	fix	mow	scratch	whiten
clear	floss	obey	seat	work
collect	fold	open	select	
comb	follow	paint	shorten	
construct	form	park	sign	

2 Hay que añadir **–d** al verbo que acaba en **–e**. Por ejemplo:

assemble → assemble**d**

assemble	declare	grate	pronounce	shave
bake	describe	hire	prune	slice
balance	dislocate	manage	raise	sneeze
barbecue	dive	measure	rake	state
bathe	dribble	microwave	recite	style
bounce	enforce	move	recycle	supervise
browse	erase	nurse	remove	translate
bruise	examine	operate	revise	type
bubble	exchange	organize	rinse	underline
change	exercise	overdose	save	unscramble
circle	experience	practice	scrape	use
close	file	prepare	serve	vote
combine	gargle	produce	share	wheeze

3 Hay que poner consonante final doble y añadir **–ed** al final del verbo. Por ejemplo:

chop → chop**ped**

chop	mop	skip	transfer
hop	plan	stir	trim
knit	occur	stop	

4 Elimine la –y final y añada **–ied** al final del verbo. Por ejemplo:

apply → appl**ied**

apply	dry	fry	study
copy	empty	stir-fry	try

Verbos irregulares

Los siguientes verbos tienen tiempo pasado y/o participio irregular.

be	was/were	been		know	knew	known
beat	beat	beaten		leave	left	left
become	became	become		let	let	let
bend	bent	bent		make	made	made
begin	began	begun		meet	met	met
bleed	bled	bled		pay	paid	paid
break	broke	broken		put	put	put
bring	brought	brought		read	read	read
build	built	built		rewrite	rewrote	rewritten
buy	bought	bought		run	ran	run
catch	caught	caught		ring	rang	rung
choose	chose	chosen		say	said	said
come	came	come		see	saw	seen
cut	cut	cut		sell	sold	sold
do	did	done		set	set	set
draw	drew	drawn		shoot	shot	shot
drink	drank	drunk		sing	sang	sung
drive	drove	driven		sit	sat	sat
eat	ate	eaten		sleep	slept	slept
fall	fell	fallen		speak	spoke	spoken
feed	fed	fed		stand	stood	stood
fly	flew	flown		sweep	swept	swept
get	got	gotten		swim	swam	swum
give	gave	given		swing	swung	swung
go	went	gone		take	took	taken
grow	grew	grown		teach	taught	taught
hang	hung	hung		throw	threw	thrown
have	had	had		understand	understood	understood
hit	hit	hit		withdraw	withdrew	withdrawn
hold	held	held		write	wrote	written
hurt	hurt	hurt				

GLOSARIO (ESPAÑOL)

El número en negrillas indica la(s) página(s) en donde aparece la palabra. El número que sigue indica la ubicación de la palabra en la ilustración y en la lista de palabras en la página. Por ejemplo, "address **1**-5" indica que la palabra "address" está en la página 1 y es el artículo número 5.

a (entrar) **129**-11
a (la autopista) **129**-13
a la derecha de **8**-9
a la izquierda de **8**-8
a través de **129**-3
a.m. (de la mañana) **16**
abadejo **50**-24
abajo **8**-2
abajo (hacia) **129**-6
abarrotería **37**-28
abdomen **86**-25
abdominales **146**-25
abedul **156**-17
abeja **30**-11d, **154**-36
abierto(a) **45**-57
abogado(a) **114**-2
abono **35**-9
abordar el avión **132**-H
abrebotellas **59**-3
abrelatas **59**-2
abrelatas eléctrico **24**-18
abreviaturas en
   los anuncios de
   empleo **118**
abrigo **67**-1,2
abrigo de invierno **67**-25
abrigo de plumas de
   ganso/acolchonado
   67-23
abrigo de punto **67**-6
abrigo para esquiar **67**-20
abrigo tejido **67**-6
abril **18**-16
abrir **31**-19
abrir el libro **6**-11
abrir una cuenta **80**-E
abrocharse el cinturón de
   seguridad **132**-K
abuela **2**-10
abuelo(s) **2**, **2**-11
aburrido(a) (estar) **47**-28
acampar **139**-A
accesorios para la
   aspiradora **32**-6
accidente (de tránsito/
   tráfico) **85**-1
acción (películas de)
   149-24
acebo **156**-24
acebo (árbol) **156**-12
aceite **53**-25, **126**-46
aceite de oliva **53**-26
aceite para cocinar
   53-25
aceite tres en uno **33**-15
aceitunas **53**-19
acelerador **127**-73
acera **40**-13
acetona **99**-32

acomodar las letras de la
   palabra **7**-58
acomodar las palabras
   7-59
acondicionador **98**-10
acondicionamiento físico
   (club de) **163**-14
acordeón **150**-26
acostarse **9**-13
acotamiento de la
   carretera **128**-16
actividades al aire libre
   139
actividades
   extracurriculares **104**
actividades manuales **134**
actividades turísticas **163**
actor **112**-2, **147**-2,16
actriz **112**-3, **147**-3,15
actuar **116**-1
acuarela **134**-14b
acuario **136**-14
acupuntor(a) **96**-15
acupuntura (recibir
   tratamiento de) **94**-8
acupunturista **96**-15
adaptador **77**-13
aderezo para ensaladas
   53-29, **60**-27
adjetivo **107**-5
administración **102**-A
administrador(a) **114**-5
administrar **116**-16
adolescente **42**-6
aduana **131**-22, **161**-3
adulto **42**-7
adverbio **107**-7
aerograma **82**-3
aeromozo(a) **132**-5
aeropuerto **131**
aerosol para matar
   insectos **33**-18
afanador(a) **102**-11,
   112-20
afección del corazón
   91-22
afeitando (*me estoy*)
   99-L
afeitar (maquinilla de)
   99-21
afeitarse **9**-4
afeitarse (crema para)
   99-20
afilado(a) **45**-67
afueras **20**-14
agalla **155**-1b
agarrador de ollas **24**-22
agarrador **27**-22
agarrar **146**-4
agencia **160**-14

agencia de carros **36**-7
agencia de turismo
   guiado **160**-14
agencia de viajes **39**-27,
   160-13
agenda **120**-6
agenda personal **120**-12
agenda rotatoria **120**-4
agente de ventas por
   teléfono **115**-31
agente de viajes **115**-33
agosto **18**-20
agotado(a) **89**-32
agotado(a) (estar) **46**-3
agradecimiento (una nota
   de) **118**-L
agricultor(a) **113**-27,
   151-2
agua **45**, **62**-B, **158**-11
agua (cuenta del) **81**-12
agua embotellada **51**-25
agua nieve (caer) **14**-13
agua oxigenada **90**-6
aguacate **48**-14
aguamala **155**-14
aguarrás **33**-22
aguaviva **155**-14
agudo (ángulo) **106**-20a
águila **154**-10
aguja **92**-4
aguja (de coser) **134**-5
aguja de gancho **134**-10
aguja de tejer **134**-8
agujetas (de zapatos)
   99-49
ahorrar agua **158**-11
ahorrar energía **158**-10
aire **126**-48
aire acondicionado
   28-28, **31**-21, **127**-67
ajedrez **135**-35
ajedrez (club de) **104**-16
ajo **49**-15
ajos (triturador/
   machacador de) **59**-16
al (autobús, subir) **129**-9
ala **154**-2a
alacena **22**-11
alacrán **154**-39
alambre **34**-24, **122**-26
alargar **72**-22
alarma (luz de) **127**-57
alarma (señal de) **127**-57
alarma contra incendios
   29-39, **40**-8
alas de pollo/gallina
   50-18
albañil **112**-10
albaricoque **48**-7

alberca **28**-25, **84**-14,
   133-16
alberca infantil inflable
   79-38
albergue para
   desamparados **20**-9
albornoz **68**-4
álbum para estampillas/
   sellos/timbres **135**-25
alcachofa **49**-27
alcalde **84**-9
alcaldía **40**-7, **84**-D
alcantarilla **40**-10
alcantarilla (boca de la)
   41-38
alcanzar **146**-18
alce **152**-1
alcohol **93**-10
alérgica (reacción) **91**-7
alergista **96**-5
alergólogo(a) **96**-5
aleta(s) **145**-16, **155**-1a
alfalfa **151**-31
alfarería (hacer) **134**-J
alfiler **134**-2
alfiler de gancho **100**-9,
   134-7
alfiler de seguridad
   100-9, **134**-7
alfiletero **134**-3
alfombra **21**-23, **23**-12
alfombra de baño **26**-35
alfombrilla **21**-23
alfombrilla de baño
   26-35
alfombrilla de goma
   26-32
álgebra **105**
algodón **71**-17, **151**-33
alhajero **23**-21
alicates **34**-16
aliño para ensaladas
   53-29, **60**-27
alisadora de pelo/cabello
   98-14
alisar con la plancha **10**-4
alitas de pollo/gallina
   50-18, **64**-4
almacén **37**-18, **121**-11
almacén de música **38**-13
almacén de ropa de
   maternidad **38**-10
almacenaje (estante/
   armario de) **119**-25
almádena **122**-1
almejas **50**-32
almidón en aerosol **73**-20
almocafre **35**-20
almohada **23**-3

almohadilla de tinta **120**-28

almohadilla eléctrica **94**-9

almohadilla estéril **90**-5

almohadilla para la mesa de cambiar pañales **25**-9

almorzar **9**-19

almuerzo **9**-16

alquilar un coche/carro **163**-8

alquiler **81**-6

alrededor de **129**-4

altavoces **76**-27

altavoz **21**-16

altavoz (sistema de) **4**-14

alternador **126**-38

alto(a) **42**-14, **44**-5,27, **72**-7, **130**-1

altoparlante(s) **4**-14, **21**-16, **76**-27

altura **106**-1,18b

alud **159**-13

alumbrado **40**-15

aluminio (papel de) **54**-12

alumno(a) **4**-3

alzar la mano **6**-16

amamantar **100**-E

amante de asolearse **138**-14

amante de broncearse **138**-14

amarillo **65**-4

ambientales (problemas) **158**

ambulancia **84**-8

americana **66**-11

amigo(a) **45**

amo(a) de casa **113**-37

amoniaco **32**-14

amoníaco **32**-14

ampolla **88**-18

añadir **58**-10

analgésico sin aspirina **90**-14, **95**-5

análisis **94**-16

análisis de sangre **94**-15

anaranjado **65**-3

ancho(a) **44**-21, **72**-4,15, **106**-2

anchura **106**-2

anciano(a) **42**-10

andadera **25**-18, **94**-13

andador **25**-18

andamio **122**-12

andar en patineta **140**-F

andén **124**-16

anémona de mar **155**-25

anestesia **93**-F

anestesiólogo(a) **97**-17

anestesista **97**-17

anfibios **155**

anfitrión **62**-2

anfitriona **62**-1

angosto(a) **44**-22, **72**-16

anguila **155**-7

ángulo agudo **106**-20a

ángulo obtuso **106**-20b

ángulo recto **106**-19b

anillo **70**-1

anillo de compromiso **70**-2

anillo de matrimonio **70**-3

animadores(as) **104**-6

animales marinos **155**

aniversario **18**-27

año **18**-1

anoche **19**-11

anochecer (al) **19**-6,14

anochecer (ayer al) **19**-10

anochecer (mañana al) **19**-18

anotador(a) de datos **112**-22

anotar la orden **62**-C

anotar las observaciones **110**-E

antena **126**-14

antena de televisión **27**-29

antena parabólica **27**-28

anteojos para sol **67**-26

anteojos protectores **123**-3

antiácido en tabletas **95**-8

antílope **153**-44

antipasto **64**-10

antiséptico bucal **98**-4

antojitos **52**

anuario **104**-10

anuncio clasificado **118**-3

anuncio de empleo **118**-3

anuncios **119**-a

anuncios para apartamentos/ departamentos **28**-1

apagar las luces **7**-42

apagón **85**-13

aparador **22**-3

aparcamiento **28**-23

aparejo **139**-16

apartamentos (edificio de) **20**-1

apellidos (paterno y materno) **1**-4

aperitivos **52**, **64**

apio **49**-1

apóstrofe **107**-12

apoyabrazos **127**-82

apretado(a) **44**-30

aptitudes **118**-H

aquifolio **156**-12

araña **154**-33

arañazo **89**-40

arándanos **48**-31

arandela **34**-26

árbol **156**-1

árbol de fruta **151**-29

arbusto **35**-G, **156**-23,26

arce **156**-18

archivador **119**-18

archivar **116**-12, **119**-e

archivero **119**-18

archivista **119**-17

arcilla **134**-23

arco **141**-S

arco y flecha **141**-43

ardilla **152**-31

ardilla de tierra **152**-32

ardilla listada **152**-30

ardilla rayada **152**-30

área de abordaje **131**-14

área de entrega de mercancía **74**-7

área de juegos para niños(as) **137**, **137**-16

área de picnic **137**-3

área de reclamo de equipaje **131**-15, **161**-2

área de retiro de equipaje **131**-15

área de trabajo **119**-D

área para comer al aire libre **137**-3

área postal **82**-21

arena **137**-23

aretes **70**-4, **71**-12

aretes de pinza/de presión **71**-13

aritmética **105**

armadillo **152**-20

armador(a) **112**-6

armadura (de la cama) **23**-25

armar **116**-2

armar modelos **135**-M

armario **22**-11, **24**-5, **73**-22, **100**-22

armario de almacenaje **119**-25

armario de artículos de oficina **119**-24

armónica **150**-27

arnés **139**-16

arnés de soporte **123**-7

aro **79**-21

aromatizante ambiental **26**-25

arpa **150**-8

arquitecto(a) **112**-4

arreglando el pelo/ cabello (me estoy) **98**-K

arreglar **117**-22, **99**-M

arreglar la mesa **63**-H

arrendador(a) **28**-5

arrendajo **154**-2

arrendatario(a) **28**-4

arriba **8**-1

arriba (hacia) **129**-5

arriendo **81**-6

arroyo **109**-9

arroz **53**-7, **64**-21, **151**-34

arrugada (ropa) **73**-18

arrullar **100**-G

arte **103**-19

arte (galería de) **136**-2

arterias **87**-68

artes industriales **103**-15

artes marciales **141**-P

artículo **107**-4

artículo de revista **108**-10

artículo periodístico **108**-11

artículos de oficina **120**

artículos para el bebé **54**

artículos para el hogar **54**

asado **64**-13

asador **27**-24

asalto **85**-11

asar **58**-22

asar a la parrilla **58**-17,23

ascensor **29**-32, **74**-5, **133**-18

ascensor de carga **121**-14

asesinato **85**-12

asfixiarse **90**-17c

asiento **6**-10, **127**-84, **132**-J

asiento (de niños) para automóvil **25**-22

asiento (tomar) **6**-10

asiento central **132**-9

asiento con ventanilla **132**-8

asiento de pasillo **132**-10

asiento del excusado **26**-27

asiento elevador **62**-7

asilo **20**-8

asilo para pobres **20**-9

asistente **4**-2

asistente (del dentista) **93**-25

asistente administrativo **119**-22

asistente de enfermero(a) **97**-14

asistente de salud **113**-35

asistente de salud en casa **113**-36

asistente digital personal **77**-8

asistente médico **114**-8

asma **91**-18

asociación de estudiantes **104**-7

áspero(a) **44**-44

aspersor **35**-12

aspiradora **32**-5

aspiradora de mano **32**-8

aspirina **90**-13, **95**-1

asqueado(a) (estar) **47**-19

asta **152**-1a

campo de juego de
  béisbol **142**-2
campo de lacrosse **142**-8
campo de sófbol **142**-4
caña de pescar **145**-25
canal de desagüe **27**-26
canapé **21**-14
canario **152**-42
canasta **26**-1, **143**-23
canasta de papeles **4**-19
canasta de picnic **139**-22
canasta para la ropa sucia
  26-16, **73**-4
canasta para pan **62**-9
canastilla para pan **62**-9
cáncer **91**-19
cancha de baloncesto/
  básquetbol **142**-12
cancha de tenis **137**-10
cancha de voleibol
  142-14
candela **22**-17
candelero **22**-18
candil de techo **22**-10
cangrejo **155**-20
cangrejos **50**-31
canguro **25**-30, **112**-7,
  153-62
cano **43**-34
caño **27**-27
canoa **145**-3
canoa (navegar en) **145**-B
cañón **109**-12
canoso **43**-34
cansado(a) (estar) **46**-1
cantante **147**-12
cantante de ópera **147**-9
cantar **117**-26
cantimplora **139**-11
caparazón **155**-26a
capataz **113**-31
capitán **132**-2
capó del motor **126**-8
capote **67**-12
capote corto **67**-17
cápsula **95**-16
cápsula comprimida
  95-17
capullo **154**-28a, **157**-37
cara **9**-6, **86**-4
caracol **155**-22
caramelo **55**-10
carapacho **155**-26a
caravana **125**-14
carbón **158**-3
cárcel **40**-12
carcomas **30**-11a
cardenal **89**-42, **154**-3
cárdigan **71**-6
cardiólogo(a) **96**-1
cardiopulmonar
  (resucitación) **90**-15
careta (de hockey) **143**-18

careta (de lacrosse)
  143-14
cargador de baterías/de
  pilas **76**-13, **77**-5
cargar **100**-D
caricaturas animadas
  149-22, 35
caries **88**-17, **93**-G
carmelita **65**-5
carmín **99**-47
carnada **145**-29
carne (asada) (bocadillo/
  emparedado/sándwich
  de) **61**-28
carne (de vaca) asada
  52-1
carne adobada **52**-6
carne en salmuera **52**-6
carne en salmuera
  (bocadillo/emparedado/
  sándwich de) **61**-26
carne molida **50**-2
carne molida (pastel/
  budín de) **64**-12
carne para asar **50**-4
carne para guisar **50**-3
carne salpresa **52**-6
carnero **151**-27
carnes **50**
carnet de identificación
  83-5
carnicero(a) **112**-13
caro(a) **45**-61
carpa **139**-1
carpa dorada **152**-41
carpeta **5**-27, **120**-19
carpeta con espiral **5**-26
carpeta de felpa **120**-5
carpintero(a) **31**-K, **112**-14
carreta para equipaje
  131-18, **133**-5
carrete (de pescar)
  145-26
carretera(s) **45**, **128**,
  128-6
carretilla **35**-8, **55**-3,8,
  122-4
carretilla de helados/
  mantecados **41**-28
carretilla para equipaje
  131-19
carricoche (de bebé)
  25-21
carriel **70**-22
carril central **128**-14
carril de entrada **128**-10
carril de salida **128**-20
carril derecho **128**-15
carril izquierdo **128**-13
carriola **25**-20
carrito **55**-3,8
carrito de camarero(a)
  133-22
carrito de juguete **79**-14

carrito de postres **63**-20
carrito de recamarero(a)
  133-22
carrito manual **121**-19
carrito para equipaje
  131-18,19, **133**-5
carrizos **54**-4, **60**-20
carro **45**
carro (entrada para el)
  27-16
carro de tres puertas
  125-2
carro deportivo **125**-4
carro híbrido **125**-5
carrusel de equipaje
  131-16
carta(s) **11**-7, **62**-8, **82**-1,
  108-13, **119**-f, **135**-34,O
cartelera **4**-13
cartero(a) **70**-19,21,
  82-28, **114**-4
cartilla para medir la vista
  92-7
cartón **56**-6
cartón de jugos **51**-21
cartón de seis artículos
  56-15
cartucho de papel **55**-13
cartucho de tinta para
  impresora **120**-26
cartucho de tinta para
  máquina de escribir
  120-25
cartucho de videojuego
  76-34
cartulina para actividades
  manuales **79**-28
casa **20**-2
casa (de granja) **151**-1
casa (llegar a) **10**-16
casa de ancianos **20**-8
casa de juguete **79**-37
casa de muñecas **79**-10
casa de reposo **20**-8
casa flotante **20**-12
casa móvil **20**-7
casa prefabricada **20**-7
casa remolque **122**-21
casa rodante **20**-7,
  122-21
casado(a) **44**-47
casas (de dos o tres
  plantas) en hileras **20**-4
cascada (pequeña)
  109-23
cáscaras de papa rellenas
  64-6
casco **139**-19, **140**-9
casco de béisbol **143**-3
casco de construcción
  123-1
casco protector **143**-11
casero(a) **28**-5
caseta de peaje **128**-3

caseta para
  herramientas **27**-19
casetera **76**-26
casilla postal **27**-2, **29**-31
casillero **102**-Fa
casillero postal **27**-2,
  29-31
castaño **43**-31
castillo de arena **138**-12
castor **152**-14
catálogo **83**-2
catálogo de monedas
  135-27
catálogo en línea **83**-1
catarata (grande) **109**-23
catarina **154**-25
catarinita **154**-25
catarro **88**-8
catsup **53**-15, **60**-23
cazadora **67**-4
cazo **59**-7
CD **76**-22, **83**-17
cebo **145**-29
cebolla **49**-36
cebolleta **157**-39
cebollín **49**-37
cebollino(a) **49**-37
ceda el paso **130**-13
ceja **86**-6
cellisquear **14**-13
celoso(a) (estar) **47**-31
cemento **122**-11a
cempasúchil **157**-43
cena **9**-17, **162**-a
cenar **9**-20
centavo **17**-1
centavos (cinco) **17**-2
centavos (diez) **17**-3
centavos (veinticinco)
  17-4
Centígrados **14**-21
centímetro **106**-8
centro **106**-21a
centro comercial **39**-23
centro de fotocopias
  36-16
centro de reciclaje/
  reutilización **84**-16
centro de revelado **39**-17
centro para personas
  mayores **84**-H
centro recreativo **84**-E
cepillando el pelo/cabello
  (me estoy) **98**-J
cepillando los dientes (me
  estoy) **98**-A
cepillarse el pelo/el
  cabello **9**-8
cepillarse los dientes **9**-3
cepillo **98**-13, **126**-10
cepillo (del inodoro)
  26-23
cepillo de carpintero
  34-18

gira en autobús/
guagua **163**-3
giradiscos **76**-21
girasol **157**-52
giro **82**-14
giro postal/
telegráfico **81**-4, **82**-14
gis **5**-32
globo del mundo **4**-16
globo terráqueo **4**-16
gobierno **103**-5
gofres **61**-10
gogles **145**-12
golf **141**-M
golf (bola de) **141**-30
golf (palos de) **141**-29
golf (pelota de) **141**-30
goma **120**-13,30
goma (de llanta) **126**-6
goma (neumático) **126**-6
goma de borrar **5**-22
goma de masticar **55**-9
goma de pegar **33**-16
goma para armar
modelos **135**-30
goma sintética **120**-31
gordo(a) **42**-17, **44**-13
gorila **153**-61
gorra **67**-8
gorra de baño **145**-13
gorra de béisbol **67**-10
gorra de esquiar **67**-19
gorra(o) de baño **98**-8
gorrión **154**-14
gorro de esquiar **67**-19
gospel **148**-7
gotas para los ojos **95**-10
gotear **30**-1
gotera **27**-26, **30**-5
gotero **110**-15
GPS (Sistema de Posición
Global, aparato de)
139-14
grabadora de cintas
magnetofónicas **76**-17
gradas **102**-la
gradería **102**-la
grama **35**-A
grande **44**-9, **71**-36, **72**-5
granero **151**-7
granizar **14**-12
granja **20**-10
granjero(a) **113**-27, **151**-2
grapa **120**-15
grapadora **120**-2
grifo **24**-11, **26**-7
grifo (cabello/pelo) **43**-29
grillo **154**-37,41
gripe **91**-12
gris **43**-34, **65**-16
grúa **122**-15
grúa (camión) **125**-13
grúa (con plataforma
movible) **122**-16

grueso(a) **44**-23, **72**-11
grulla **154**-18
grupo **7**-38
guagua **41**-33, **124**-A
guajolote **50**-20, **52**-20,
151-11
guante (de béisbol)
143-6
guante de hockey **143**-19
guante de receptor **143**-7
guante de sófbol **143**-9
guantera **127**-70
guantes **67**-21, **93**-23
guantes de boxeo **141**-45
guantes de jardín **33**-17
guantes de látex **123**-11
guantes enteros **67**-24
guapo(a) **45**-53
guardabarros **126**-5
guardafango **126**-5
guardapolvo **66**-19
guardar cama **94**-1
guardar el libro **6**-15
guardar la ropa
(limpia) **73**-I
guardar su equipaje de
mano **132**-I
guardería infantil **36**-9,
84-18,G, **100**-19
guardería infantil (auxiliar
de) **112**-17
guardia de seguridad
80-11, **102**-7, **115**-23,
131-8
guarnición **64**
güero **43**-32
guerra (películas de)
149-25
guía **74**-1, **135**-33
guía (volante) **127**-59
guillotina **119**-16
guineo **48**-4
güira(o) **49**-14
guisante **49**-16
guisar **58**-20
guitarra **11**-9
guitarra (acústica) **150**-5
guitarra eléctrica **150**-6

haba **49**-18
habichuelas
coloradas **49**-20
habichuelas tiernas **49**-17
habilidades **118**-H
habitación **45**, **133**-24,
162-c
habitación accesible para
discapacitados(as)
162-4
habitación con vista
162-5
habitación doble **162**-2
habitación para no
fumadores(as) **162**-3

habitación sencilla **162**-1
hablar **117**-27
hablar sobre su
experiencia laboral
118-I
hablar sobre sus aptitudes
y habilidades **118**-H
hacendado(a) **113**-27
hacer **116**-5
hacer banca en línea
81-18
hacer ejercicio **11**-11,
94-5
hacer el almuerzo **9**-16
hacer el balance de las
cuentas **81**-16
hacer el desayuno **9**-15
hacer gárgaras **94**-3
hacer inventario **117**-30
hacer la cama **9**-10
hacer la cena **9**-17
hacer su depósito **81**-25
hacer su tarea **6**-21
hacer sus deberes **6**-21
hacer un cheque **81**-17
hacer un depósito **80**-A
hacer un retiro **80**-B
hacer una pregunta **6**-17
hacer una presentación
119-b
hacer una reservación en
un restaurante **163**-7
hacerle algunas preguntas
sobre su salud **92**-E
hacha **34**-3, **139**-5
hacia abajo **129**-6
hacia arriba **129**-5
hacienda **20**-10
halcón **154**-9
hambre (tener) **46**-7
hamburguesa **60**-1
hamburguesa con
queso **60**-2
hámster **152**-38
hardware (de
computadora) **78**
harina **53**-35
harina preparada para
bizcocho **53**-37
harto(a) (estar) **47**-19
hatchback **125**-2
hebilla de cabello **70**-12
hebilla para el pelo/
cabello **98**-18
Heimlich (la maniobra
de) **90**-17
helada (caer una) **14**-13
heladería **38**-6
helado **52**-18, **60**-14,
64-26
helado de yogur **60**-15
helar **14**-26
helecho **156**-27
hemorragia nasal **88**-16

heno **151**-5
herido(a) **91**-1, **93**-B
hermana **2**-8, **45**
hermano **2**-9
hermanos(as) **2**
herramientas (caja de)
34-17
hervidor **24**-23
hervir **58**-16
hibisco **157**-59
hidrante **40**-5
hiedra venenosa **156**-31
hielera **138**-21
hielo (bolsa de) **93**-16
hielo (máquina de
hacer) **133**-19
hielo (pista de) **142**-10
hiena **153**-54
hígado **50**-9, **87**-57
higiene **103**-10
higienista dental **93**-21
higo **48**-12
hija **2**-5
hijo(s) **2**, **2**-6
hilo **71**-21, **134**-4
hilo (carrete de) **134**-4
hilo de dientes **98**-3
hilo dental **98**-3
hilo dental (estoy usando
el) **98**-B
hilo para tejer **134**-9
hinchazón **89**-49
hinchazón del
abdomen **89**-30
hip hop **148**-11
hipertensión **91**-23
hipo **88**-20
hipopótamo **153**-59
hipoteca (pago de la)
81-7
hipotenusa **106**-19d
hipótesis **110**-B
hisopo **100**-15
historia **103**-3
historia clínica **93**-4
historial clínico **93**-4
hockey (jugador(a) de)
142-9
hockey sobre hielo
142-E, **143**-E
hogar **21**-5
hogar (artículos para
el) **54**
hogaza(s) de pan **56**-11
hoja **7**-60, **156**-2,9
hoja clínica **97**-10
hoja de navaja **99**-22
hojas **35**-E
hojuelas de maíz **52**-27
holgado(a) **44**-29
hombre(s) **42**-8
hombre de negocios
112-11
hombro **86**-23

máquina de coser **134**-1
máquina de escribir **119**-12
máquina de estampillas **82**-27
máquina de fax **77**-9
máquina de hacer hielo **133**-19
máquina de radiografías **92**-9
máquina de rayos X **92**-9, **131**-9
máquina expendedora de pasajes/boletos **124**-23
máquina para sellos **119**-7
máquina universal **141**-52
maquinilla de afeitar **99**-21
maquinista **114**-3
maraquita **25**-17
maravilla **157**-43
marcador **5**-34
marcadores **79**-26
marco (de la cama) **23**-25
maremoto **159**-7
mareo (tener) **89**-28
margarina **51**-8
margarita **157**-42
margen de la carretera **128**-16
mariapalito **154**-34
mariposa **154**-29
mariquita **66**-28, **154**-25
mariscos **50**
maromas **146**-28
marrano **151**-16
marrón **43**-31, **65**-5
marsopa **155**-13
marsopla **155**-13
Marte **111**-15
martes **18**-8
martillo **34**-1
marzo **18**-15
más **105**
más allá de **129**-8
máscara **93**-22, **123**-10
máscara (de béisbol) **143**-5
máscara (de bucear) **145**-19
máscara (de hockey) **143**-18
máscara (de lacrosse) **143**-14
máscara (de nadar) **145**-14
máscara de esquiar **67**-22
mascarilla **93**-22, **123**-10
mascarilla de oxígeno **132**-14
mascarilla filtrante **123**-12
mascotas (comida para) **54**

masilla **79**-30
masking tape **33**-9
mata **21**-21, **156**-28
matacucarachas **33**-19
matamoscas **33**-2
matasellos **82**-22
matemáticas **103**-1, **105**
material **71**
material (tela) **75**-7
material (tipos de) **71**
materias **103**
matraz **110**-5
mayo **18**-17
mayonesa **53**-24, **60**-25
mayor **42**-13
mayor (persona) **44**-4
mazo **56**-4, **122**-1
mazo de hule **34**-2
mecánico(a) **30**-E, **114**-7, **114**-19
mecano **79**-3
mecanografiar **117**-33
mecedora **100**-21
mecer **100**-G
mechero de Bunsen **110**-11
mechudo **32**-9
media libra **57**, **111**-23, **126**-13
mediano(a) **71**-35
medianoche **16**
medias **68**-12,19,23, **71**-9
medias cortas **71**-10
medias de nailon/nylon **71**-16
medias deportivas **71**-11
mediaslunas **146**-29
medicina (facultad de) **101**-12
medicinas **91**-9
médico(a) **93**-6, **97**-11
medidas **106**
medidor de gasolina **127**-54
medio(a) **105**
medio ambiente (problemas del) **158**
medio fondo **68**-17
medio galón **56**-20
medio tiempo **118**-5
mediodía **16**
medir **92**-A
medirle y pesarle **92**-A
medusa **155**-14
mejilla **86**-14
mejillones **50**-33
melena **153**-55a
melocotón **48**-2
melón **48**-15,16
melón de agua **48**-17
melón verde/dulce/chino/ de Indias **48**-16
membrete **120**-22
memoranda **108**-18

memorándum **108**-18
menos **105**
mensáfono **77**-7
mensaje instantáneo **108**-20
mensaje por correo electrónico **108**-19
mensajero(a) **114**-9
mentón **86**-21
menú **62**-8
menudo **50**-8
mercadillo **136**-10
mercado de pulgas **136**-10
Mercurio **111**-12
merendar al aire libre **139**-E
merendero **37**-24, **53**-12, **137**-3
mero **50**-23
mes **18**-2
mesa **4**-6, **22**-1, **24**-34, **62**-5, **63**-E
mesa abatible **132**-16
mesa de billar **141**-32
mesa de cama **97**-8
mesa de centro **21**-22
mesa de comedor **22**-1
mesa de conferencias **119**-4
mesa de noche **23**-19
mesa de reconocimiento **92**-6
mesa de reuniones **119**-4
mesa para cambiar pañales **25**-7
mesa para jugar pimpón/ ping-pong **140**-26
mesa para merendar **137**-6
mesera **62**-11, **115**-37
mesero **62**-12, **115**-36
meseta **109**-11
mesilla **21**-26
mesita **21**-26, **23**-19
metales (instrumentos) **150**
meteoro **111**-9
meter la ropa en la lavadora **73**-B
meter la ropa en la secadora **73**-D
meterle a la costura **72**-23
método científico **110**
metro **33**-1, **40**-20, **106**-9, **124**-C
mezcladora de cemento/ mortero **122**-11
mezcladora eléctrica **24**-4
mezclar **58**-12
mezclilla **71**-18
mezquita **84**-K

microbús **125**-10
microcomputadora **78**-11
microfilm **83**-24
micrófono **76**-18
microondas **24**-21
microscopio **110**-1
miedo (tener) **47**-27
miércoles **18**-9
milla **106**-11
minibús **125**-10
miniván **125**-10
minutero **59**-24
mirar la pantalla **7**-43
mirilla **29**-34
misterio (películas de) **149**-20
mitones **67**-24
mocasines **69**-16,27
mochila **70**-24,25
mochila de excursión **70**-25, **139**-10
modelo para armar **79**-18
módem **78**-14
módulo de computadora **119**-20
mofeta **152**-11
mofle(r) **126**-23
moisés **25**-28
mojado(a) **45**-55, **130**-15
mojada (ropa) **73**-10
molde de hacer galletas **59**-29
molde para bizcochos/ hornear/pasteles **59**-34
molde para tartas **59**-26
moldeador de pelo/ cabello **98**-14
molestar (a uno(a), no) **165**-17
molesto(a) (estar) **46**-16
molinillo de alimentos **24**-32
mollete **61**-35
mondador **59**-4,27
mondar **58**-5
mondongo **50**-8
moneda suelta **17**
monedero **70**-18
monitor **5**-37, **78**-3
monitor con control de signos vitales **97**-7
monitor de bebé **25**-2
monitor de llegadas y salidas **131**-5
mono **25**-8, **43**-32, **66**-19,21,25, **152**-24
monopatín **79**-35, **140**-10
monopatín (andar en) **140**-F
monopolio **135**-38
montacarga **121**-13
montador(a) **112**-6
montaje (cadena de/línea de) **121**-4

trotar **140**-A
trucha **50**-26, **155**-1
truenos **14**-14
truenos (tormenta de) **14**-15
trusas **68**-8
tsunami **159**-7
tuba **150**-19
tuberculosis **91**-24
tubería de agua principal rota **85**-15
tubo **56**-17, **122**-29
tubo de ensayo **110**-8
tubo de escape **126**-22
tubo de respiración **145**-15
tuerca **34**-27
tulipán **157**-54
túnel **128**-1
túnica **66**-23
turbado(a) (estar) **47**-22
turista **163**
turista (gestiones del) **164**
turquesa **65**-9
tuza **152**-32
TV **21**-8

UFO **111**-31
un cuarto **105**
un solo sentido **130**-7
uña **87**-43
uña del dedo del pie **87**-51
uñas (*me estoy arreglando las*) **99**-M
ungüento **95**-11, **100**-13
ungüento antibiótico **90**-7
unidad de disquete **78**-6
unidad de pared **21**-15
uniforme **66**-15
uniforme (de béisbol) **143**-4
uniforme de lucha libre **141**-47
unión de carriles **130**-12
universidad **101**-8,9
universo **111**
Urano **111**-18
urgente **82**-6
URL **135**-41
urraca azul **154**-2
usar **117**-34
usar el Internet **135**-Q
usar el ordenador **11**-14
usar la computadora **11**-14
usar la Internet **135**-Q
usar señales de mano **130**-26
usar un teléfono celular/móvil aquí **164**-9

uso del cajero automático **81**
uvas **48**-24
uvas (jugo de) **51**-19
uvas pasas **48**-28

vaca **151**-26
vaciarse los bolsillos **132**-B
vacío(a) **45**-60
vagón **79**-34
vagoneta **79**-34, **125**-6
vajilla **22**-12
vajilla de loza **22**-12
vajilla de porcelana **22**-12
valija **131**-4
valla **27**-32, **109**-5
van **125**-9
vandalismo **85**-19
vapor (cocer al) **58**-18
vapor (rejilla para cocer al) **59**-14
vaqueros **71**-18
vaquita de mar **155**-17
vara de una yarda **33**-1
varicela **91**-17
varilla del aceite **126**-39
vaso **22**-31, **26**-10
vaso de precipitados **110**-7
vaso para el agua **63**-27
vasos de cartón **54**-2, **60**-19
vasos desechables **54**-2
váyase **165**-17
veces a la semana (dos) **19**-24
veces a la semana (tres) **19**-25
vecino(a) **28**-9
vecinos(as) (hijos(as) de los) **45**
vegetales **35**-B, **53**-10
vegetales congelados **52**-19
vegetales enlatados **53**-10
vegetales mixtos **64**-23
vehículo autobomba **84**-4
vehículos (tipos de) **125**
vehículos de cortesía del hotel **161**-8
vejiga **87**-66
vela **22**-17, **145**-22
vela (ir de) **145**-A
velear **145**-A
velero **145**-1
velocidad (letrero de límite de) **128**-9
velocímetro **127**-55
venado **152**-3
venas **87**-67
venda **90**-12

venda elástica **90**-12
vendar la herida **93**-C
vendedor(a) **114**-20, **138**-5
vendedor(a) ambulante **41**-40
vendedora automática **119**-26
vender **117**-23
veneno **91**-8
venenoso(a) **123**-15
veneras **50**-30
venoclisis **97**-6
venta de patio **136**-9
ventana **21**-13, **27**-10, **32**-D
ventana trasera **126**-15
ventanilla **124**-12
ventanilla(s) de alquiler de coches/carros **161**-7
ventanilla(s) de renta de coches/carros **161**-7
ventanilla(s) de servicio rápido **41**-41
ventas (programas de) **149**-40
ventila **127**-62
ventilador **26**-17
ventisca de nieve **159**-4
ventoso **14**-7
Venus **111**-13
ver a un especialista **94**-7
ver la televisión/tele **11**-1
veranda **27**-23
verano **19**-28
verbo **107**-2
verde **65**-10
verde claro **65**-11
verde oscuro **65**-12
verduras **53**-10
verduras (frutas y) **55**-20
verduras enlatadas **53**-10
vereda **128**-12
verja de seguridad **29**-46
verruga **88**-19
vértice **106**-19a
vertir **58**-9
vertir el agua **62**-B
vesícula biliar **87**-58
vespa **125**-20
vestíbulo **29**, **133**-7
vestido **45**, **66**-8
vestido de baño **69**-10, **145**-11
vestido de chaqueta **66**-12
vestido de dos piezas **66**-12
vestido de etiqueta **66**-29
vestido de fiesta **66**-29
vestido de maternidad **66**-18
vestido de noche **66**-29

vestido de tres piezas **66**-13
vestido formal **66**-29
vestidor **102**-Ha, **121**-3
vestir **100**-F
vestirse **9**-5
vestirse de manera apropiada **118**-E
veterinario(a) **115**-35
vez a la semana (una) **19**-23
vía **124**-17
vía de peatones **128**-25
viaje **160**
viaje con la familia **160**-2
viaje de estudios **160**-9
viaje de negocios **160**-1
viaje en avión **132**
viaje en barco **160**-7
viaje en lancha **160**-7
viaje en tren **160**-6
viaje guiado **160**-4
viaje para esquiar **160**-8
víbora de cascabel **155**-37
vida real (programas sobre la) **149**-33
video en blanco **76**-9
videocámara **76**-11
videocasete en blanco **76**-9
videocasetera **21**-9, **76**-10
videocentro **39**-28
videocinta en blanco **76**-9
videocintas **83**-18
videograbadora **21**-9, **76**-10
videojuego **76**-34
videojuego manual **76**-35
videoreproductora **76**-10
vieiras **50**-30
viejo(a) **44**-2,4
viento **14**-7
viento (energía eólica) **158**-7
viento (instrumentos de) **150**
vientre **86**-25
viernes **18**-11
viga **122**-30
viga de balance **141**-39
viga de equilibrio **141**-39
vigilar **116**-15
villa **20**-16
vinagre **53**-28
vincha **69**-3
viñetas animadas **149**-22,35
viola **150**-2
violencia de pandillas **85**-20
violeta **65**-13, **157**-56

The bold number indicates the page(s) on which the word appears. The number that follows indicates the word's location in the illustration and in the word list on the page. For example, "address **1**-5" indicates that the word address is on page 1 and is item number 5.

gill **155**-1b
giraffe **153**-56
girder **122**-30
girl **42**-5
give a presentation **119**-b
give *you* a shot of anesthetic **93**-F
give *you* a shot of Novocaine™ **93**-F
glass **22**-31
global warming **158**-18
globe **4**-16
glove compartment **127**-70
gloves **67**-21, **93**-23, **143**-6
glue **33**-16, **120**-30, **135**-30
glue stick **120**-29
go bird-watching **135**-N
go away **165**-17
go in **164**-8
go on **31**-13
go on a diet **94**-4
go online **135**-Q
go over the answers **6**-23
go shopping **163**-11
go sightseeing **163**-1
go straight **130**-23
go to a club **163**-16
go to a fitness club **163**-14
go to a health club **163**-14
go to a park **163**-12
go to an Internet cafe **163**-15
go to an interview **118**-G
go to a museum **163**-13
go to bed **9**-13
go to school **10**-10
go to the board **6**-7
go to the store **10**-15
go to work **10**-9
goat **151**-12
goggles **123**-3, **145**-12
gold **65**-18
goldfish **152**-41
golf **141**-M
golf ball **141**-30
golf clubs **141**-29
good **44**-31
goose **154**-15
gopher **152**-32
gorilla **153**-61
gospel music **148**-7
government **103**-5
gown **66**-29
GPS device **139**-14
graduate school **101**-10
graduated cylinder **110**-12

grandchildren **2**
granddaughter **2**-12
grandfather **2**-11
grandmother **2**-10
grandparents **2**
grandson **2**-13
grape juice **51**-19
grapefruit **48**-19
grapefruit juice **51**-17
grapes **48**-24
graph paper **5**-29
grasshopper **154**-37
grate **58**-4
grater **59**-17
gray **43**-34, **65**-16
Greek salad **64**-8
green **65**-10
green bean **49**-17
green onion **49**-37
green pepper **49**-31
grill **27**-24, **58**-23, **137**-5
grizzly bear **152**-7
grocery store **37**-28
ground beef **50**-2
group **7**-38,39
grow **116**-14
guard **116**-15
guest **133**-10
guest room **133**-24
guidance counselor **102**-4
guidance office **102**-D
guided tour **160**-4
guinea pig **152**-40
guitar **11**-9, **150**-5
gum **55**-9
gums **86**-19
gurney **97**-22
gutter **27**-26
gym **84**-11, **102**-H
gymnasium **102**-H
gymnastics **141**-Q
gynecologist **96**-2

hacksaw **34**-5
haddock **50**-24
hailing **14**-12
hair **43**, **86**-2, **98**-G,K
hair brush **98**-13
hair dryer **26**-14, **98**-11
hair gel **98**-16
hair salon **38**-1
hairclip **98**-19
hairdresser **113**-34
hairnet **123**-9
hairspray **98**-15
half **105**
half dollar **17**-5
half past **16**
half slip **68**-17
half-gallon **56**-20
halibut **50**-23
hall **133**-20

hallway **29**, **102**-F, **133**-20
ham **50**-13, **52**-4
ham and cheese sandwich **61**-25
hamburger **60**-1
hammer **34**-1
hamper **26**-16
hamster **152**-38
hand **6**-16, **87**-38
hand drill **34**-14
hand in your homework **6**-25
hand lotion **99**-34
hand signals **130**-26
hand towel **26**-19
hand truck **121**-19
hand vacuum **32**-8
handbag **70**-21
hand-held video game **76**-35
handicapped-accessible room **162**-4
handicapped parking only **130**-16
handkerchief **70**-16
handsaw **34**-4
handsome **45**-53
handstand **146**-30
"handyman" **31**-J
hang clothes on the clothesline **73**-E
hang up clothing **73**-H
hanger **73**-23
happy **46**-10
hard **44**-40,42
hard hat **123**-1
hardware store **38**-2
harmonica **150**-27
harness **139**-16
harp **150**-8
has no pulse **90**-15a
hat **67**-3
hatchback **125**-2
hatchet **139**-5
have breakfast **9**-18
have dinner **9**-20
have lunch **9**-19
hawk **154**-9
hay **151**-5
hazardous **123**-19
hazardous waste **158**-15
hazy **14**-4
head **56**-9, **86**-1
headache **88**-1
headboard **23**-2
headlight **126**-2
headphones **76**-31
headrest **127**-83
health **103**-10
health club **38**-3, **163**-14
health-care aide **113**-35
health-care attendant **113**-35

hearing impaired **42**-23
heart **87**-56, **92**-G, **135**-34c
heart attack **91**-6
heart disease **91**-22
heat wave **14**-18
heater **127**-66
heating and air conditioning service **31**-L
heating bill **81**-11
heating pad **94**-9
heating system **31**-20
heatstroke **91**-4
heavy **42**-17, **44**-13,15, **72**-11
hedge clippers **35**-17
hedge trimmer **35**-18
heel **87**-49
heels **69**-14, 72
height **42**, **92**-A, **106**-1
Heimlich maneuver **90**-17
helmet **123**-1, **139**-19, **140**-9
help each other **6**-28
help wanted sign **118**-1
hen **151**-20
hen house **151**-19
herbal tea **51**-30
hibiscus **157**-59
hiccups **88**-20
high **44**-27, **72**-7
high blood pressure **91**-23
high chair **25**-27, **62**-6
high heels **69**-14
high school **101**-4
high-top sneakers **69**-20
high-tops **69**-20
highway **128**-5
hiking **139**-B
hiking boots **69**-25, **139**-15
hill **109**-2
hip **86**-31
hip hop **148**-11
hippopotamus **153**-59
hired hand **151**-6
historic site **136**-6, **163**-10
history **103**-3
hit **146**-1
hockey **142**-E, **143**-E
hockey glove **143**-19
hockey mask **143**-18
hockey player **142**-9
hockey puck **143**-16
hockey rink **142**-10
hockey skates **143**-20
hockey stick **143**-17
hoe **35**-6
hold **100**-D
holly **156**-12,24

NÚMEROS, DÍAS DE LA SEMANA, MESES DEL AÑO

Cardinal Numbers

1	one
2	two
3	three
4	four
5	five
6	six
7	seven
8	eight
9	nine
10	ten
11	eleven
12	twelve
13	thirteen
14	fourteen
15	fifteen
16	sixteen
17	seventeen
18	eighteen
19	nineteen
20	twenty
21	twenty-one
22	twenty-two
30	thirty
40	forty
50	fifty
60	sixty
70	seventy
80	eighty
90	ninety
100	one hundred
101	one hundred (and) one
102	one hundred (and) two
1,000	one thousand
10,000	ten thousand
100,000	one hundred thousand
1,000,000	one million
1,000,000,000	one billion

Ordinal Numbers

1st	first
2nd	second
3rd	third
4th	fourth
5th	fifth
6th	sixth
7th	seventh
8th	eighth
9th	ninth
10th	tenth
11th	eleventh
12th	twelfth
13th	thirteenth
14th	fourteenth
15th	fifteenth
16th	sixteenth
17th	seventeenth
18th	eighteenth
19th	nineteenth
20th	twentieth
21st	twenty-first
22nd	twenty-second
30th	thirtieth
40th	fortieth
50th	fiftieth
60th	sixtieth
70th	seventieth
80th	eightieth
90th	ninetieth
100th	one hundredth
101st	one hundred (and) first
102nd	one hundred (and) second
1,000th	one thousandth
10,000th	ten thousandth
100,000th	one hundred thousandth
1,000,000th	one millionth
1,000,000,000th	one billionth

Days of the Week

Sunday
Monday
Tuesday
Wednesday
Thursday
Friday
Saturday

Months of the Year

January	July
February	August
March	September
April	October
May	November
June	December